IMAGES
of America

SUGAR VALLEY VILLAGES

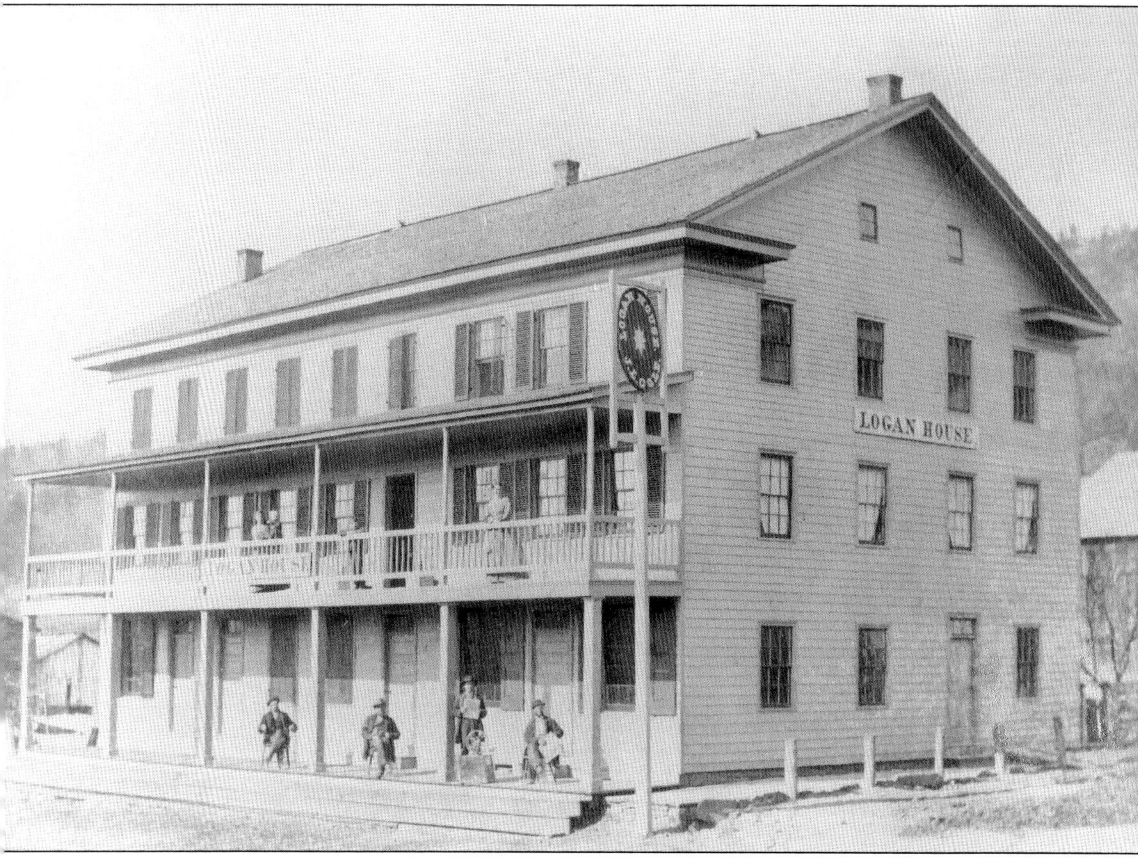

A landmark building, the Logan House was a very popular hotel at the main intersection in the heart of Logansville (renamed Loganton in 1888) during the second half of the 1800s until its destruction in the great fire that devastated much of the borough on June 19, 1918. St. Paul's Evangelical Lutheran Church, which is still active today, was erected at the site within a few years of the conflagration. (Courtesy of John W. Harbach Sr.)

On the Cover: The White Deer & Loganton Railway—which was about 24 miles long from the village of White Deer in Union County west through Sugar Valley to Loganton in Clinton County—began passenger service with a first arrival in Loganton on May 10, 1907. The Loganton Depot, shown here, was dismantled when the line was discontinued in 1916. The wood was used to build the home of Andrew and Hattie Snook, which burned down in 1972. (Courtesy of Kenneth and Peggy Karstetter.)

IMAGES
of America

SUGAR VALLEY VILLAGES

David Ira Kagan and
John W. Harbach Sr.

ARCADIA
PUBLISHING

ISBN 978-0-7385-7469-1

Published by Arcadia Publishing
Charleston, South Carolina

Printed in the United States of America

Library of Congress Control Number: 2010938067

For all general information, please contact Arcadia Publishing:
Telephone 843-853-2070
Fax 843-853-0044
E-mail sales@arcadiapublishing.com
For customer service and orders:
Toll-Free 1-888-313-2665

Visit us on the Internet at www.arcadiapublishing.com

To Gloria Harbach, whose uncountable hours of genealogical and historical research on Sugar Valley added much to this book.

Contents

Acknowledgments		6
Introduction		7
1.	Earning a Living	11
2.	Recording Valley Scenes	27
3.	Worshipping the Lord	41
4.	Traversing the Land	57
5.	Receiving an Education	67
6.	Witnessing Historical Moments	85
7.	Enjoying Free Time	95
8.	Posing for Posterity	111

Acknowledgments

No local history book consisting primarily of old photographs could ever become a reality without those who clicked the cameras to record special events, family reunions, workplaces, school and church gatherings, and other daily activities and everyday sights. Just as important are those who saved these images through the years. So, first of all, we wish to thank the people who, through the latter half of the 1800s, the 1900s, and into the 2000s, did this for Sugar Valley.

Next, our gratitude goes to Gloria Harbach, whose years of detailed research into Sugar Valley's past allowed us to include birth and death dates, marriage and family data, full names and correct spellings, and interesting specific information about people's lives and their communities.

We also thank the following for access to photographs from their private collections and for information about those images: Mildred Bixel, Christine Brungard, John and Verna Carey (their Meyer Estate collection), Ralph Embick, Ernest Geisewite, William and Betty Harbach, Mary Lamey Hoffer (our special gratitude to her for sharing her extensive knowledge of Sugar Valley's history), Kenneth and Peggy Karstetter, Perry and Jane Klinefelter, Floyd and Gladys Lamey, Anne McCloskey, Hilera Miller, Rilla Seyler, Theora Smith, Tama Thompson, Nathan Walizer, Yvonne and Steve Weaver, and Geraldine Bower Wynn.

In addition, we acknowledge the Clinton County Historical Society (in Lock Haven) and its staff—specifically, executive director Anne M. McCloskey, curator Lou Bernard, and administrative assistant Jane Cryder.

Furthermore, the existence of the Pennsylvania Room of Lock Haven's Annie Halenbake Ross Library was a boon to our research. Its collection of books on Clinton County's history provided us with information for our captions and introduction.

Finally, we thank the members of the Sugar Valley Historical Society for their endorsement and their encouragement of our effort to provide a lasting tribute to the people, places, and events of this unique north central Pennsylvania valley's past.

Unless otherwise noted, all images in this book appear courtesy of coauthor John W. Harbach Sr., who gathered photographs from many other people and whose collection will one day go to the Sugar Valley Historical Society Museum.

INTRODUCTION

Until after the Revolutionary War, Native Americans are the only people—aside from trappers, hunters, and explorers—known to have frequented the roughly 20-mile-long and 2-mile-wide limestone-floored north central Pennsylvania valley later known as Sugar Valley. One Native American in particular, an Iroquois named Chief Tah-gah-jute (given the English name Chief James Logan, honoring the 18th-century secretary of the province of Pennsylvania), reputedly had dealings with white men who visited the valley early on, the most notable being a man named Peter Pence. Logan's name was later given to two communities in Sugar Valley—Logan Mills and Logansville—and to its later Clinton County division, Logan Township.

It is believed that three of the very earliest white settlers in Sugar Valley were John Christopher Culby, Rudolph Karstetter, and John Kleckner. Culby, a Revolutionary War veteran, arrived around 1784, settling along Fishing Creek (the valley's east-west waterway) by what would become the village of Logan Mills. Karstetter came around 1800 and is credited with being the first settler in what later became Greene Township (named after Capt. Harry Greene, reputedly slain in the area in 1801 by Native Americans). Karstetter built a home at what would later be Logansville. Kleckner, also arriving around 1800, settled in the same area and is known as the builder of the first gristmill in the future Greene Township.

Logansville (at first named Alpine), which was to become Sugar Valley's largest community, was laid out on the north side of the valley in 1840 by John Kleckner's son Col. Anthony Kleckner and surveyor John L. Eckel. It was incorporated as a borough in 1864. A post office, the valley's first, had already been established there in 1829, with Colonel Kleckner appointed postmaster. Colonel Kleckner's son-in-law Levi Conser became a successful general merchandiser in Logansville beginning in 1863.

The Honorable George A. Achenbach was elected to serve in the Pennsylvania House of Representatives both in 1860 and 1874. Before that, from 1838 until 1851, he served as the second postmaster of the Sugar Valley Post Office. Yet another prominent 19th-century resident was Dr. Jonathan Moyer, who began practicing medicine in Logansville in 1842.

Logansville flourished in the mid-1800s and had a population of 414 in 1870. In 1872, the Patriotic Order Sons of America Washington Camp 202 was established, and in 1873, the Independent Order of Odd Fellows Lodge 829 was instituted. The Logan House became a popular resort hotel with nearby Sulphur Spring and its reputed healing mineral waters drawing visitors from as far away as Philadelphia. The community boasted three general stores, two churches, a graded school, three sawmills, a gristmill, John Gerstung's pottery factory (his works, embossed with a "Sugar Valley, Pa." trademark, are said to have made Sugar Valley famous), and three physicians. In 1888, the community's name was changed to Loganton.

Loganton entered the 20th century promisingly as the commercial center of Sugar Valley. The White Deer & Loganton Railway began passenger service on May 10, 1907. The 24-mile-long railroad, connecting the village of White Deer in Union County west through Sugar Valley to

Loganton (with regular stops at White Deer Junction, Mile Run, Carroll, and Loganton, and with flag stops at eight other locations along the route), also transported mail, lumber, and various types of freight. Unfortunately, the railroad was never extended west beyond the borough, and it shut down in 1916.

Even worse was the disastrous fire of June 19, 1918, which destroyed well over half of the community's buildings. Loganton, however, survived that tragic day. Two replacement churches were erected within three years (St. Paul's Evangelical Lutheran and Albright United Methodist are both still active today) and businesses and houses were rebuilt. In 1926, the borough gained electricity and a four-year high school. Important Loganton businesses in the first half of the 1900s included the Loganton National Bank (chartered in 1909), the Sugar Valley Mutual Fire Insurance Company, John Guiswite's creamery, the Morris Funeral Home, the Greningers' general merchandise store, and Harry Kauffman's Pequea Fishing Tackle Works, which employed 72 women in 1948.

Four very helpful organizations also arose in Loganton in the first half of the 1900s. The first was the Loganton Community Club in 1925; its fundraisers greatly aided the development of the borough through the years. In 1938, area sportsmen organized the Southern Clinton County Forest, Fish, and Game Association. The Sugar Valley Vocational High School Mothers' Association, formed in 1939, raised money both for the school's band and for community charities. Finally, the major organization originating in the 1940s was the Sugar Valley Volunteer Fire Company, which began operating on October 1, 1946.

Today, the Loganton Country Store, located at 21 East Main Street, could be seen as a symbol of the community's determination to endure. At that same site, John Brown had started his general store in 1888. After the terrible fire of 1918, W.H. Greninger rebuilt another general store on the same site. After 1940 and for many years, it was Cora Schrack's store. Now, after more than 120 years, the residents of Loganton and Sugar Valley's other communities continue to be served there.

In the 21st century, Loganton provides for the valley's residents, educating their children at its Sugar Valley Elementary and Sugar Valley Rural Charter Schools. In addition, it is the only valley community still to have a post office, though the office's name changed from Sugar Valley to Loganton in 1888.

The other communities—Eastville, Carroll, Sugar Grove (later known as Bull Run), Rosecrans, Centerville (sometimes called Schracktown), Greenville (later renamed Greenburr), Booneville, Logan Mills, and Tylersville—all arose in the 1800s. Greene Township, formed in 1840, encompassed the first five; Logan Township, organized in 1839, included the last four.

Eastville, Bull Run, and Greenburr (in that order, from east to west) lie along the so-called "winter road," which runs along the south side of the valley at the base of Brush Valley Mountain. Carroll, Loganton, Centerville, and Booneville (in that order, from east to west) lie along the "summer road," running along the north side of the valley at the base of Sugar Valley Mountain. The road names reflect the fact that the snow melts first on the north side of the valley because of its exposure to the winter sun. Rosecrans is on top of Sugar Valley Mountain, about two miles directly north of Loganton. Logan Mills is along Fishing Creek, roughly in the center of the valley and just west of Booneville and Greenburr. Finally, Tylersville is farthest west, located where the summer and winter roads merge.

By 1883, Eastville, so named because of its location at the eastern end of settlements in Sugar Valley, consisted of about a dozen dwellings, two or three sawmills, a blacksmith shop, and a church. One of this area's earliest settlers was Frederick Friedley, who built an iron ore furnace (later known as the Deborah Furnace) along Fishing Creek in 1829. Later in that century, a limekiln was erected at the site. A third industry, the art of pottery making, peaked in the 1840s and 1850s with resident Joseph Kemmerer's fine red and Delft blue clay crocks and other wares.

Eastville's Sugar Valley Church of the Brethren was constructed in 1881, and a one-room schoolhouse, the Franklin School, was erected in 1899. The school closed in 1954, but the church remains active to this day.

Finally, mention must be made of Eastville's general store from the first half of the 1900s. It was owned by Charles C. Brungard, and even as far back as 1919, this popular little valley store had a sign out front advertising gasoline for automobiles.

The hamlet of Bull Run (originally called Sugar Grove because of the many sugar maple trees in the area) lies along Bull Run Stream, which flows north down from a gap through Brush Valley Mountain. The community's one-room school was constructed in 1899, closed in 1955, and has been maintained as a historical site since 1976. It is fully furnished with old desks, a clock, and other classroom items, and the Sugar Valley Historical Society holds its meetings and special events there.

Greenburr, rumored to have originally been named Greenville because its first houses arose in the mid-1800s among the many green trees in the area, became Greenburr upon its designation as a postal village in 1882.

Three of Greenburr's leading 19th-century citizens were John B. Rowe (the first postmaster and a Logan Township justice of the peace for many years), his son, the Reverend A.D. Rowe (who also became the superintendent of Clinton County's common schools), and Samuel Kahl (a leading politician of Logan Township).

By the late 1890s, the community had about 20 dwellings, approximately 100 residents, two churches, the post office, and one school (existing as far back as 1875). In the first half of the 1900s, the community boasted two general stores—Lamey's and Bressler's. Today, aside from the two-street hamlet's homes, only Trinity United Methodist Church remains, still offering regular Sunday services.

Carroll, about five miles directly east of Loganton and two miles north of Eastville, was named after early-1800s resident William Carroll. In 1853, Carroll became the third valley community to have its own post office (with Henry Barner as its first postmaster), which operated until 1918. By 1890, Carroll had approximately 15 dwellings, a store, the post office, a blacksmith shop, and a few minor industries. Carroll also had its own brass band (organized in 1897), Washington Camp 520 of the Patriotic Order Sons of America, and one of only two Sugar Valley passenger station communities for the White Deer & Loganton Railway.

About a mile west of Loganton on the summer road is Centerville, named so because it is roughly located in the center of Sugar Valley. Nearby, just to the south, the first church in Sugar Valley was built around 1806. It was a union church, serving Lutheran and Reformed congregations, erected on land donated by Jacob Kahl. Just west of the church, the first school in Sugar Valley was constructed in 1824. Centerville was also known as Schracktown, named after the Schracks, who were longtime farmers in the area. In 1977, the 950-acre Schrack Farm, with its nine silos, was designated a century farm (a farm that has been continuously owned by the same family for 100 years or more).

Booneville, another mile west of Centerville, was named in honor of John and Ralph Boone, who laid out the village in 1866. A general store was started shortly afterward by Henry Wolf and Samuel R. Boone, which lasted into the second half of the 1900s. It was last run by Harry, then his son Ralph, and finally grandson Elwood Welshans. In 1868, the valley's first band, the Booneville Cornet Band, was organized. Booneville became the sixth valley postal village in 1870 (with Henry M. Schwenck appointed the first postmaster) and lasted until 1937. By the mid-1870s, the community contained about 25 dwellings, two churches, a shoe repair shop, a tannery, two sawmills, a blacksmith's shop, and a schoolhouse. In 1926, Booneville resident Samuel Ilgen brought electricity to Sugar Valley, having constructed a power plant near his home.

Booneville today has an active church, St. John's Lutheran, erected in 1900. Its brick edifice replaced a frame structure that was built in 1854 and torn down in 1890. Down the road toward Greenburr, just on the south side of Fishing Creek, is the Booneville Campground, which is the site of yearly summer church picnics and other gatherings since the late 1800s and continuing to today.

The mountaintop hamlet of Rosecrans emerged about the time George Wagner returned to his farm in the area after the Civil War. He named the community Rosecrans in honor of Union major general William Starke Rosecrans, under whom he had served. Wagner and then his daughter

Matilda "Tillie" Wagner Kreamer ran a general store there for many years. The Rosecrans Post Office was established in 1863, with Thomas Furst as postmaster. It was discontinued in 1914.

Two other well-known Rosecrans area residents were Samuel Motter and Prince Farrington. In the second half of the 1800s, Motter gained a reputation as a trapper, fisherman, and eccentric adventurer. Farrington was a legendary bootlegger during Prohibition. He purchased a farm at Rosecrans as a cover-up for his stills. Today, two churches continue to serve the area—Mount Pleasant Bible and Loganton Wesleyan.

Logan Mills is known for a great hunter, a gristmill, a covered bridge, and a church. In the early 1800s, pioneer settler Philip Schreckengast became known as the greatest hunter in Sugar Valley, reportedly killing about 400 deer, 100 wolves, and 75 bears during his lifetime. Col. Anthony Kleckner really got the community going, building a gristmill along Fishing Creek around 1840, which continued operating into the 1960s; the structure is still standing. Also in 1840, under postmaster George Rearick, Logan Mills became the valley's second postal community. It remained in service until 1939.

In the village's heyday, from 1840 to 1939, in addition to the gristmill and post office, a school (built in 1820), a church (erected in 1879 along winter road), a store (owners through the years included William Bartges, Thomas Ilgen, Daniel Moyer, Abraham Nearhood, and Elmer Emig), Frank Eiseman's blacksmith's shop, two water-powered sawmills, and a cider press existed. The covered bridge over the creek by the mill was constructed in 1874 and is still traversed by modern-day traffic; Sugar Valley residents celebrate it as the only remaining covered bridge in Clinton County. St Paul's Evangelical United Brethren Church still exists today but holds only special services.

Farthest west in Sugar Valley is Tylersville. Records show that a one-room schoolhouse existed in the area as of 1828. Squire Michael D. Rockey is credited with naming the community at the beginning of the 1840s in honor of John Tyler, president of the United States at that time. Another important early resident was Isaac Frantz, who erected a sawmill and a gristmill on Fishing Creek and who served as a judge. West of Tylersville, Michael Kettner operated another gristmill. Tylersville became the fourth postal village in 1854, with Barnet Roff as its postmaster. The last postmaster was Ruth Rogers, who was appointed in 1971.

In the second half of the 1800s and early 1900s, Tylersville boasted quite a few businesses, including Samuel Spangler's tavern, David Gingerich's tavern and hotel, James S. Bierly's cigar factory, Emanuel Grimes's tailoring establishment and confectionery shop, Samuel Glantz's funeral parlor, Reuben McKee's and Joseph Eilert's potteries, Andrew Albright's and James S. Bierly's blacksmith shops, and Erwin Schreckengast's Keystone Broom Factory and Keystone Hennery. General store owners through this period included Barnet Roff, Jacob Spangler, Jonathan Shaffer, Samuel Greninger, and William Harter. In 1901, Washington Camp 418 of the Patriotic Order Sons of America was organized. Today, the only center of activity in this once-prosperous community is St. John's United Church of Christ.

Sugar Valley in the early 21st century is still a quiet, unpolluted place to live. No factories or industries belch smoke into the air or pour pollutants into the water, and the steady traffic of nearby Interstate 80 passes by harmlessly and noiselessly way up on the mountaintop, sparing the valley. Residents of and visitors to Sugar Valley witness a primarily rural land that often echoes the soft clip-clop of the horses, a sound that became a part of the valley when the Amish started arriving in the early 1970s to farm the sweet land where hosts of sugar maples once grew.

One

Earning a Living

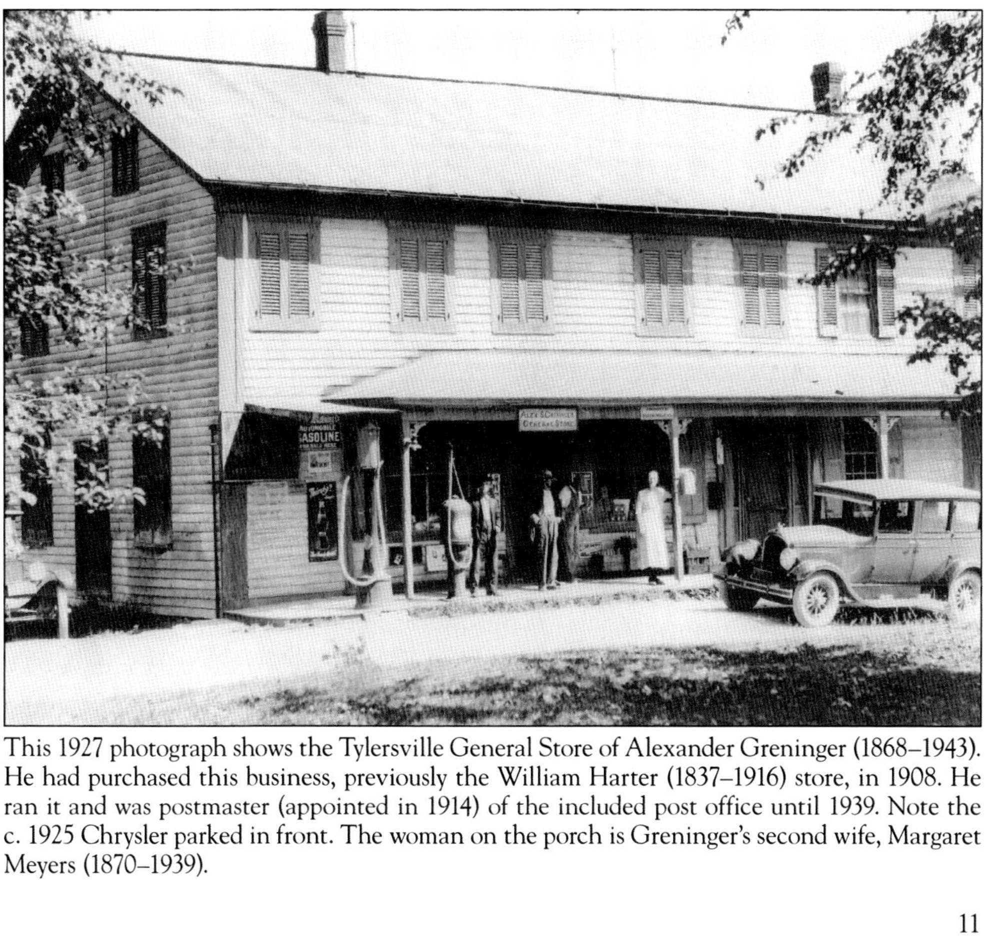

This 1927 photograph shows the Tylersville General Store of Alexander Greninger (1868–1943). He had purchased this business, previously the William Harter (1837–1916) store, in 1908. He ran it and was postmaster (appointed in 1914) of the included post office until 1939. Note the c. 1925 Chrysler parked in front. The woman on the porch is Greninger's second wife, Margaret Meyers (1870–1939).

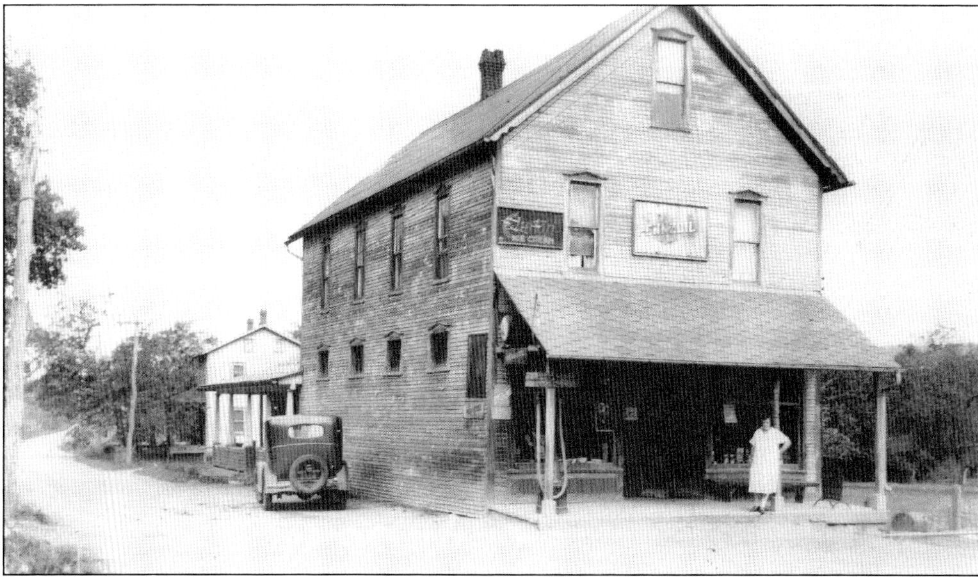

Shown around 1932, the Bressler General Store in Greenburr also served as the post office under postmaster Adam Bressler (1886–1958) from 1924 to 1942. An advertisement for A.C. Bressler & Son read, "Paints and Spouting. Service guaranteed. Give us a try."

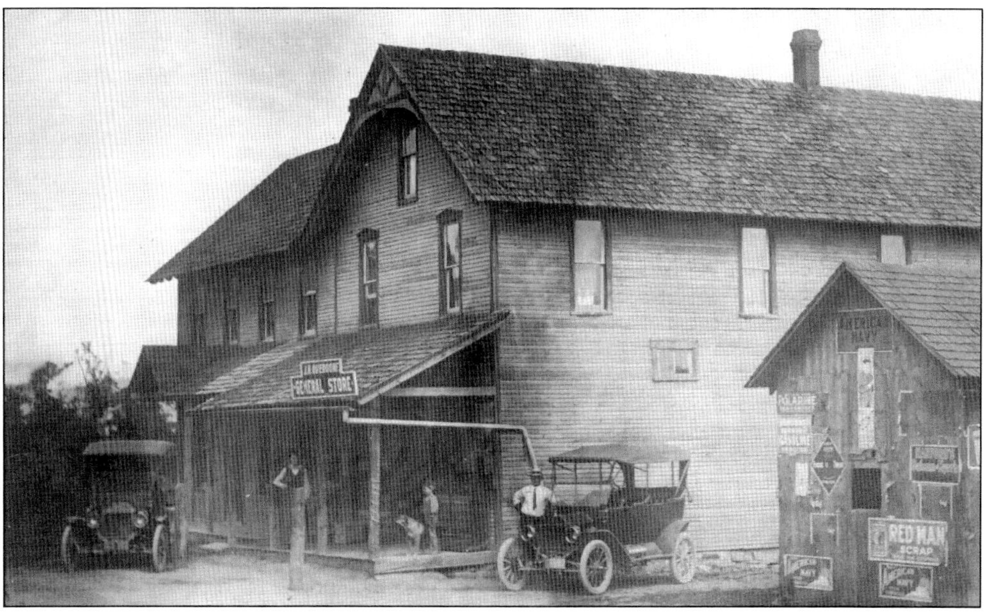

James Overdorf (1868–1937) was the proprietor of the Overdorf General Store in Carroll, shown around 1915. He was also postmaster at that location from 1909 to 1918, when the post office was discontinued. Jacob Kohlberger (1892–1973) ran the store next, until about 1940.

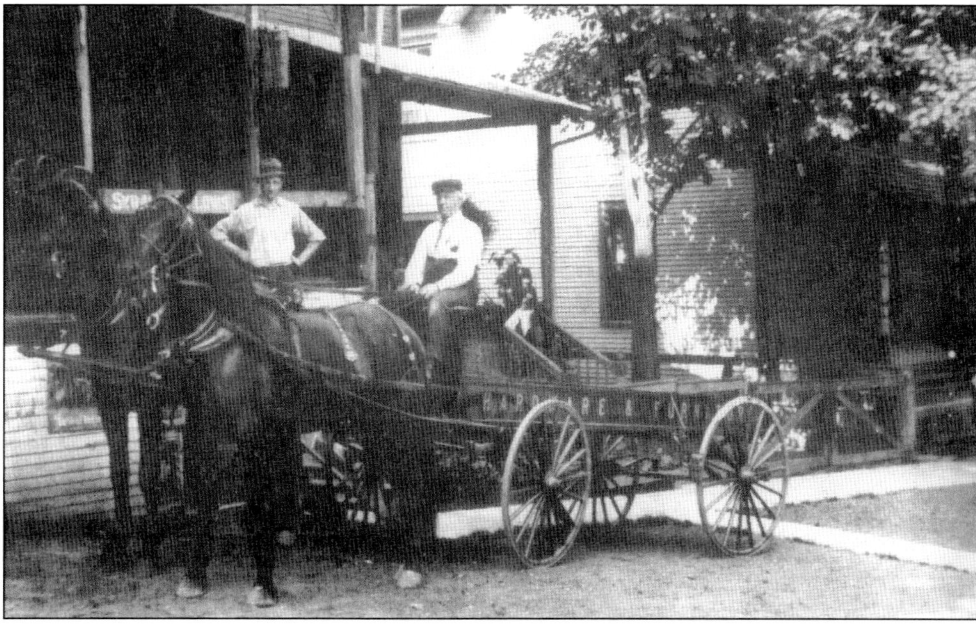

Lee Morris (1888–1973), on the porch, and his father, Elmer Morris (1861–1923), on the wagon, pose in front of their Loganton E.E. Morris & Sons' Hardware Store, which partially burned in the great fire of 1918. Note the sidewalk, which was put in before the streets were paved.

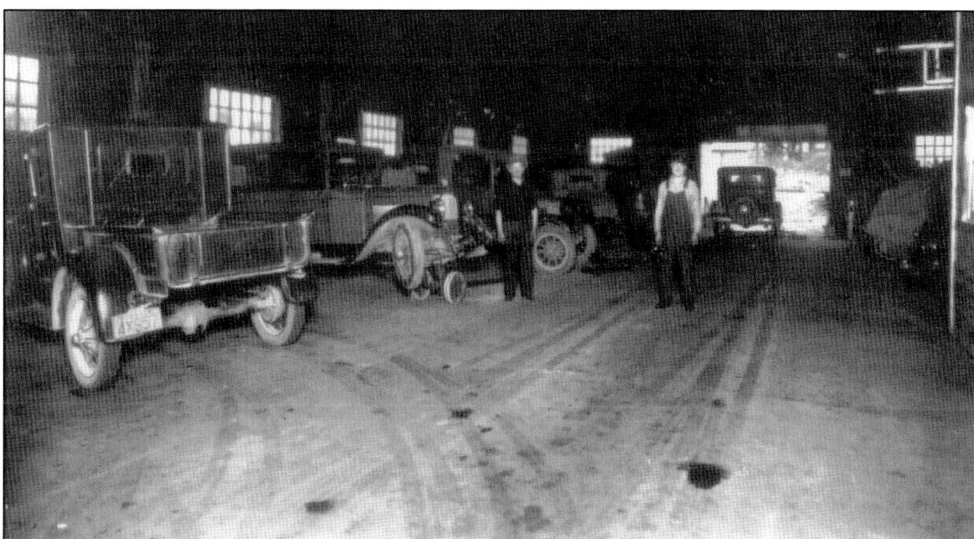

In 1932, Chauncey Royer's Garage of Loganton was at 11 East Main Street. After Royer (1890–1963) retired, his son-in-law Cleston Albright (1909–1978) took over, also selling Chevrolets. Harry Smith (1922–1999) was a well-known mechanic there, and he ran the garage after Albright. Finally, Earl Weaver took charge, renamed it Weaver's Garage, and has continued as the owner to the present. (Courtesy of Ralph Embick.)

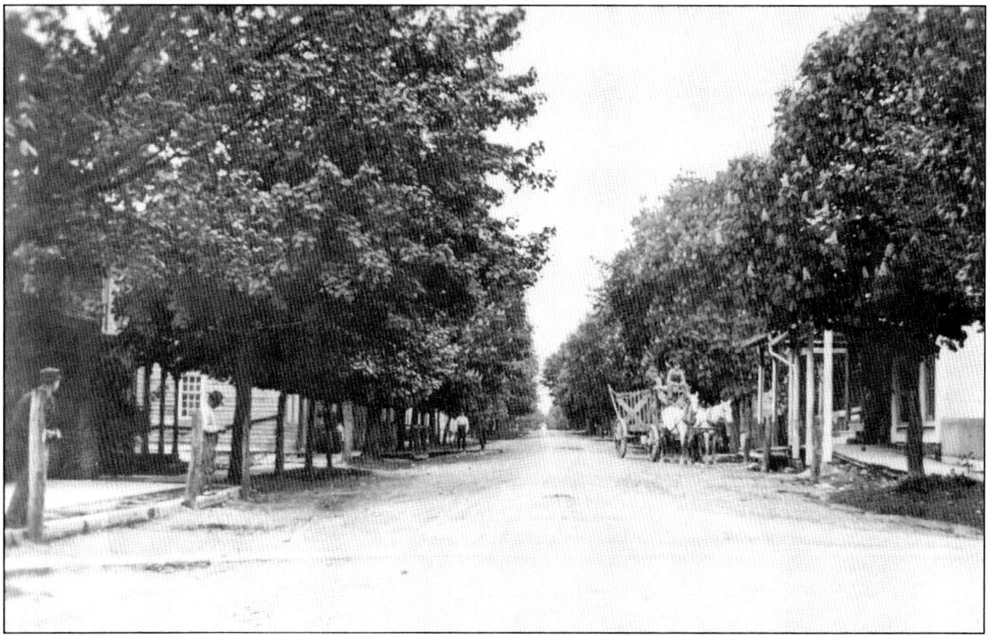

Many years ago, this wagon, drawn by two white horses, stopped in front of Samuel Stamm's (1835–1905) store in Loganton. (Courtesy of Yvonne and Steve Weaver.)

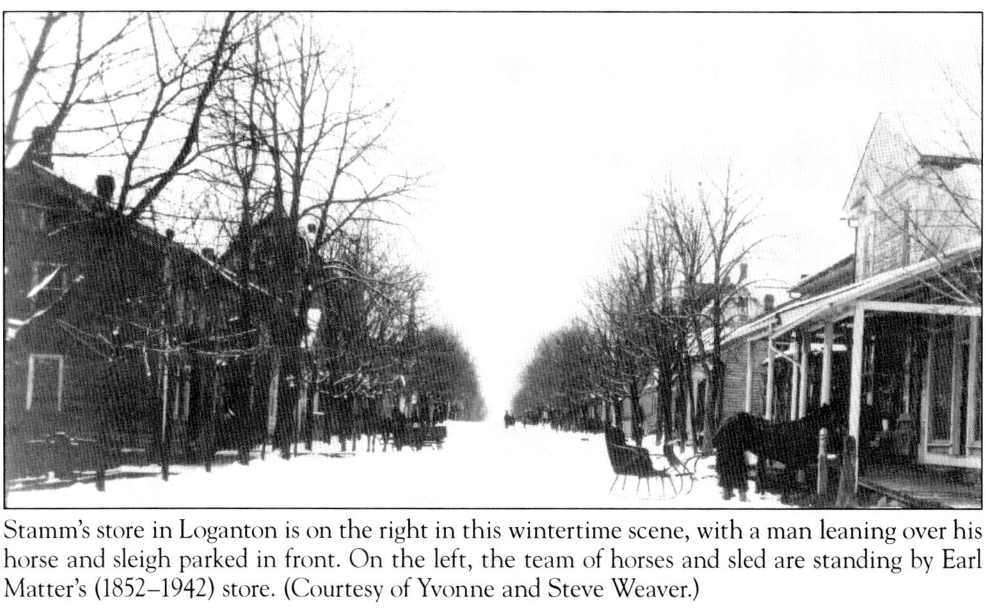

Stamm's store in Loganton is on the right in this wintertime scene, with a man leaning over his horse and sleigh parked in front. On the left, the team of horses and sled are standing by Earl Matter's (1852–1942) store. (Courtesy of Yvonne and Steve Weaver.)

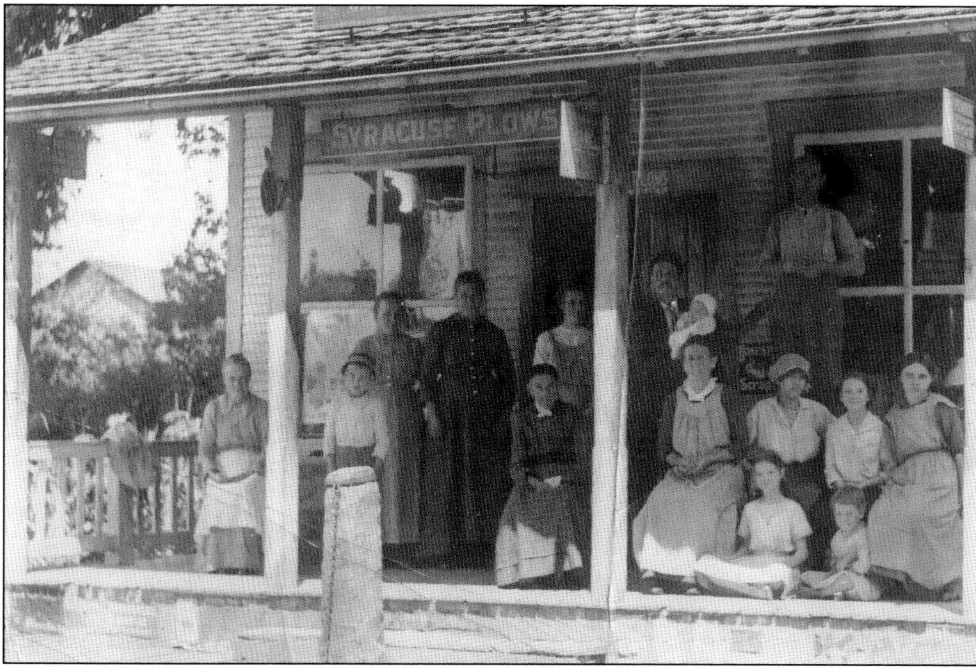

In front of Harvey Lamey's Greenburr General Store in 1917 are, from left to right, (first row, children with legs crossed) Rhea Bechtol and Gordon Adams; (second row) Emma Warntz, Dean Schade (boy standing), Anna Bartges Lamey (Harvey Lamey's mother), Lydia Shaffer, unidentified, Mary Bechtol, and unidentified; (third row) Cora Glantz, unidentified, Tama Lamey, Harvey Lamey (proprietor), Floyd Lamey (Tama and Harvey's son), and Newton Walizer (standing on bench).

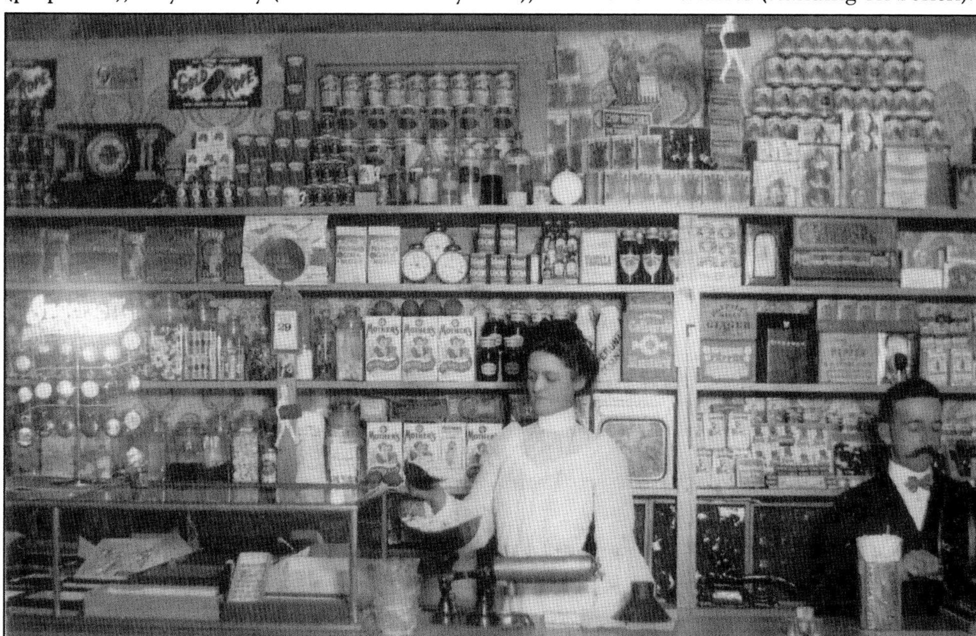

Wife and husband Tama (1880–1935) and Harvey (1869–1953) Lamey work inside their Greenburr General Store in 1914.

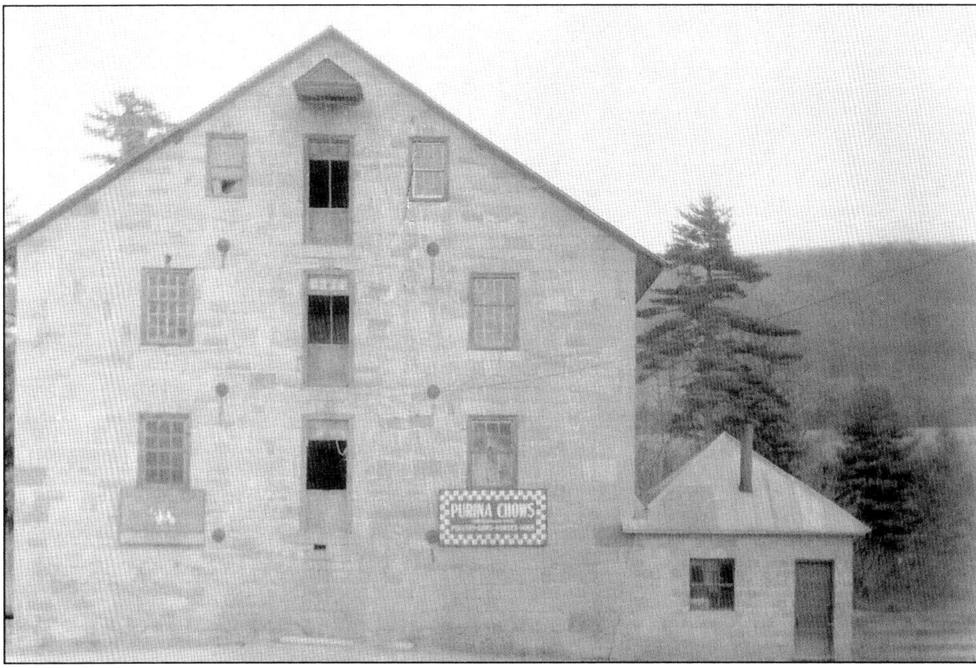

Erected around 1830 to 1840 by Col. Anthony Kleckner and powered by Fishing Creek, the gristmill at Logan Mills (shown in the early 1900s) was reputedly built from stone quarried in Brush Valley and carted over the mountain by ox sled. The Ilgen family took over after Kleckner until its closure around 1953. At one time, the flourishing mill produced flour for the Pennsylvania state prison system. The vacated mill still stands today.

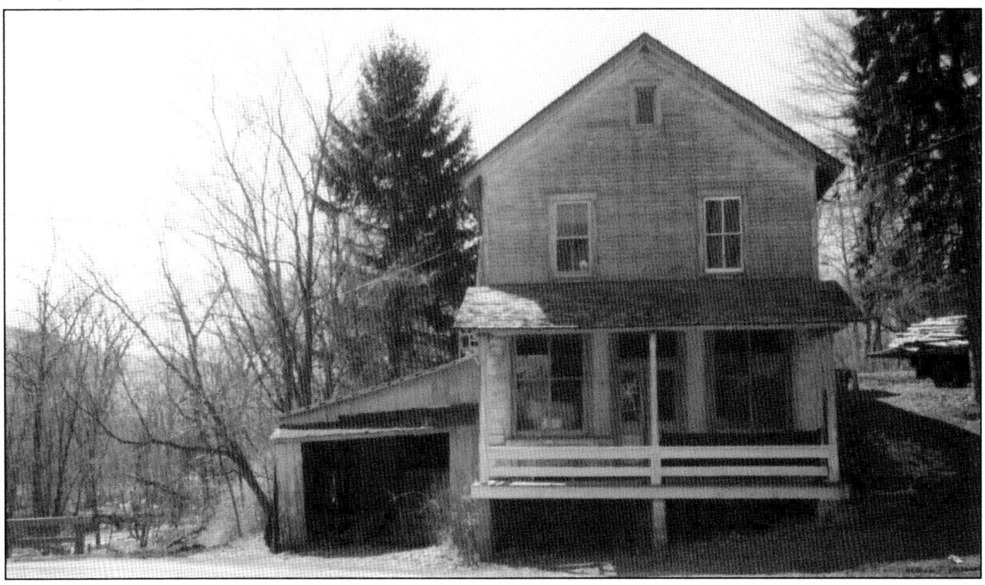

Sugar Valley's second post office was established in Logan Mills on July 1, 1840, with George Rearick appointed postmaster. It closed on April 29, 1939, when Loganton's post office established Rural Route 2. Some storekeepers through the years were William Bartges (1804–1877), Thomas Ilgen (1841–1920), Daniel Moyer (1832–1920), Abraham Nearhood, and Elmer Emig (1865–1950). The store closed some time before 1965.

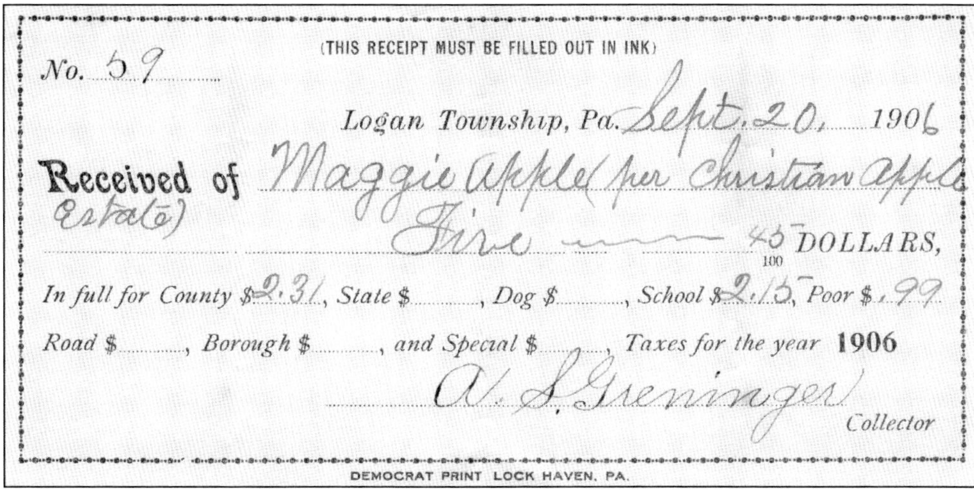

No. 59 (THIS RECEIPT MUST BE FILLED OUT IN INK)

Logan Township, Pa. Sept. 20, 1906

Received of Maggie Apple (per Christian Apple estate)

Five 45/100 DOLLARS,

In full for County $2.31, State $, Dog $, School $2.15, Poor $.99

Road $, Borough $, and Special $, Taxes for the year 1906

A. S. Greninger
Collector

DEMOCRAT PRINT LOCK HAVEN, PA.

Margaret "Maggie" Jane Apple Bierly was the daughter of pioneer Sugar Valley resident Christian Apple (on whose estate she paid taxes, as seen on this 1906 receipt). She and her husband, Adam Bierly, lived in Booneville on the north side of the highway. (Courtesy of Yvonne and Steve Weaver.)

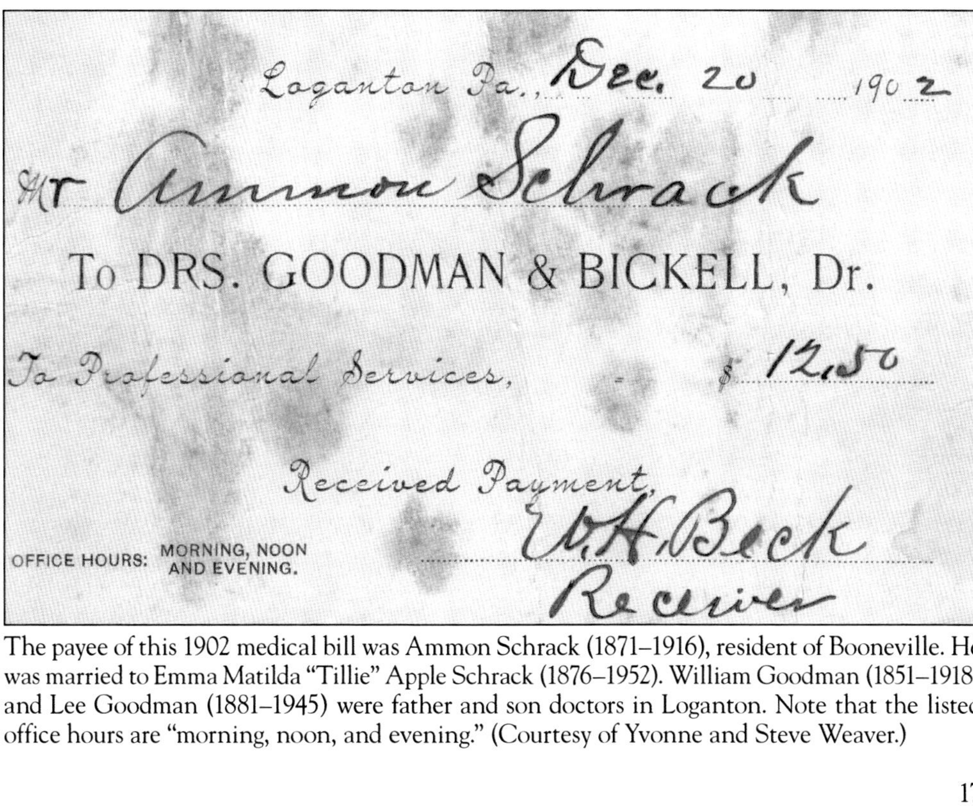

Loganton Pa., Dec. 20 1902

Mr Ammon Schrack

To DRS. GOODMAN & BICKELL, Dr.

To Professional Services, $12.50

Received Payment,
W. H. Beck
Receiver

OFFICE HOURS: MORNING, NOON AND EVENING.

The payee of this 1902 medical bill was Ammon Schrack (1871–1916), resident of Booneville. He was married to Emma Matilda "Tillie" Apple Schrack (1876–1952). William Goodman (1851–1918) and Lee Goodman (1881–1945) were father and son doctors in Loganton. Note that the listed office hours are "morning, noon, and evening." (Courtesy of Yvonne and Steve Weaver.)

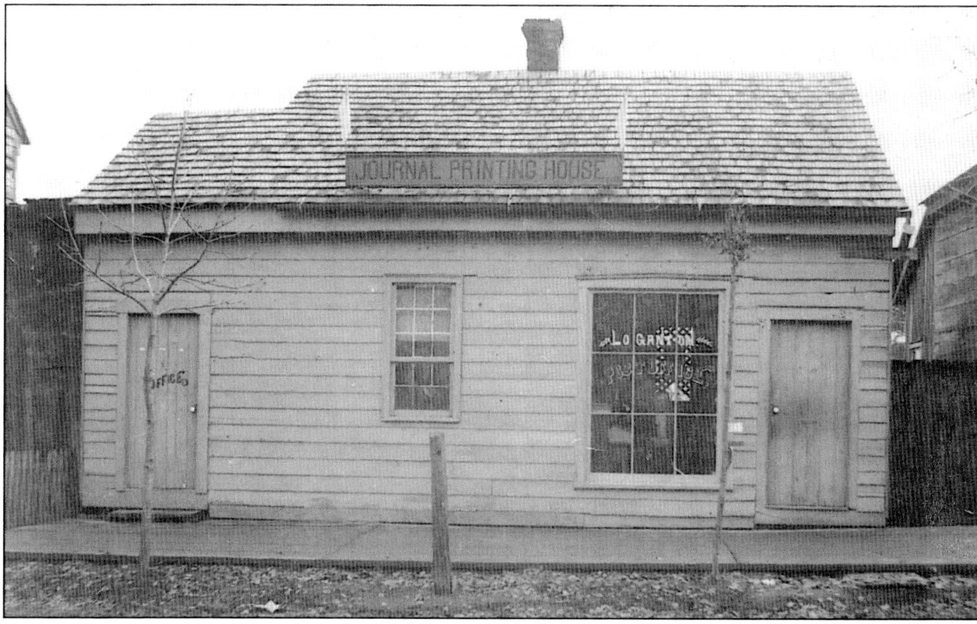

Frederick Solver (1869–1951), well-known Evangelical minister and photographer, took this pre-1900 image of the Journal Printing House in Loganton. Built by Col. Anthony Kleckner, it originally housed the community's first school and also served as the location of Solver's first sermon on August 26, 1894. It became the printing office of the *Sugar Valley Journal* and a US post office. It burned down in the fire on June 19, 1918.

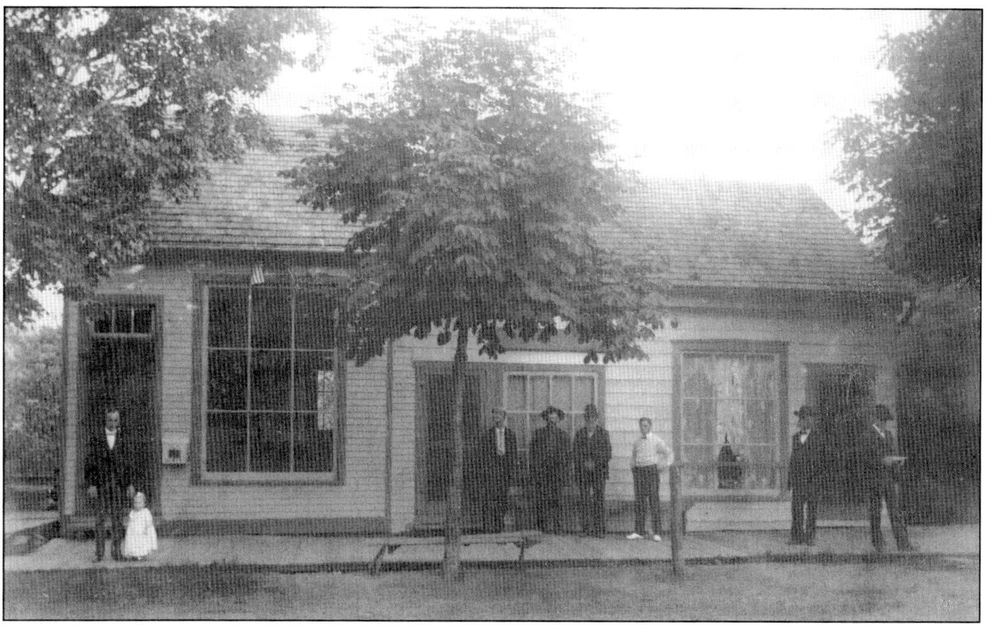

By about 1905, the Journal Printing House departed its location and the building was enlarged to accommodate the Loganton Post Office (on the left), Harry Boob's meat market (in the middle), and Anna Matter's sewing shop (on the right). From left to right are Albert Karstetter (postmaster from 1900 to 1934), his daughter Alieta Karstetter, Harry Boob, McClellan Stark, Michael Jackson "Jack" Keister (part Indian), Earl Matter, Charles Brunner, and Earl Meyer.

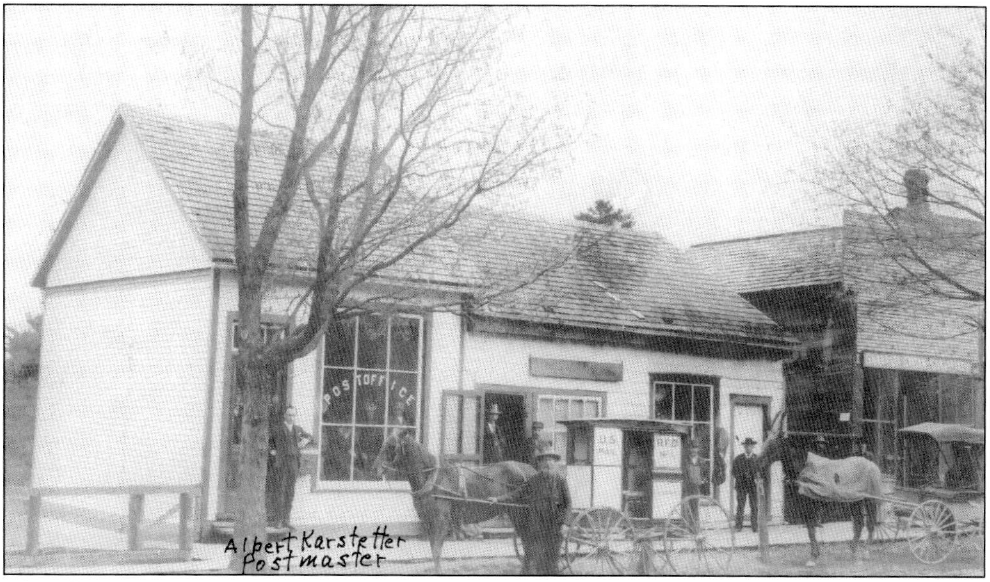

This photograph from about 1910 shows postmaster Albert Karstetter (1875–1936) standing in front of his office doorway and the first Sugar Valley Rural Free Delivery (RFD) mail carrier, Samuel C. Frankenberger (1843–1931), standing in front of his horse and wagon. Boob's butcher shop still occupies the center of the building, but on the far right, the earlier Matter sewing shop has been replaced by the saddler shop of Samuel Snyder.

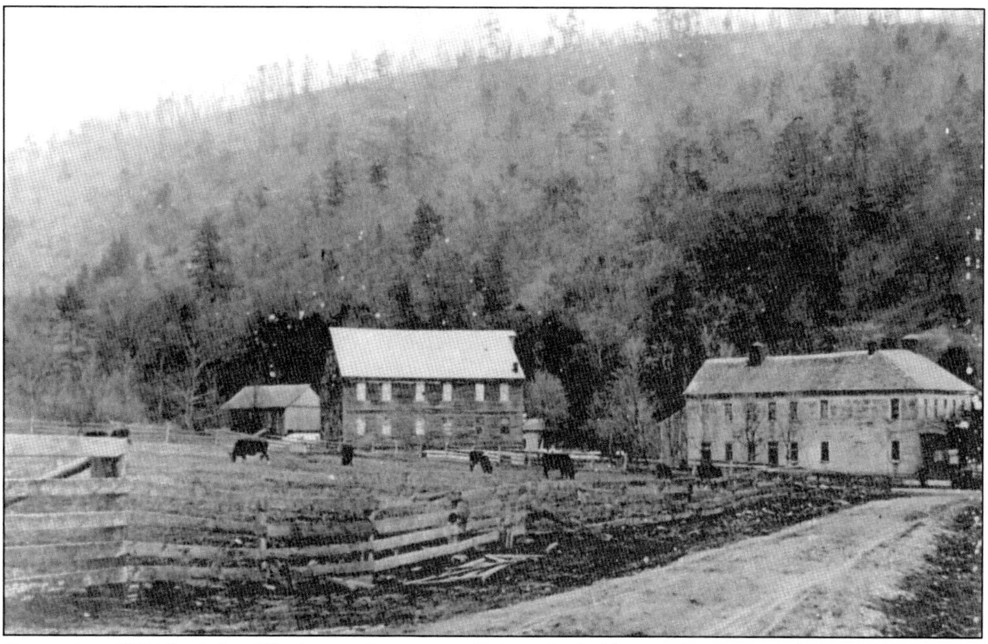

Erected in 1824 by John Kleckner, this gristmill (on the left) was the first in the Loganton area. This pre-1924 photograph also includes the combination homestead and hotel (on the right). After it was purchased in 1877 by John Morris, the mill—a victim of fire in 1890 but then rebuilt—was operated by water and steam. Earl Meyer bought it in 1912, rebuilt it after a second fire in 1923, and passed it on to his son John Meyer in 1939. William Keiser then bought it from the Meyer Estate in 1959, and it burned down yet again in 1961.

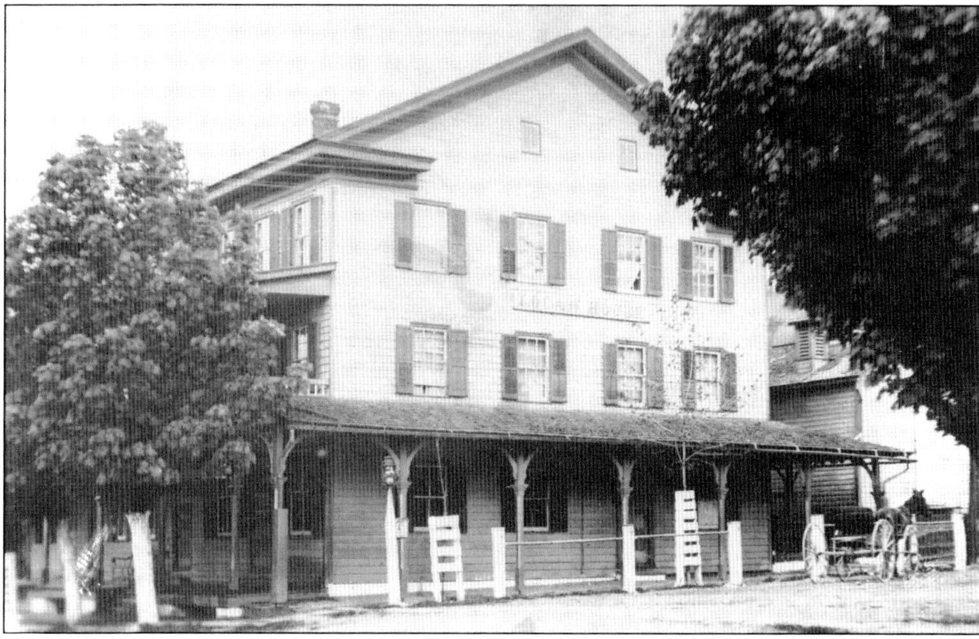

The Logan House was a favorite place for area residents to come for Sunday dinner and was a summer resort destination for people from afar, many reportedly traveling from Philadelphia. Part of the draw was the supposed medicinal properties of the nearby Sulphur Spring's mineral waters. In this 1905 photograph, the horse and buggy of mountaintop resident Samuel Motter, a legend in his own time, is outside the hotel.

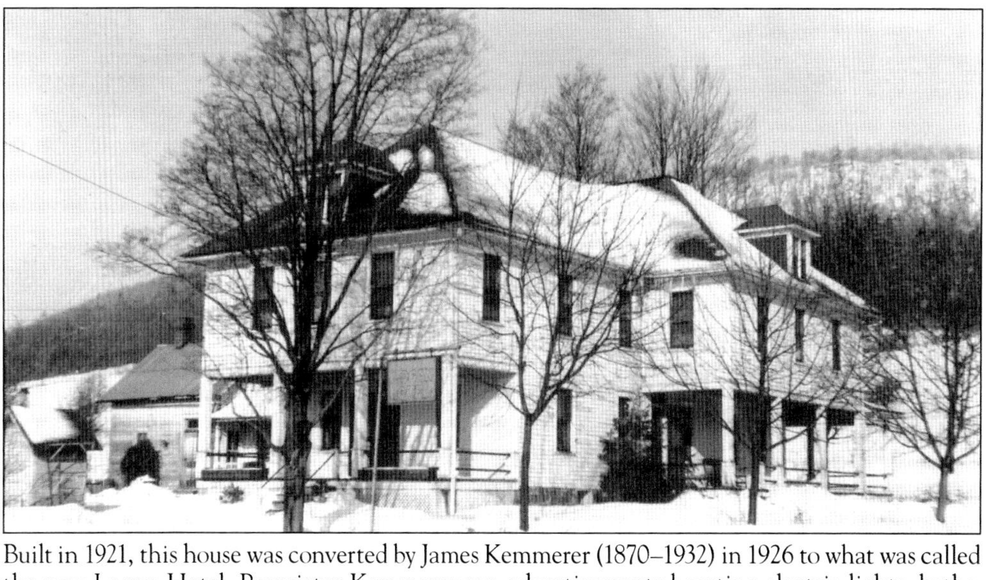

Built in 1921, this house was converted by James Kemmerer (1870–1932) in 1926 to what was called the new Logan Hotel. Proprietor Kemmerer ran advertisements boasting electric lights, baths, and heat, and that it was a "wonderful highland nature spot" where one could "forget business, care, and worry." In 1942, the hotel was purchased by Clinton County as a home for the aged. (Courtesy of Clinton County Historical Society.)

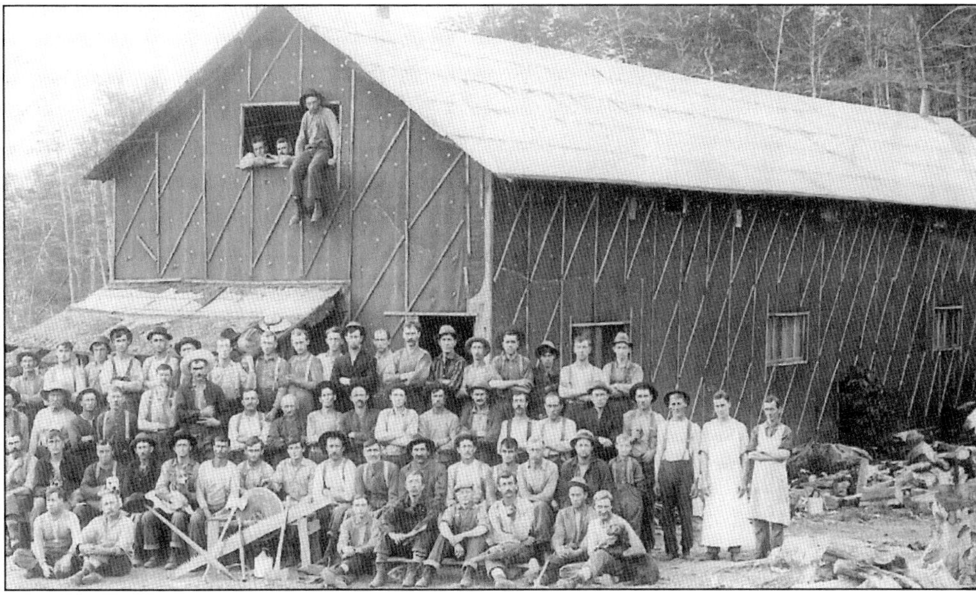

This early-20th-century lumber camp crew is possibly that of Chadwick's Sawmill in Eastville. Note that among the group there are no women. In addition to the men, there are only one young lad and four camp dogs. The tools of their trade are assembled in front.

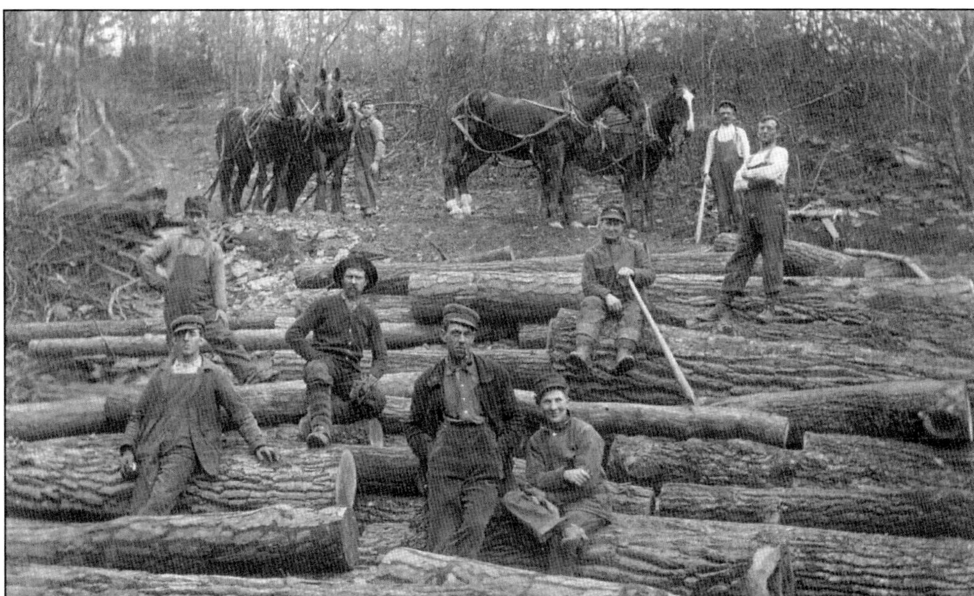

This c. 1913 postcard photograph shows a lumber crew working near Loganton. The man in the middle with the pipe is William Washburn (1877–1949). Note the man seated, holding the wooden pole. This is actually a tool called a peavey, which was very popular with lumbermen. Peaveys had iron points and hooks on their ends and were used for turning, rolling, jabbing, and hooking logs.

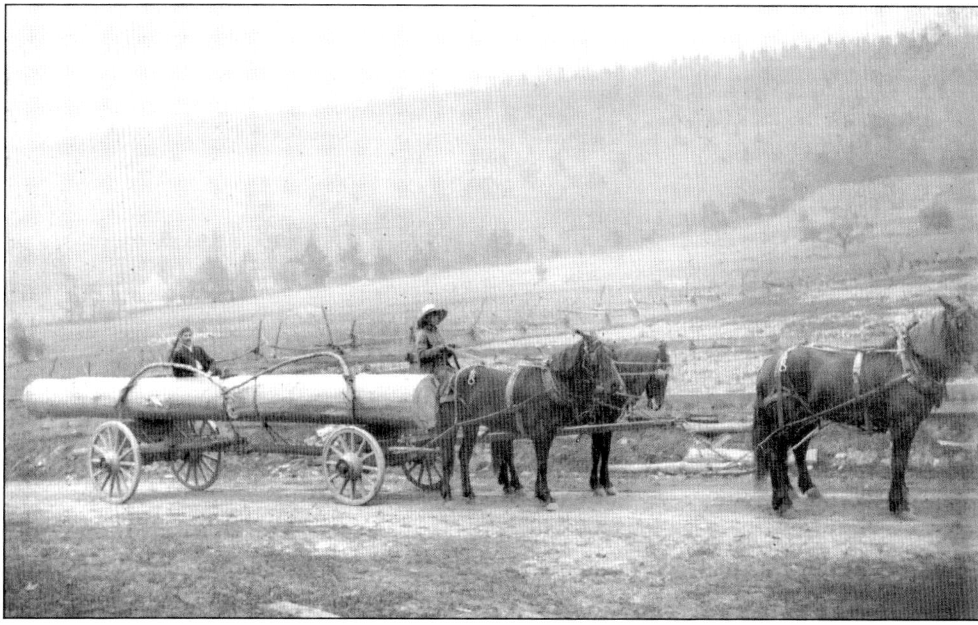

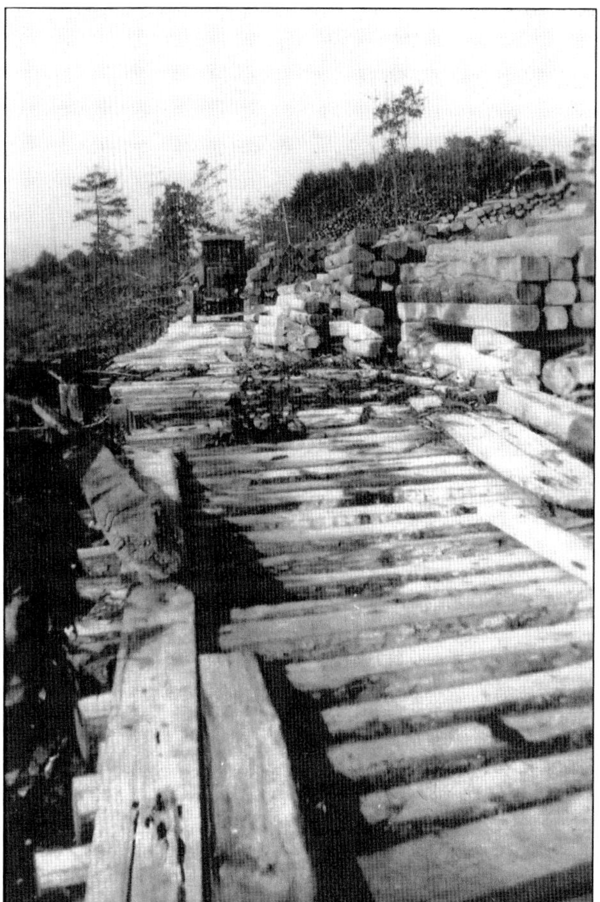

This photograph, from the late 1800s or early 1900s, shows lumber being transported and was taken about one mile west of Greenburr. In the back, with his hat on the log, is Perry Sheats (1863–1936), who played in the Booneville and Greenburr Cornet Bands in his free time. Driving the horses is John Henry "Harry" Strohecker (1878–1902).

This lumber-cutting operation from around 1915 was most likely atop the mountain, about two miles above Carroll, behind the Mount of Blessings Campgrounds near Wagner Gap. The logs were cut for mine props and shipped to Dornsife, Pennsylvania, in Northumberland County, for use in the anthracite coal mines.

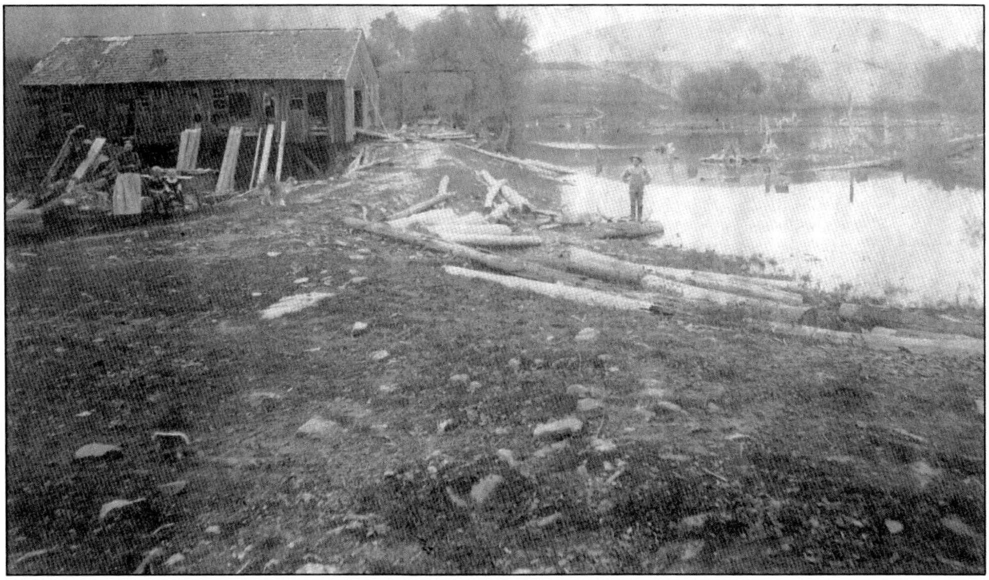

Oscar Horace Harbach owned a farm with a sawmill and pond (a backup of Fishing Creek) between Eastville and Carroll. In this image from the early 1890s, the man standing on the log is Samuel Loman (1860–?). The woman is most likely Sybilla Penticoff (1854–1929), wife of Daniel Penticoff (1852–1915), with their children Roy (1886–1971) and Nellie Penticoff (1891–1953).

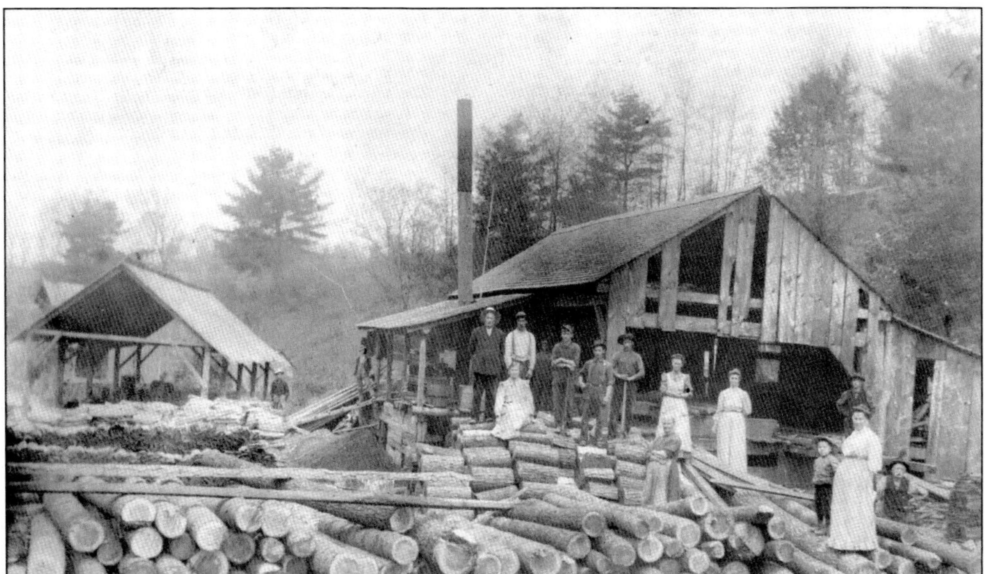

Augustus Geyer (1822–1912) and son Lewis Geyer (1861–1938), most likely the two tall men standing in the rear on the left, pose at Augustus's lumber and shingle mill, located in Hopple's Hollow, north of Loganton on a small tributary to Mill Creek. The heavy growths of pine, oak, chestnut, hickory, maple, and hemlock in Sugar Valley and its surrounding mountains allowed for the operation of up to eight or more sawmills at any one time in the valley.

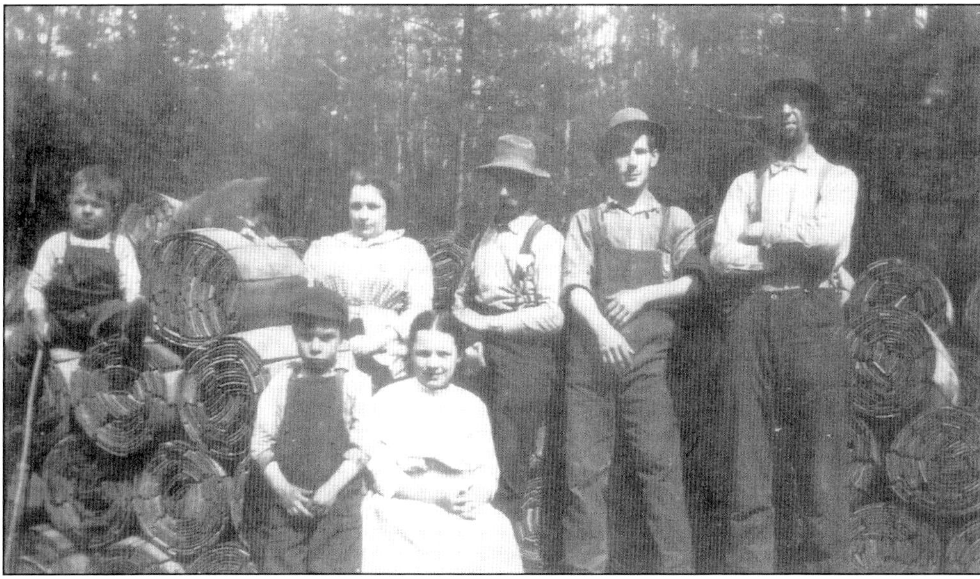

In the early 1910s, Rockey family members stand by a pile of roofing shingles, probably along Rockey Road in Greene Township. While the identities are not certain, the members included in this photograph are most likely, from left to right, son Samuel, either Harry or Charles Rockey, mother Bessie Condo Rockey, daughter Helen Rockey, father David Rockey, and two unidentified men. Both Harry and Charles were killed as children in a powder explosion.

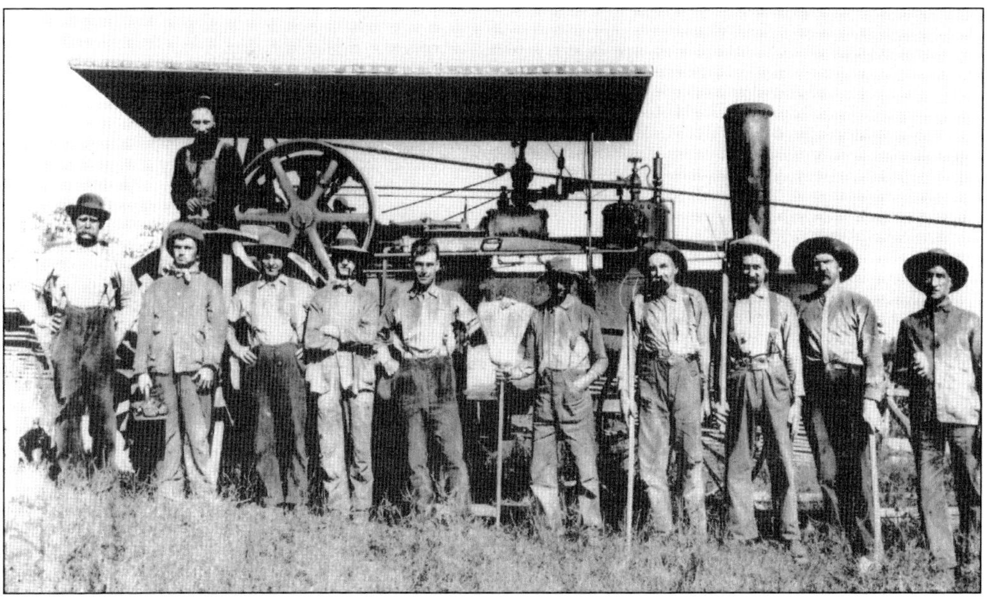

Some time between 1915 and 1920, Daniel Lamey (1871–1957), sitting on his steam engine, and his threshing crew posed for this photograph. Included in this photograph are, from left to right, John Cooper, John Herman, Ernest Cooper, Reuben Motter, Robert Cooper, George Goodman, George Fry, William Knarr, William Washburn, and Harrison Brunner.

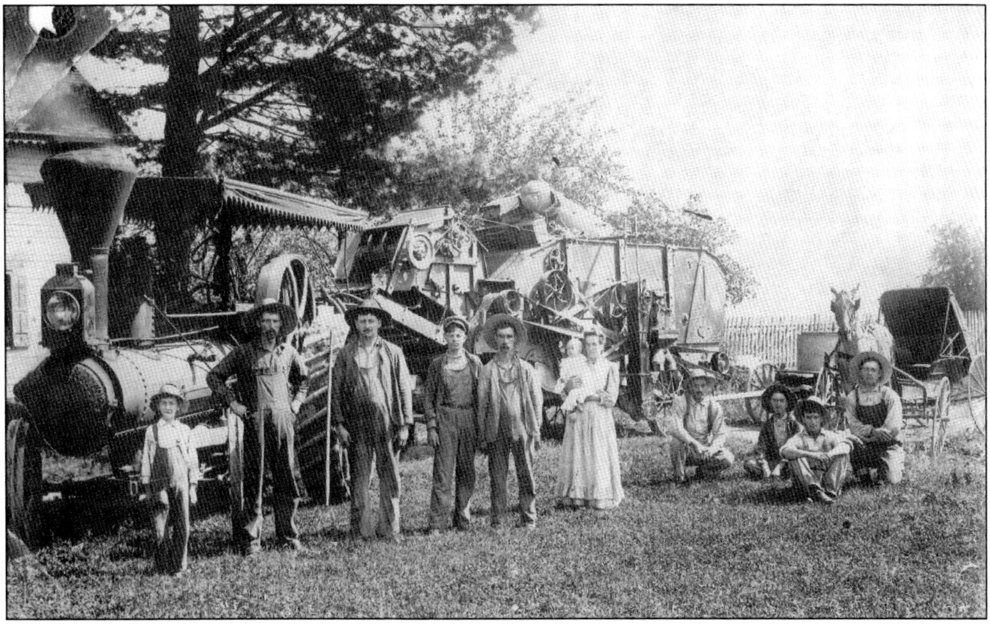

These 11 people are believed to be somewhere on Loganton Mountain near Rosecrans between approximately 1910 and 1920. The steam engine on the left powered the threshing machine (used to harvest grain crops), which is visible behind the woman holding the baby. The youth fourth from the left is Ellery Eisenhower (1894–1981).

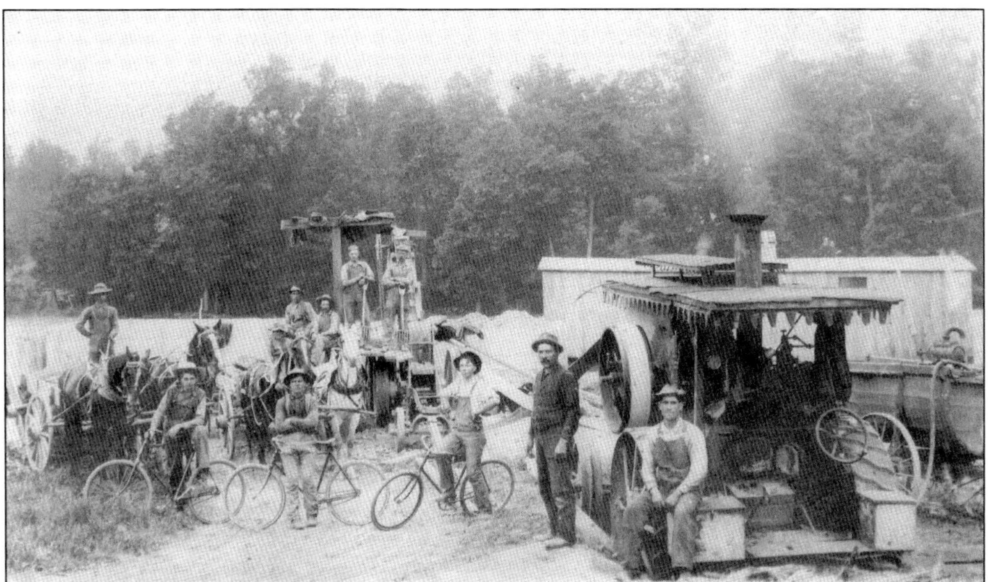

Standing in the middle in dark clothes beside this Huber steam traction engine is William Herman (1856–1928). Seated beside him is his son Silas Herman (1886–1962). Founded in 1874, the Edward Huber Manufacturing Company of Marion, Ohio, began producing affordable steam traction engines in 1880 for the nation's grateful farmers.

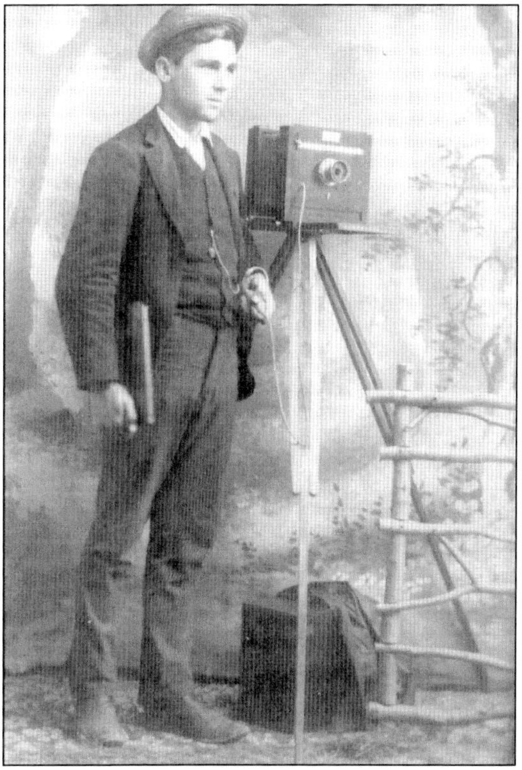

Frederick Solver (1869–1951), captured in this image in 1890, was a photographer (known for producing lantern slides), evangelical minister, artist, harpist, and mandolin player. He was married to Frances Emert in 1898 in Rosecrans. His second wife was Laura Hixson. During the latter part of his life, Solver preached in Allentown, Pennsylvania, and he is buried in that community's Greenwood Cemetery.

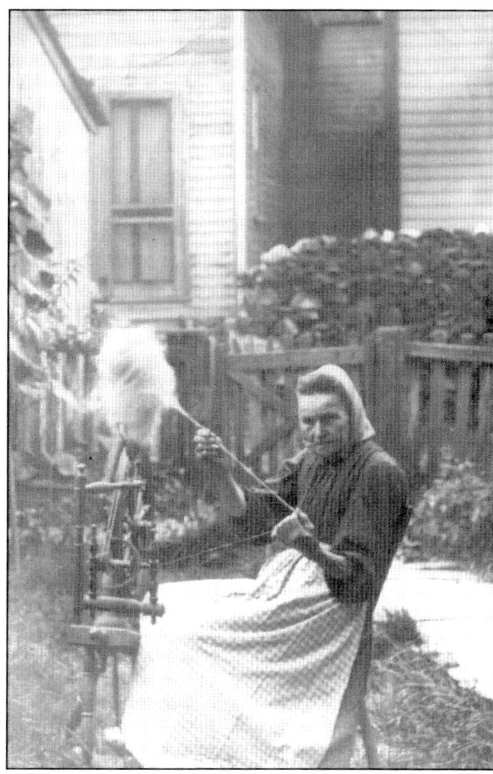

Christina (née Wolfe) Wolf (1837–1922), whose stepfather was Peter Karstetter, was married to Henry Wolf (1832–1905). They lived in Booneville. In this image, she is spinning yarn from flax. Her husband, with Samuel Boone, started a general store in Booneville shortly after the village was laid out in 1866. The store served the community for almost a century. (Courtesy of Christine Brungard.)

Two

Recording Valley Scenes

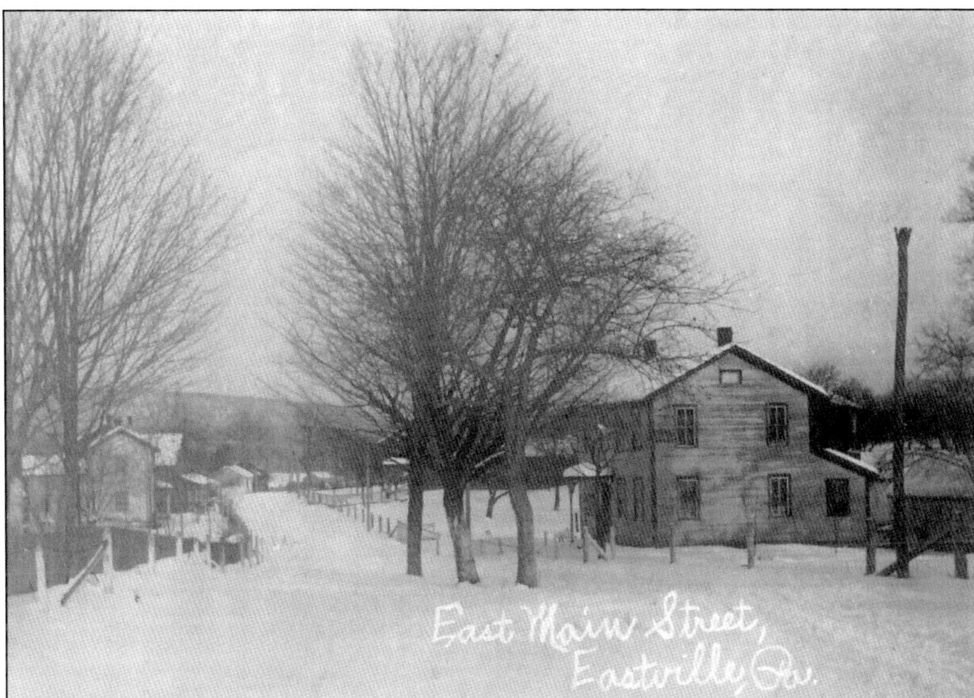

In the early 1900s, East Main Street in Eastville featured the Edgar Schwenk (1856–1935) house (on the right), the Charles Brungard (1888–1950) house and general merchandise store (first on the left), and David Geisewite's (1871–1942) home and blacksmith shop (third set of buildings on the left).

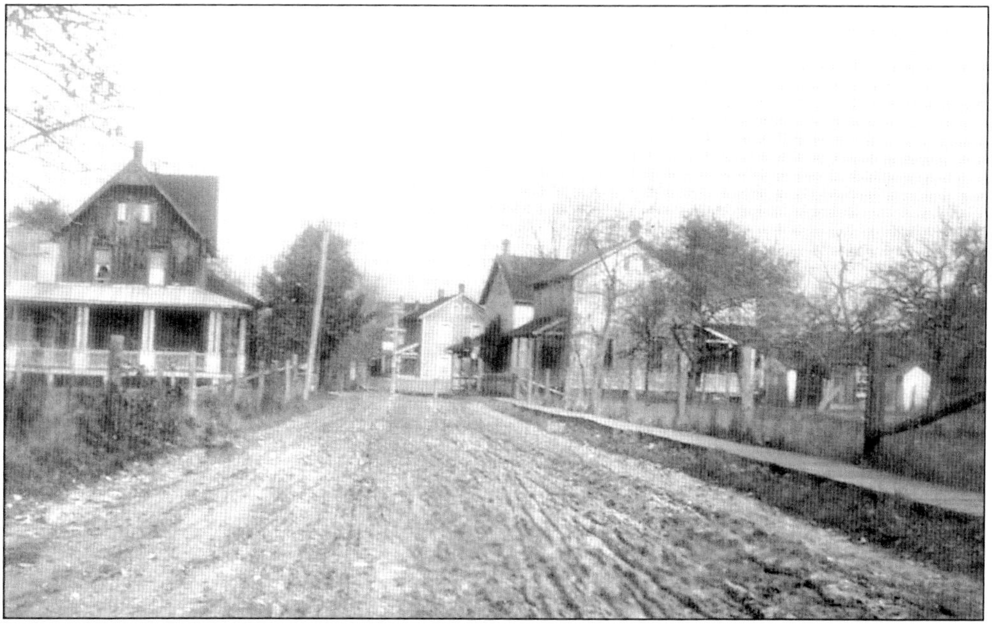

In the 1920s and early 1930s, Greenburr's main north-south street was made of dirt, but the village boasted a raised wooden sidewalk. The first large house on the far right belonged to Clyde Renninger (1884–1969). Moving down the street, the next building was Harvey Lamey's general store, and the third structure was Lamey's house (later belonging to his son Floyd).

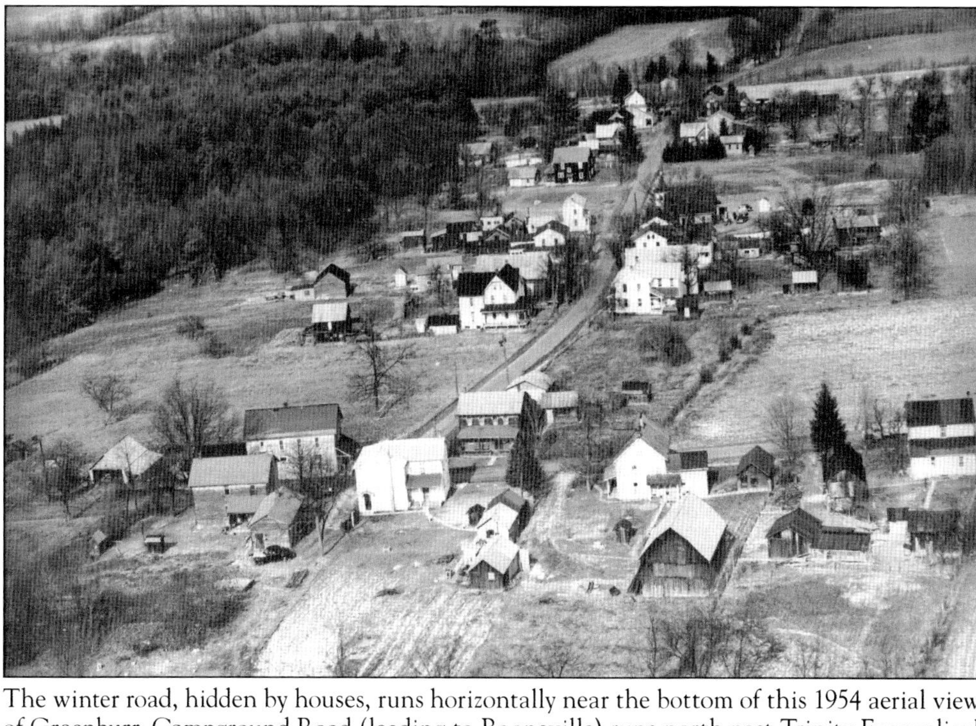

The winter road, hidden by houses, runs horizontally near the bottom of this 1954 aerial view of Greenburr. Campground Road (leading to Booneville) runs north past Trinity Evangelical United Brethren Church, the steeple of which is visible in this image. The woods on the left hide Fishing Creek.

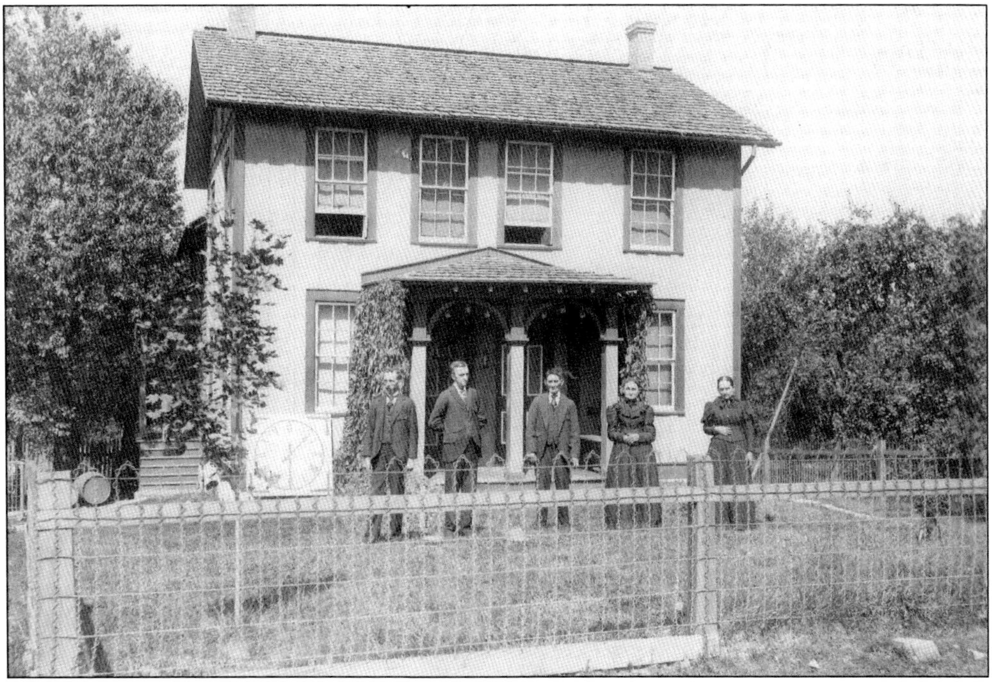

Standing in the front yard of the Lamey's Greenburr home in 1896 are, from left to right, Harvey Lamey (1869–1953), Frank Lamey (1874–1897), Michael Lamey (1829–1899), Anna Bartges Lamey (1835–1917), and Dina Lamey Emig (1867–1942).

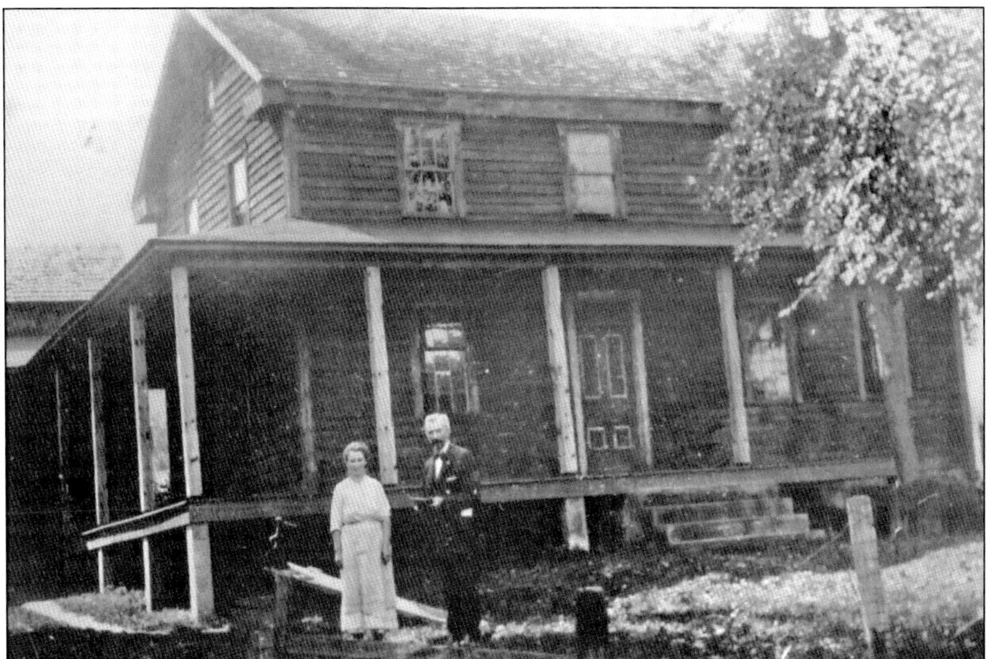

Laura Tyson (1879–1968) was the daughter of Jacob and Ellen Renninger. Her husband, Daniel Tyson (1887–1953), was a teacher and the son of Benjamin and Lovina Tyson. The Tysons stand in the front yard of their home at the west end of Greenburr on the winter road.

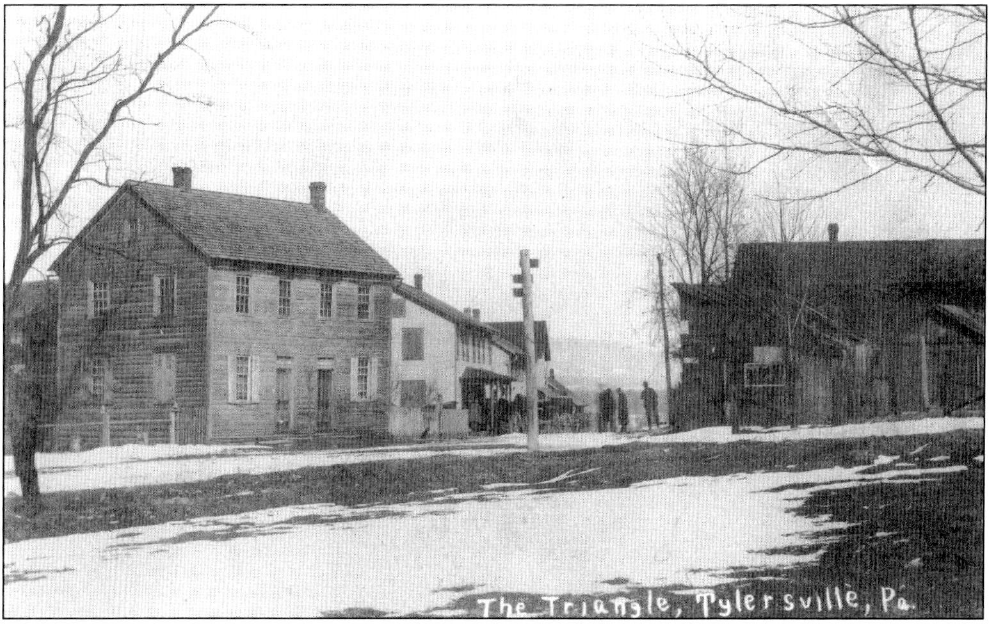

With their horses and wagons, people congregate in front of the site of Alexander Greninger's General Store in Tylersville. The photograph may actually have been taken when the store was still the William Harter Store, before Greninger purchased it in 1908. This area of the village was called "the Triangle" because Narrows Road (west to Lamar), Old Hill Road, and West Valley Road (the summer road) intersected there.

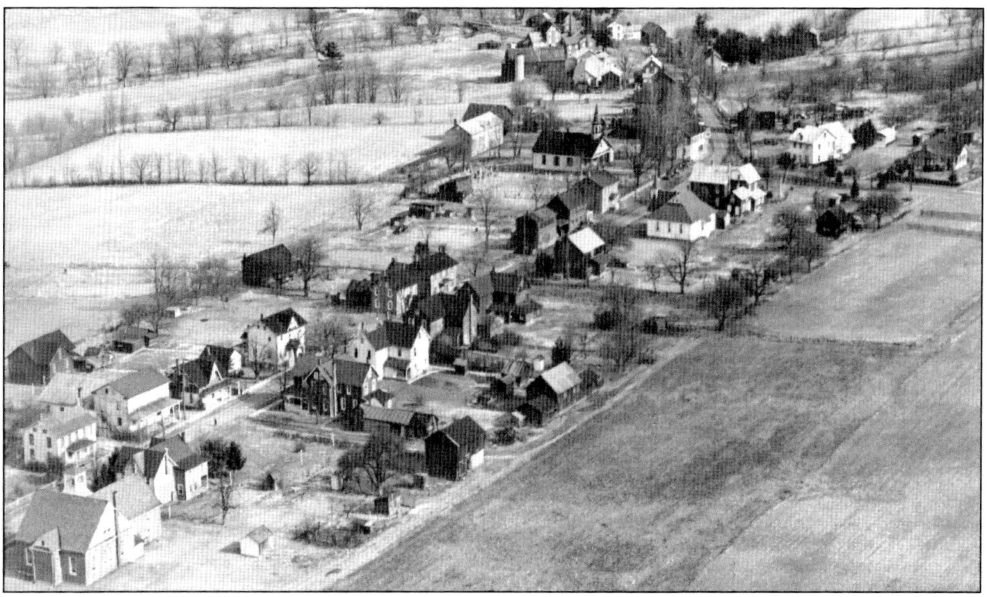

This 1960s aerial view of Tylersville shows the village when three churches still stood there. In the lower left corner is St. John's United Church of Christ, erected in 1906 and still holding services today. Farther up Narrows Road on the same side of the street is the steepled Bethel United Evangelical Church, built in 1894, closed in 1964, and finally razed in the early 1980s. Across from this is the steepled German Reformed and Lutheran Church, erected in 1841, closed in 1964, and subsequently razed.

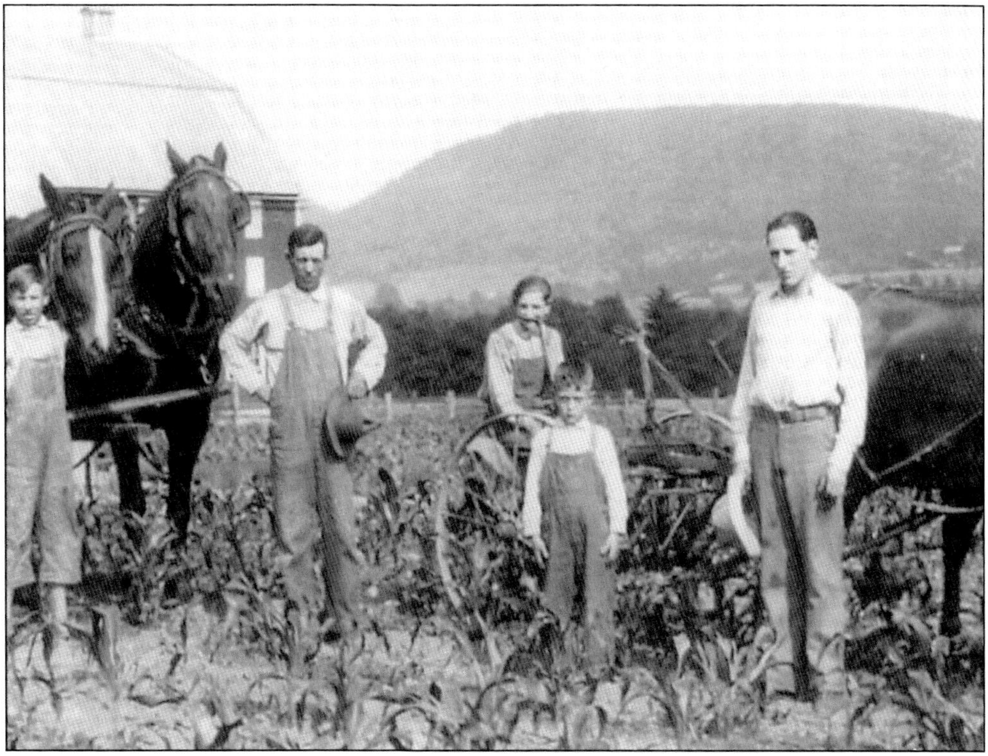

Standing in the cornfield of the Grieb family's Tylersville-area farm around 1920 are, from left to right, son Larue, father George, son Richard, and two unidentified people (on the cultivator and on the far right). Since about the 1820s, generations of Griebs owned what became a large dairy and turkey farm. After owning the farm for nearly 150 years, the Grieb family sold it to an Amish family around 1970. (Courtesy of Kenneth and Peggy Karstetter.)

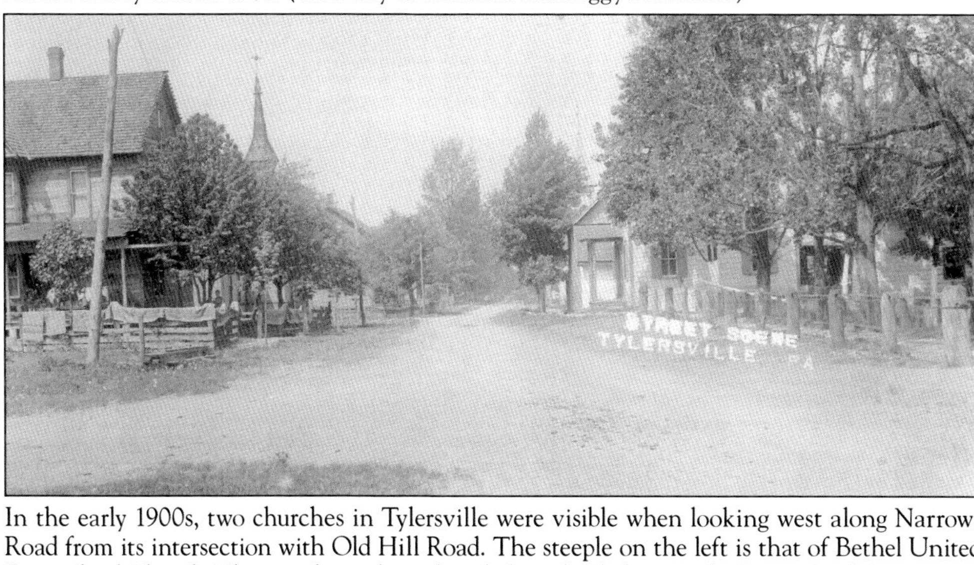

In the early 1900s, two churches in Tylersville were visible when looking west along Narrows Road from its intersection with Old Hill Road. The steeple on the left is that of Bethel United Evangelical Church. The steeple on the right is believed to belong to the Evangelical Association Methodist Church, which was erected in 1871 and dismantled in 1936 by F. Miller, who used the materials to build a private residence.

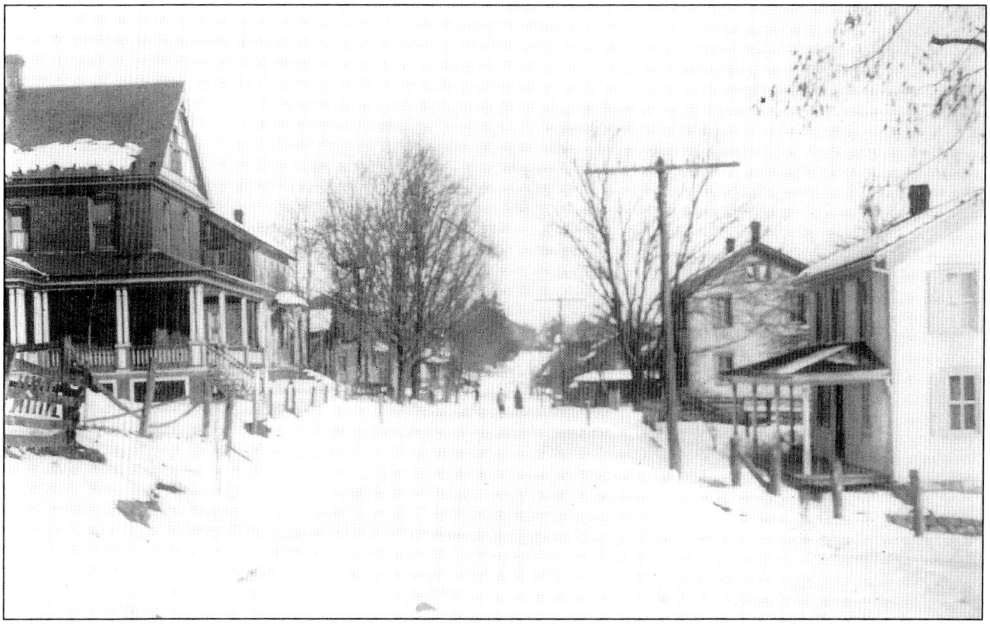

This view looks east down the main street (the summer road, now Route 880) of Booneville on a winter day long ago. Booneville was laid out in 1866, and on May 18, 1870, it became a postal village. Clinton County historian D.S. Maynard wrote that by 1875, Booneville had become "a most desirable place of residence" and that a number of retired farmers had "built fine houses there in which to spend their days." (Courtesy of John and Verna Carey.)

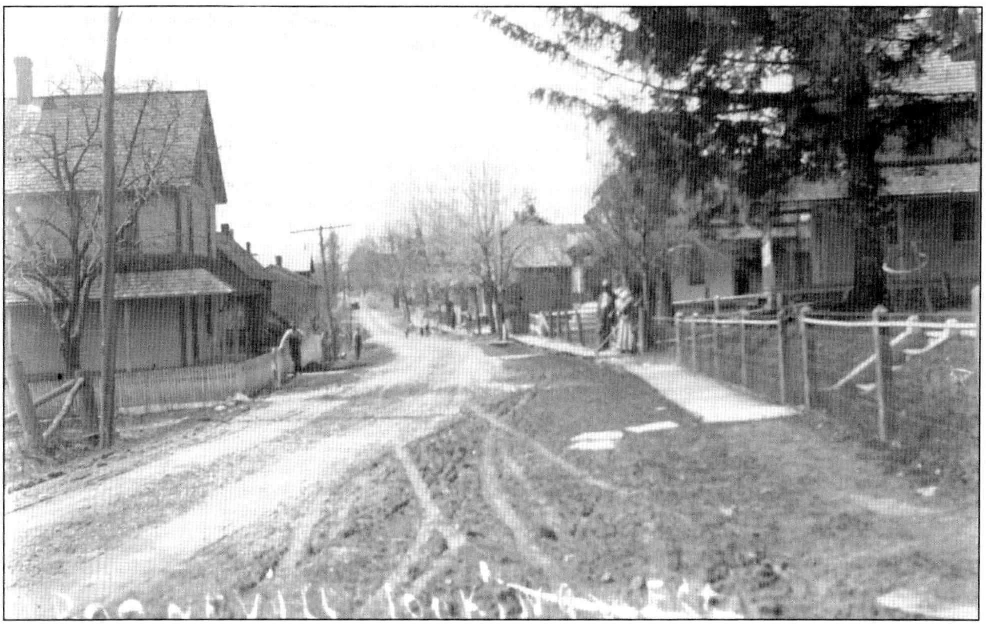

This view was shot looking west down Booneville's main street in the 1920s. During that decade, Booneville resident Samuel Ilgen lit up his community—as well as Loganton, Greenburr, and Tylersville—with an electric power plant that he built near his home. According to Ilgen, his plant "generated 20 kilovolt amperes and produced alternating current at a pressure of 2,300 volts." He also said, "Many a pole I helped put in place. It was all hard work, and I was aided by my wife."

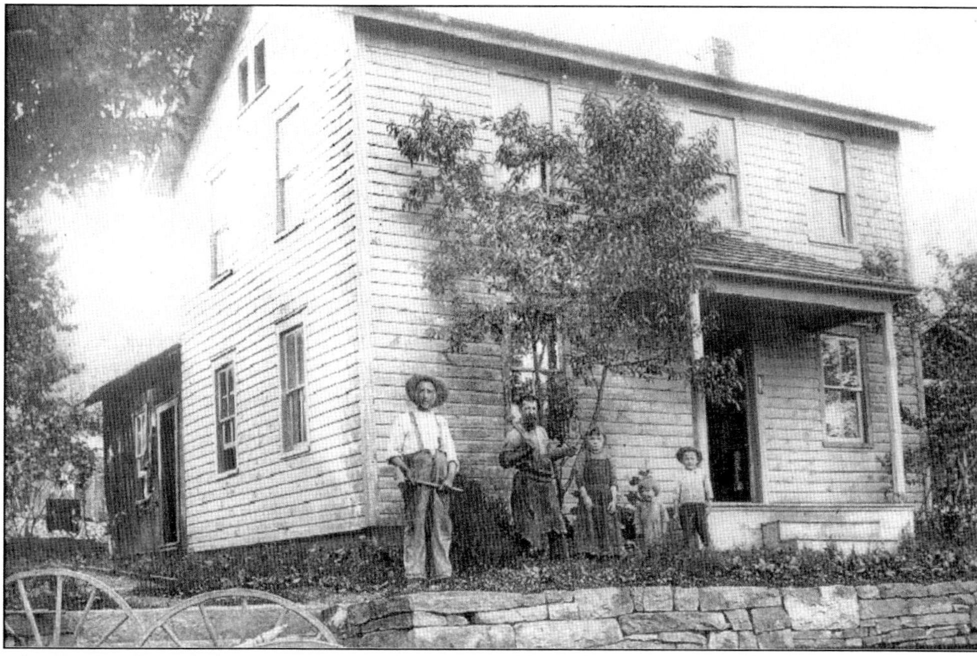

The Emanuel Bierly home (with blacksmith shop in the back) was photographed around 1900. It was located approximately in the center of Booneville, on the north side of the main street through the village. From left to right are Henry Wolf (1832–1905), Emanuel Bierly (1851–1940), Mary Bierly (1883–1963), Carrie Bierly (1890–1963), and Eurie Bierly (1886–1974). (Courtesy of Christine Brungard.)

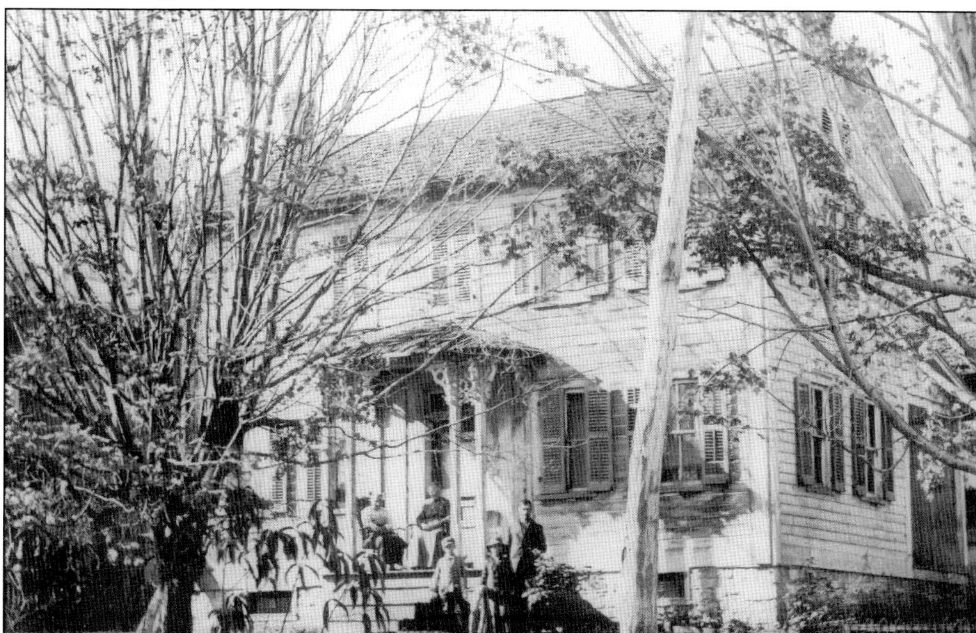

Believed to be the home of Adam Bierly (1876–1951) and his wife, Margaret "Maggie" Apple Bierly (1867–1950), this beautiful, two-story structure was located on the north side of the main street through Booneville.

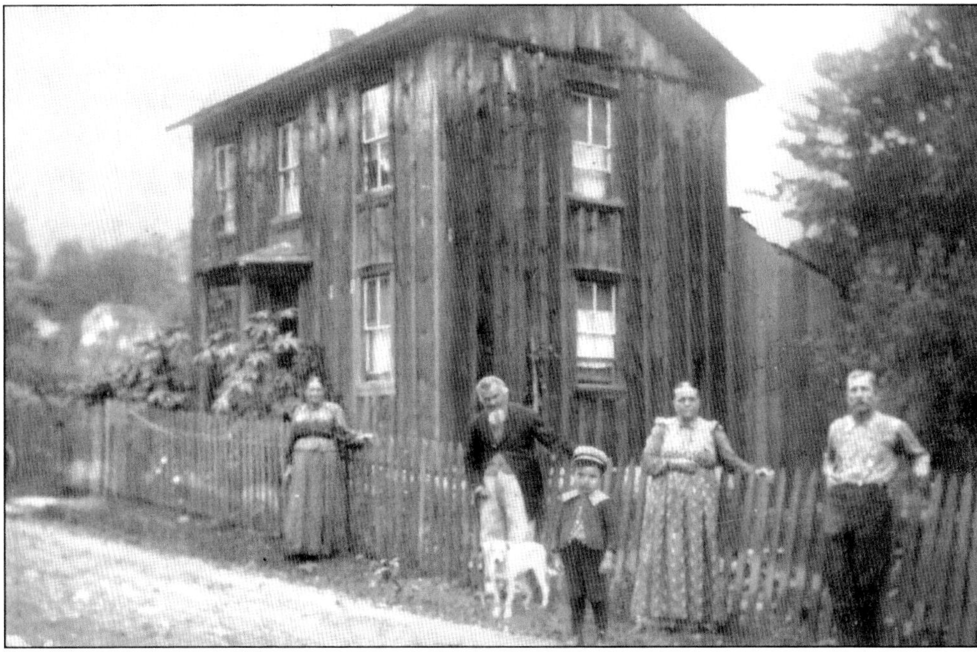

At the north end of Greenburr, on the east side of the road between that village and Booneville, was the home of Isaac Beck, photographed in 1898. Included in this image are, from left to right, daughter Salome Beck Kerstetter (1845–1898); Isaac Beck (1815–1900), who was married to Rachel Sheats; Ralph Welshans (1896–1966); most likely Beck's daughter Elizabeth Beck Kahl Bressler (1842–1908); and Joseph Herb (1848–1923), a teacher and the grandfather of Ralph Welshans.

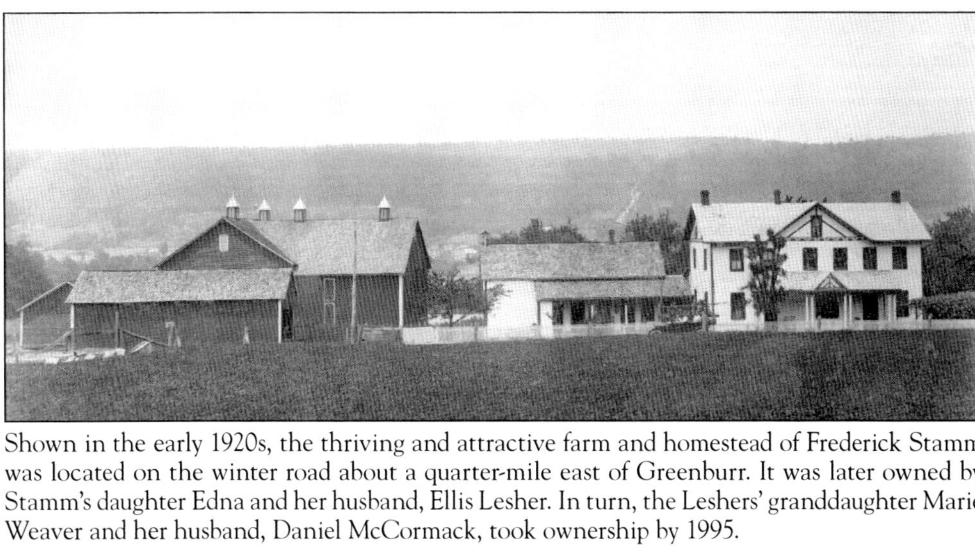

Shown in the early 1920s, the thriving and attractive farm and homestead of Frederick Stamm was located on the winter road about a quarter-mile east of Greenburr. It was later owned by Stamm's daughter Edna and her husband, Ellis Lesher. In turn, the Leshers' granddaughter Marie Weaver and her husband, Daniel McCormack, took ownership by 1995.

Sarah Eckel (1867–1939) married Charles "Jesse" Matter (1871–1945) in 1892, and they lived in this Rosecrans farmhouse (pictured, with Sarah in front). Owners that came after the Matters included Shuman Furst, Walter Wagner, Ralph Confer, and Earl Fisher. In the early 1960s, Fisher dismantled the house when the property was purchased by the city of Lock Haven for a water storage reservoir.

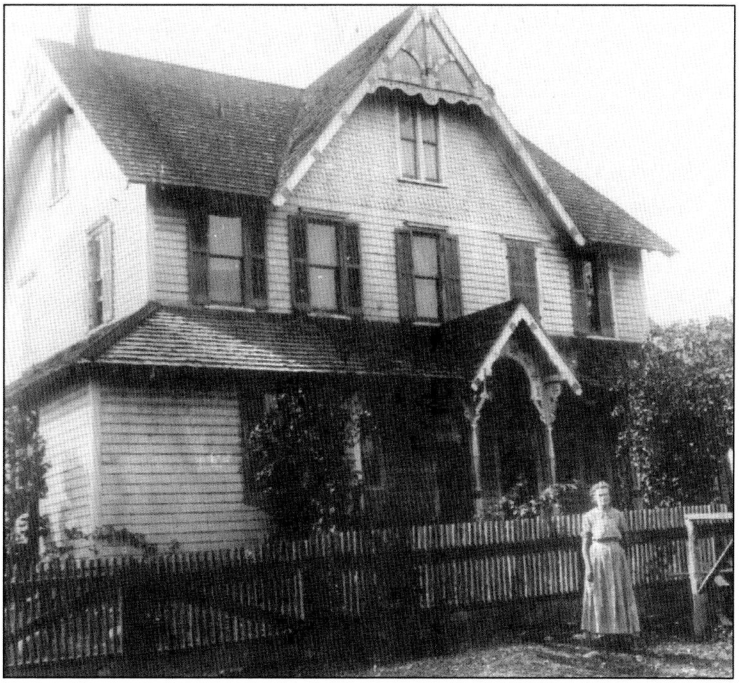

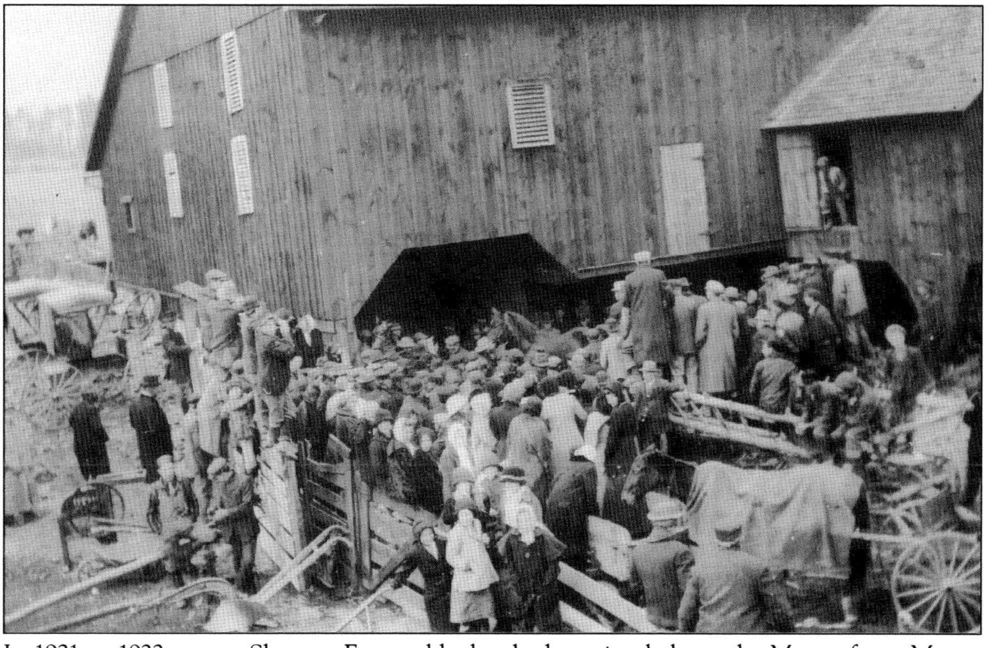

In 1921 or 1922, owner Shuman Furst sold what had previously been the Matter farm. Matter participated in the sale, as he still owned the livestock. At the headwaters of McElhattan Run, the property is now underwater, the result of a dam built there in 1964 to create a reservoir for the city of Lock Haven's water supply.

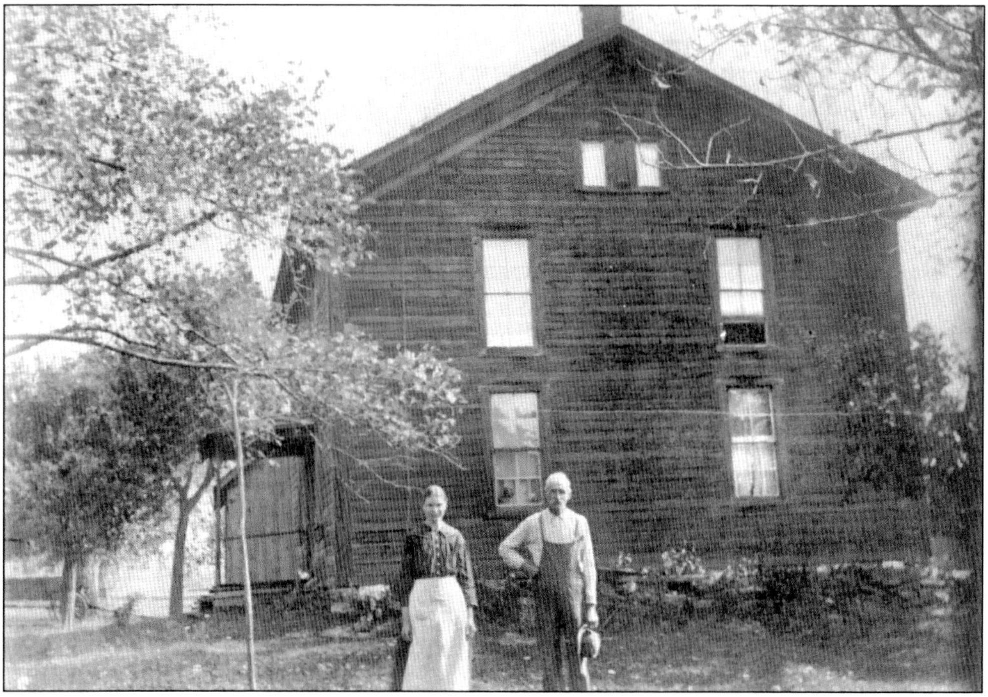

Mary Greninger (1890–1968) and her husband (whom she married in 1912), William Auman (1855–1933), were photographed some time after 1913 in front of their Rosecrans Long Run Road home, which was later occupied by Robert Weaver (1897–1976). Auman was a brick and stonemason, previously married to Elizabeth Bierly (1857–1904). After Auman's death, Mary wed Lawrence Lowry (1890–1973).

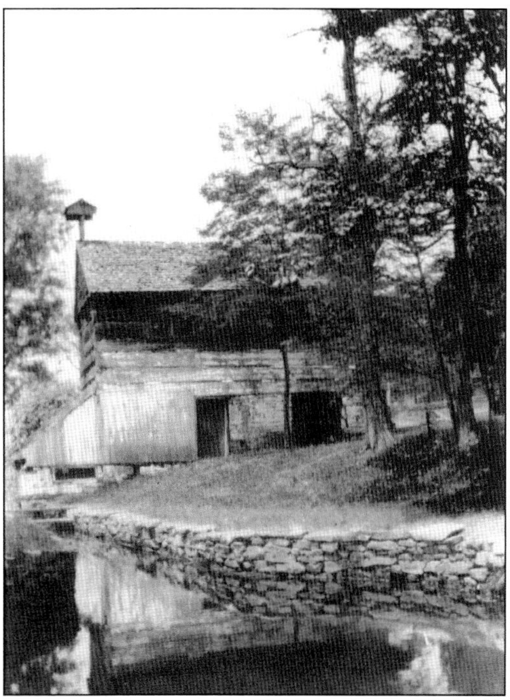

Just off the millrace waters of Zellers' Spring and immediately south of the farmhouse was this springhouse, shown between 1920 and 1925. Through the years and in chronological order, this property was the Snook farm, Zellers farm, Kemmerer farm, Sweeley farm, and finally, an Amish farm. According to historian Col. Henry Shoemaker, during an argument in 1771 with Peter Pence over Jura McEvoy (a white woman), Indian chief James Logan was shot through the hip by Pence, fell into the spring, and was crippled for the rest of his life.

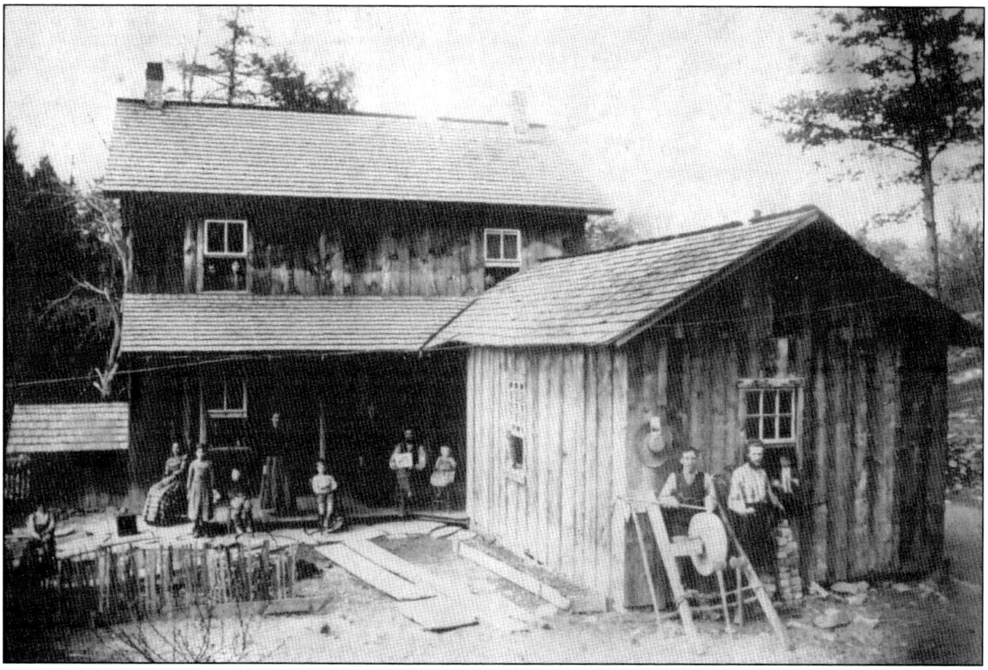

David Wolfe (1848–1918) built this home near Greenburr. He married Phoebe Greninger (1848–1921) in 1869, and she bore five sons and four daughters. Although the individuals in this c. 1870s image are unidentified, most are likely members of the large Wolfe family. Wolfe had a shingle sawmill in Wolfe's Gap that he ran with his brother William. Newton Walizer (1877–1973) subsequently lived in the house.

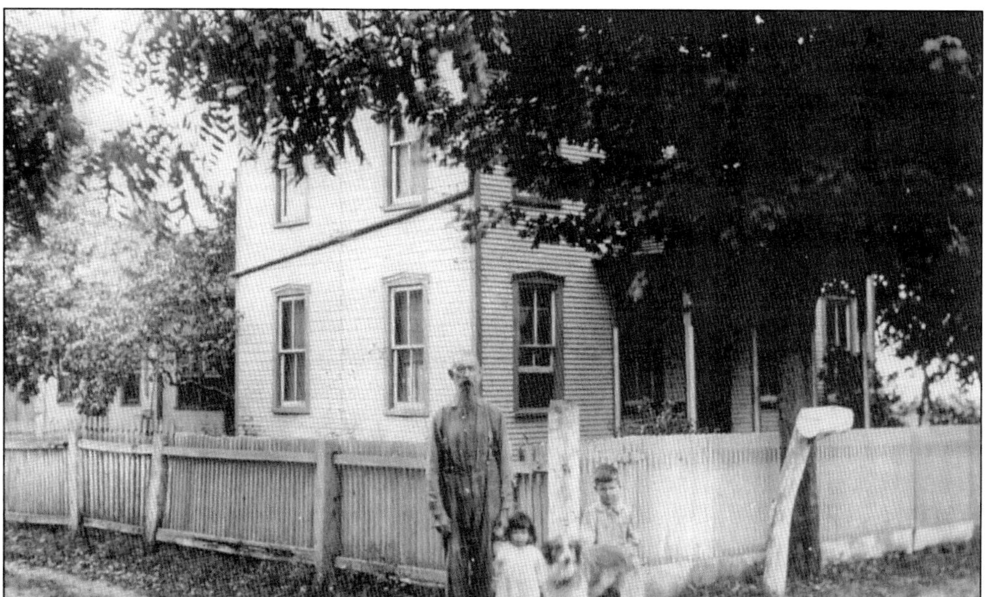

Samuel C. Frankenberger stands with his great-grandchildren Lucille and James Rockey in front of the home of his granddaughter Esther Frankenberger Rockey, who was married to Walter Rockey Sr. The Rockeys' house was about 1.5 miles east of Loganton, on the south side of the summer road.

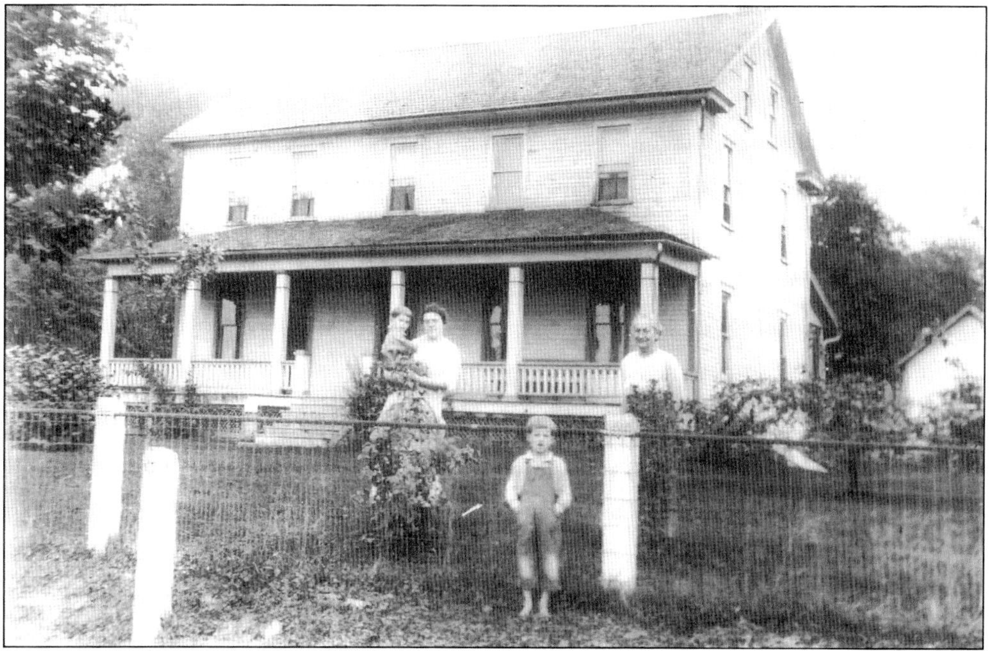

This farmhouse stood just east of Loganton. It burned to the ground on June 19, 1942, along with seven other buildings on the farm. The farmlands were later owned by Forrest Lamey Sr. and were then sold and split in the 1970s between Amish farmers and Lamey relatives (this area is now known as Lameytown). In this photograph from around 1919 are, from left to right, Bruce, Mabel, John W., and Mary Frankenberger.

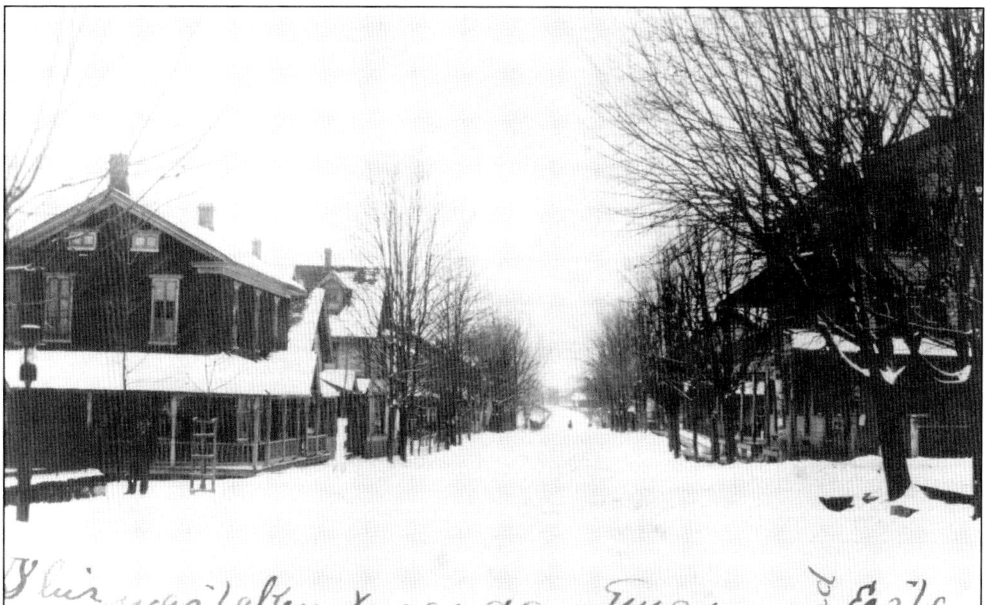

Taken on Christmas Day 1908, this view looking west down Loganton's snow-filled main street includes the Logan House on the right and the Dr. Goodman residence on the left. By this time, Loganton had become the commercial center of Sugar Valley, with the Loganton National Bank to open in the spring of the following year on March 1, 1909.

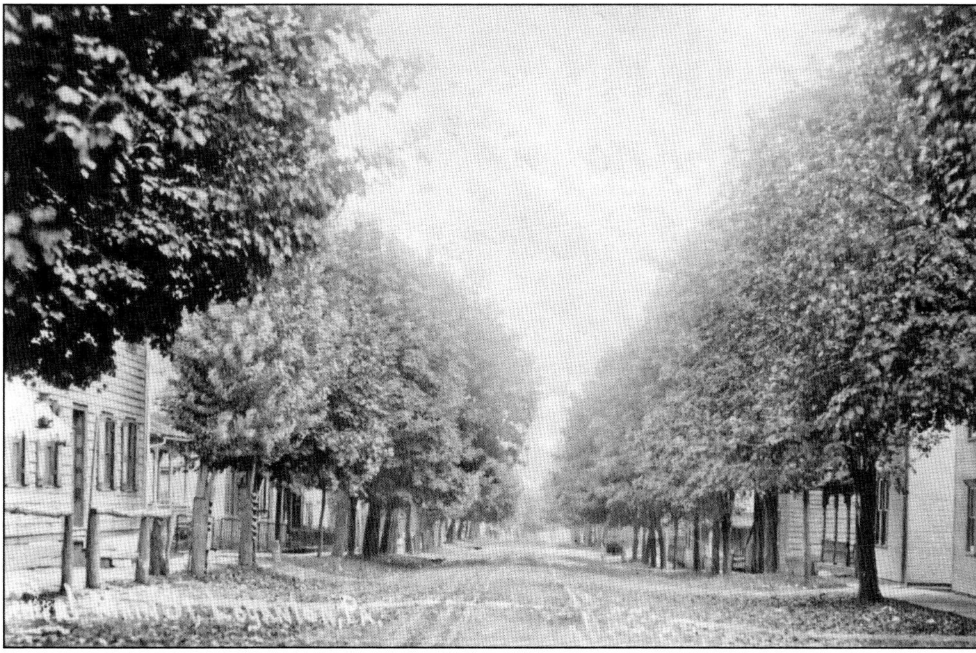

This photograph, taken in the spring of 1908, was shot in front of John Brown's store, looking east down Loganton's beautiful, tree-lined main street. Loganton was flourishing with the White Deer & Loganton Railway servicing the community, the post office expanding to offer RFD and parcel post service, and plans set to establish a two-year high school in the borough, which became a reality in 1910.

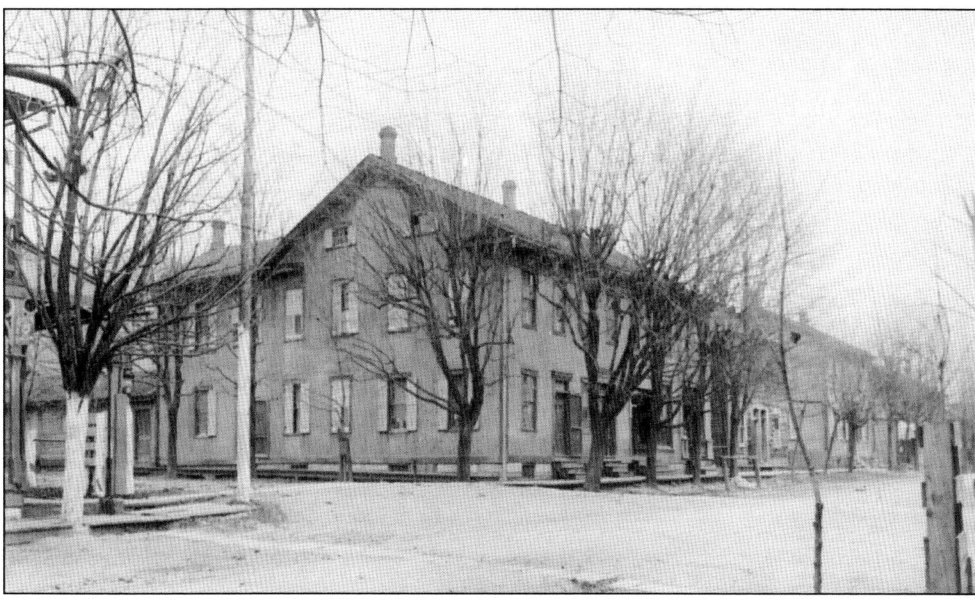

The great fire that devastated much of Loganton on June 19, 1918, broke out in the Clair Kemmerer Bakery housed in the E.M. DeLong building in the center of this photograph. Possibly started by a defective flue or a chimney spark, the fire jumped across Mill Street to the Logan House (the eastern ends of its first- and second-story porches are visible). Both structures were completely destroyed.

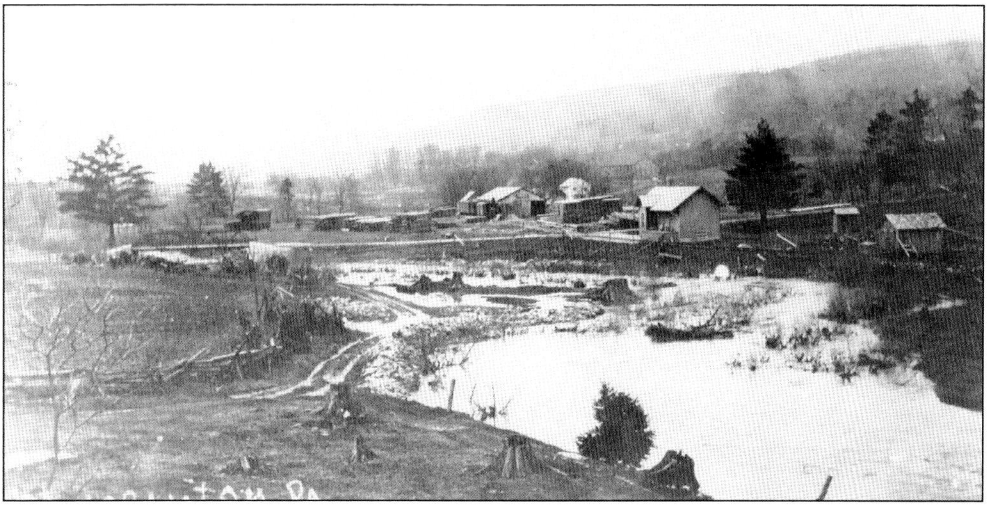

This 1908 image shows the Loganton Depot (the building with the loading platform) of the White Deer & Loganton Railway. The station was located just off South Mill Street, across this road from the sawmill complex (note all the piled lumber), and just north of the bridge that can be seen crossing over Fishing Creek. (Courtesy of Ralph Embick.)

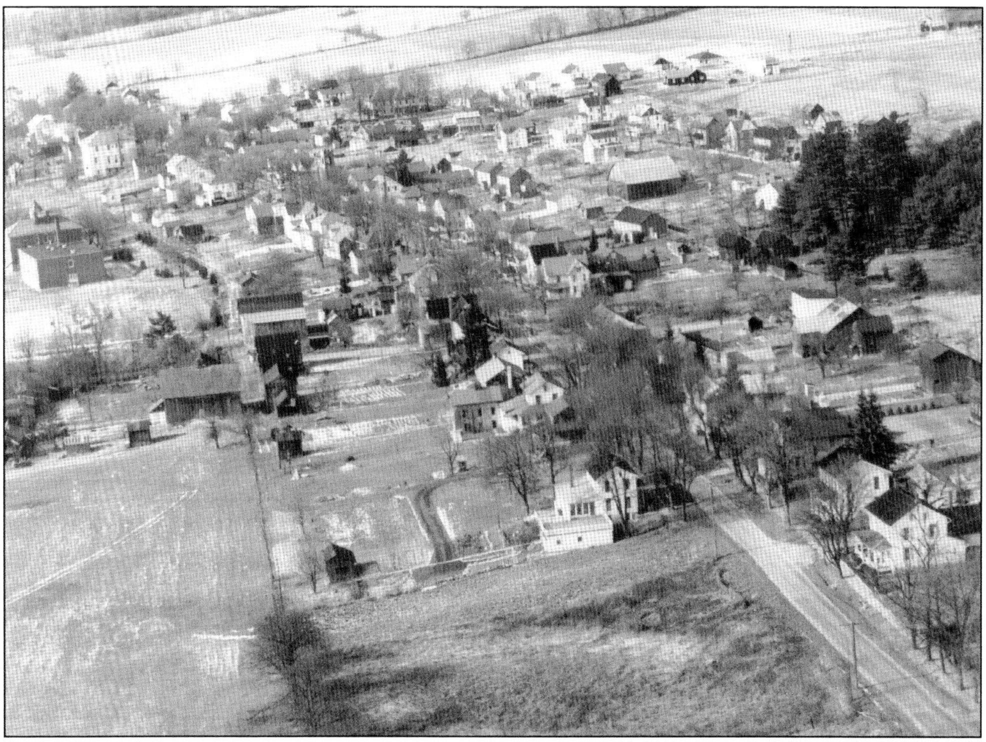

In this aerial view of Loganton, looking from east to west, Loganton High School (upper left, with the bell tower) can be seen with its first addition—the flat-roofed rectangular building with a chimney that was completed on October 7, 1939—but not its second addition, which included room for the primary grades and was completed on September 6, 1955. Therefore, it is possible to date this image to between 1939 and 1955. Valley Road (the summer road), visible coming from the lower right corner of this image, is Loganton's main street.

Three

Worshipping the Lord

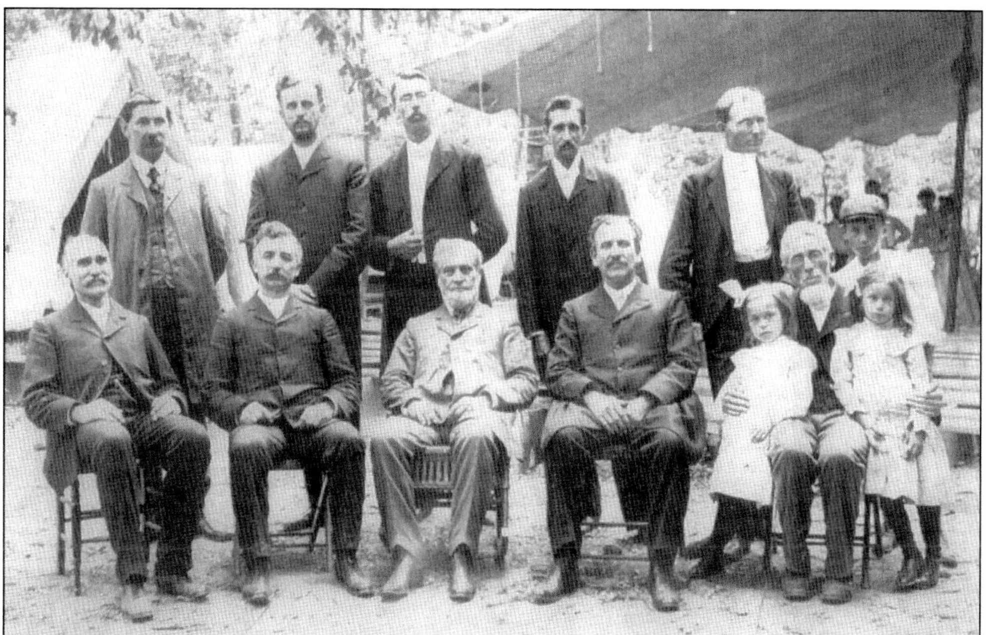

One summer around 1895, ten Sugar Valley ministers posed in front of their Booneville Campground tabernacle tent. Included in this photograph are, from left to right, the following: (first row) ? Rotan, E. Bailey, W. Swangler, ? Hollenbaugh, H. Greninger, and his three grandchildren, Evelyn Loos, Leslie Greninger (boy standing behind), and Esther Greninger; (second row) M. Kennelly, ? Finkbinder, C. Redeker, ? Crouch, and ? Ryder. Greninger was minister at St. Paul's (Miller's) Church in Logan Mills from 1874 to 1895.

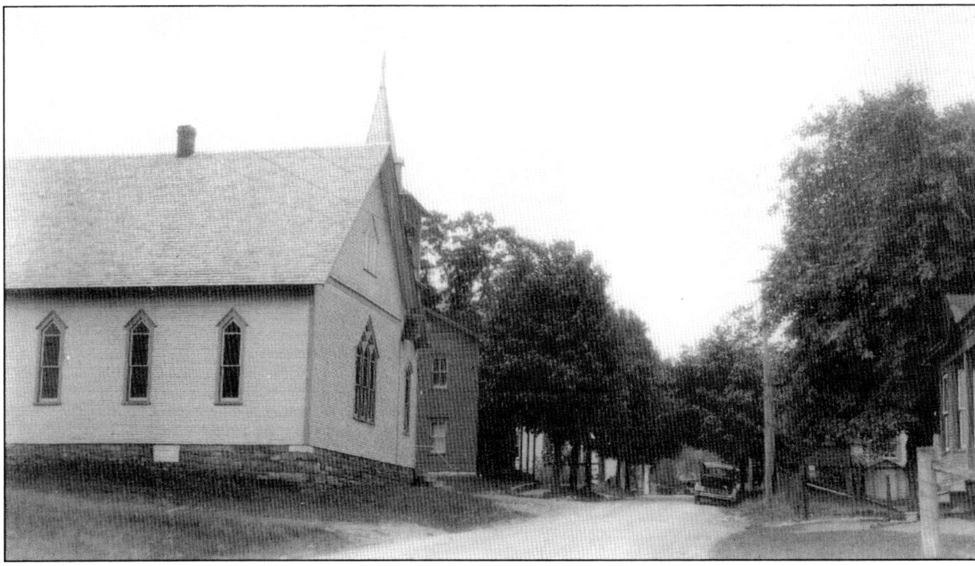

The frame Trinity United Evangelical Church in Greenburr was built in 1898 with the congregation led by Rev. C. Garret. Fire caused by an overheated flue destroyed the church on January 20, 1941. To replace it, a brick house of worship was erected on the same site. A dedication ceremony was held on December 7, 1941, the same day the Japanese attacked Pearl Harbor. It was conducted by Rev. Thurman Husler, the church's pastor from 1940 to 1950.

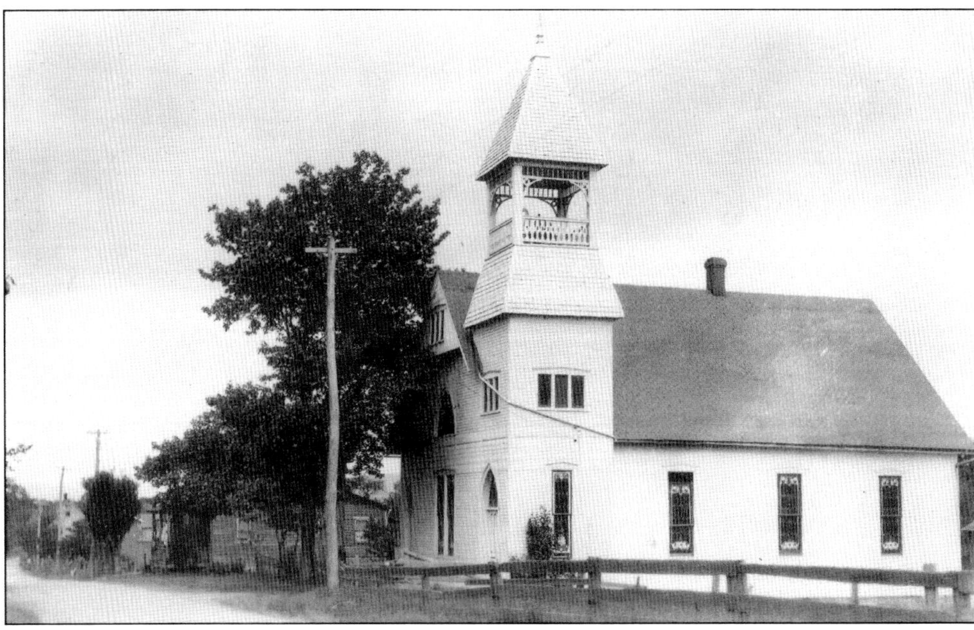

Greenburr's Emanuel Reformed Church was established in 1867. The cornerstone was set during a dedication in 1869. The church was originally built for the use of both Lutheran and Reformed congregations. Some families who attended since the beginning were the Meyers, Tysons, Lameys, Wolfes, Gharets, and Kahls. Closed in the 1940s, it was purchased by Lynn Frazier of Loganton and dismantled in 1962.

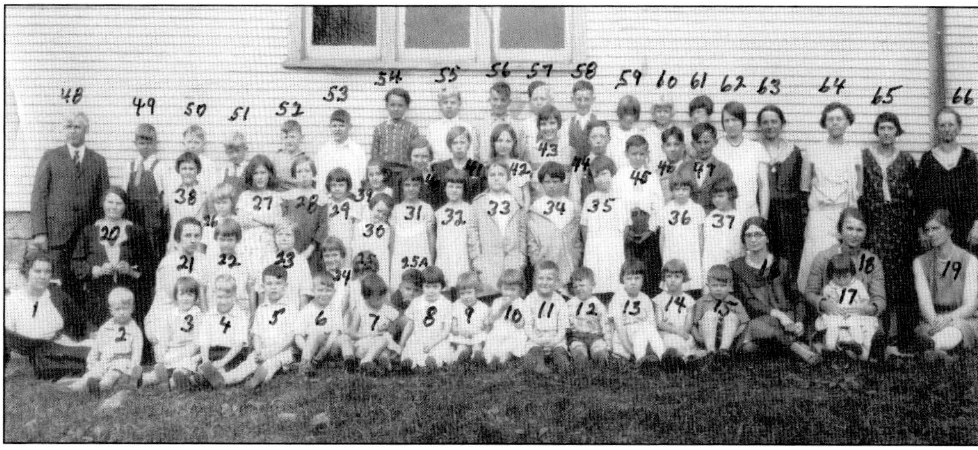

Members of Greenburr's Trinity United Evangelical Church Bible School posed for this c. 1933 photograph. Those included in this image are identified by number from lowest to highest and are as follows: Welshans, Brungard, Lamey, Fiedler, Wolfe, Fiedler, Ilgen, Ilgen, Lesher, Lesher, Welshans, Bressler, Wolfe, Bartges, Bressler, Geary, Schreckengast, Walizer, Sheats, Kahl, Stamm, Welshans, Schrack, Lamey, unidentified, Adams, Miller, Lamey, Schrack, Adams, Douty, Douty, Lehman, Overdorf, Bierly, Schreckengast, Karstetter, Schreckengast, Overdorf, Bressler, Schrack, Bletz, Showers, Meyer, Smith, Miller, Meyer, Welshans, Rev. Lester Fuhrman, Sheats, unidentified, Sheats, Day, Bierly, Douty, Lesher, Fiedler, Bletz, Stecher, Yarrison, Shaffer, Welshans, Smith, Emig, Harbach, Douty, and Florence Fuhrman (reverend's wife).

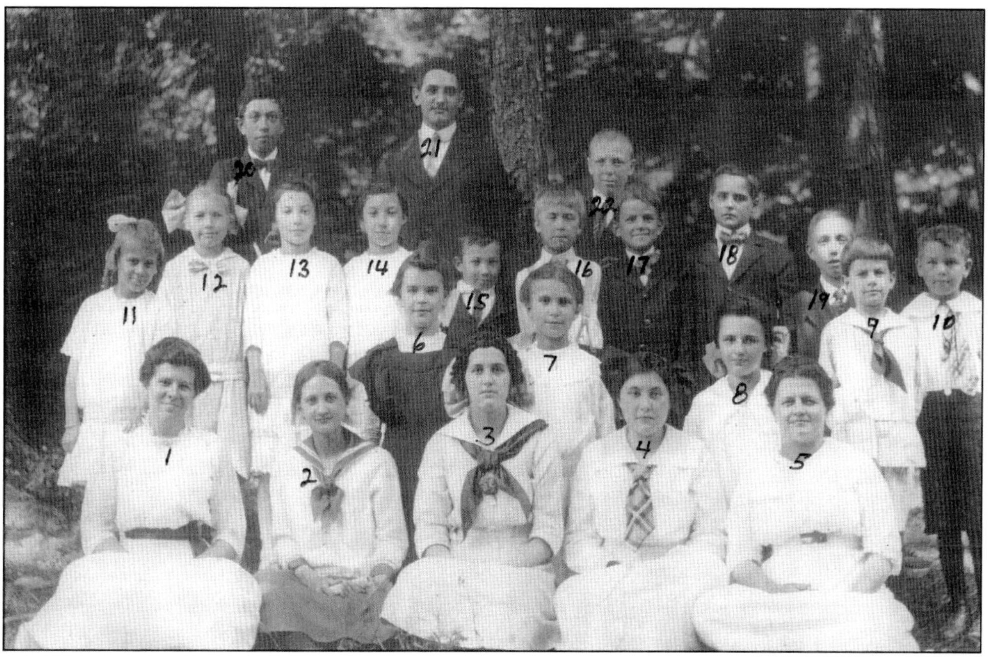

Joint Sunday school members of Greenburr Trinity United Methodist and Emanuel Reformed Churches who posed for this c. 1916–1917 photograph are, from left to right, (first row) M. Bechtol, C. Confer, D. Lamey, M. Schreckengast, and unidentified; (second row) R. Adams, H. Tyson, E. Stamm, Glenn Adams, and D. Shade; (third row) two unidentified, Mary Lebo, Martha Lebo, R. Lebo, C. Walizer, Gordon Adams, unidentified, and H. Lebo; (fourth row) E. Tyson, G. Schade, and R. Schade.

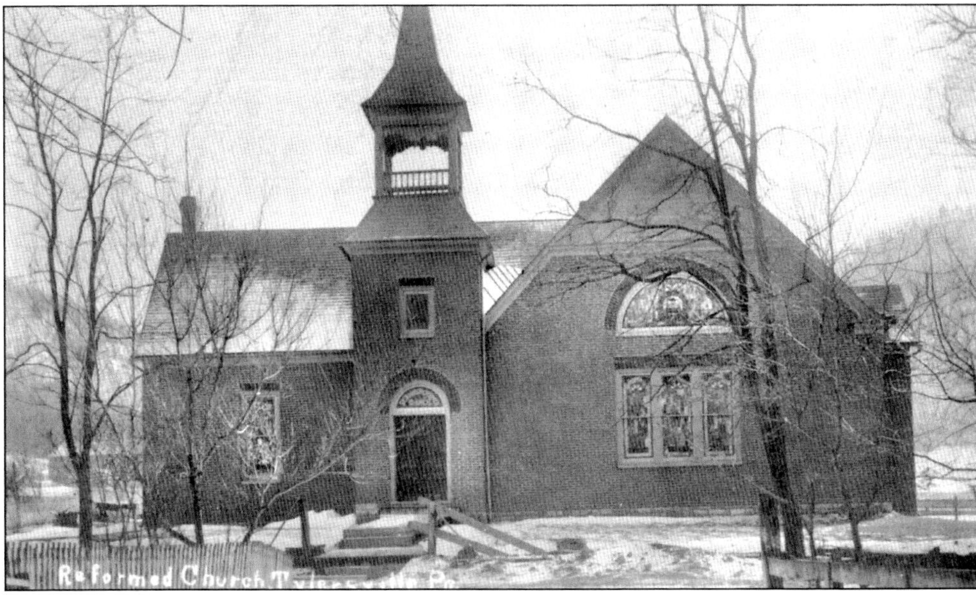

This image of the Tylersville Reformed Church was taken about two years after its construction in 1906, following the division of the Lutheran and Reformed congregations. In 1957, it merged with the Congregational Christian Church to form the United Church of Christ. In 1965, an addition to the church school was completed. Services at St. John's United Church of Christ have continued into the 21st century.

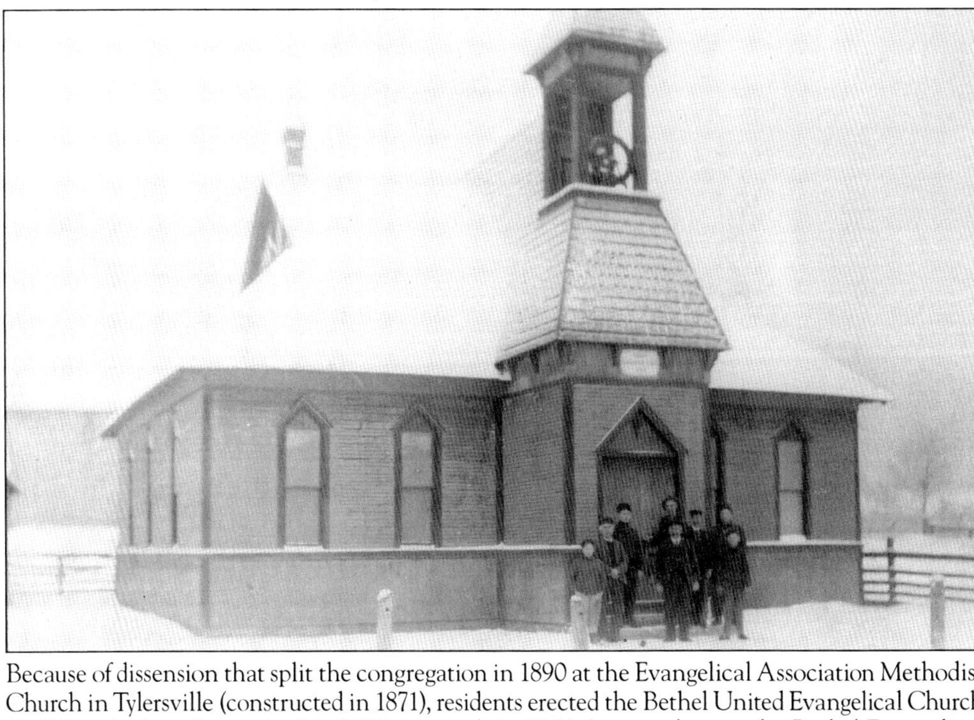

Because of dissension that split the congregation in 1890 at the Evangelical Association Methodist Church in Tylersville (constructed in 1871), residents erected the Bethel United Evangelical Church in 1894, which is shown in this 1908 postcard. In 1964, known then as the Bethel Evangelical United Brethren Church, it closed. The congregation then went to Trinity Evangelical United Brethren Church in nearby Greenburr for services.

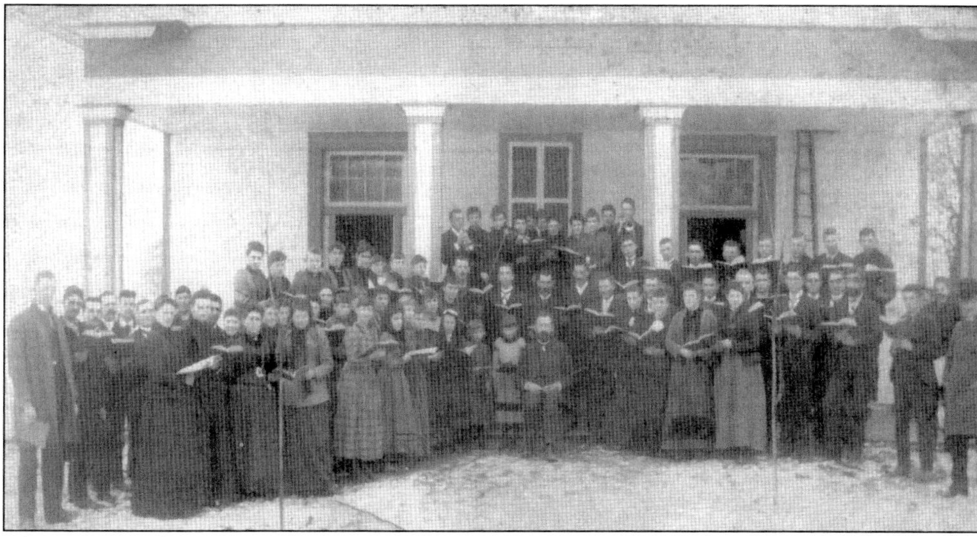

This group of choir members and musicians gathered in front of Tylersville's German Reformed and Lutheran Church, most likely some time between 1890 and 1900. Families that attended the church in the 19th century included the Ilgens, Spanglers, Ruhls, Becks, Glantzes, Bierlys, Mechtleys, Smiths, and Rockeys. The two ministers serving between 1883 and 1910 were J.R. Brown and Frank Wetzel.

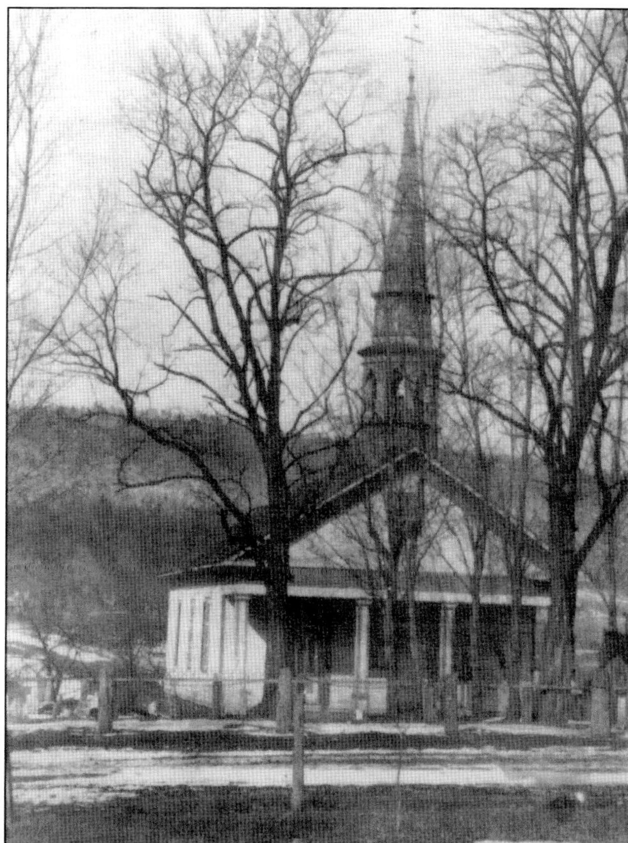

In the late 1830s, Paul Frantz donated land in Tylersville for the construction of the German Reformed and Lutheran Church. Begun in 1840, with labor and timber provided by residents of the community, it was completed the following year and dedicated on August 9, 1841. The church was remodeled between 1871 and 1872. Dwindling membership led to the end of services in the late 1950s, the church's official closure in 1964, and finally the razing of the building.

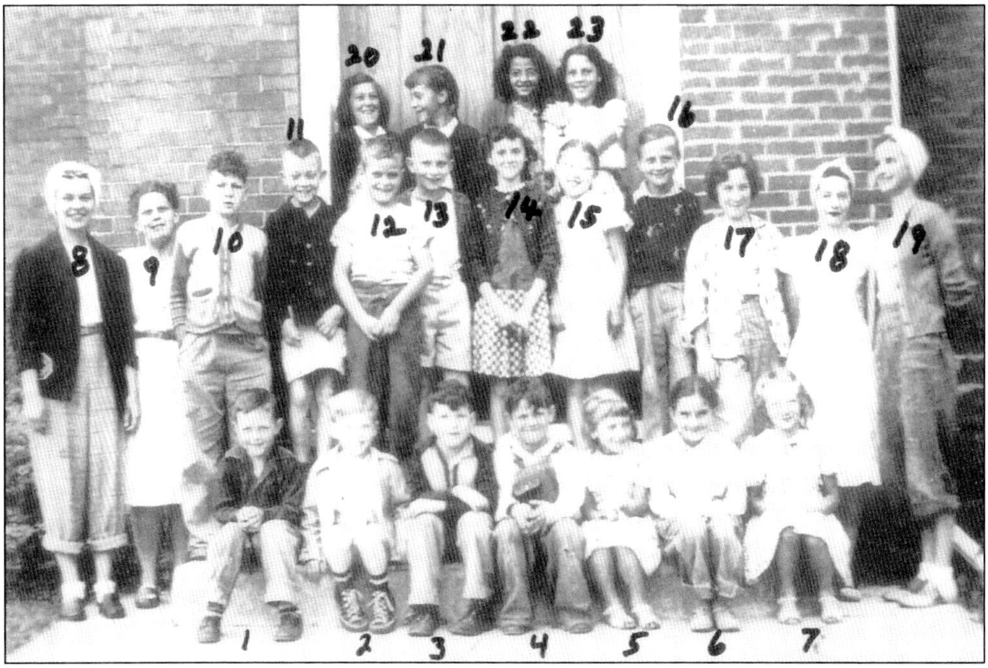

The June 1948 Tylersville Reformed Vacation Bible School photograph includes, from left to right, the following: (first row) John Bock, Leon Grieb, Ralph Beck, Richard McCaleb, Eleanor Grieb, Julia Miller, and Laura Grieb; (second row) Margaret Frantz, Mrs. Donald Schlicher (preacher's wife), Karl Beck, David Overdorf, Karl Miller, Robert Keene, Nancy Klinefelter, Barbara Mays, Perry McCaleb, Adelia Miller, Janet Greninger, and Jane Klinefelter; (third row) Gail Ilgen, Carol McCaleb, Vivian Weaver, and Catherine McCaleb. Tylersville Reformed Church later became St. John's United Church of Christ.

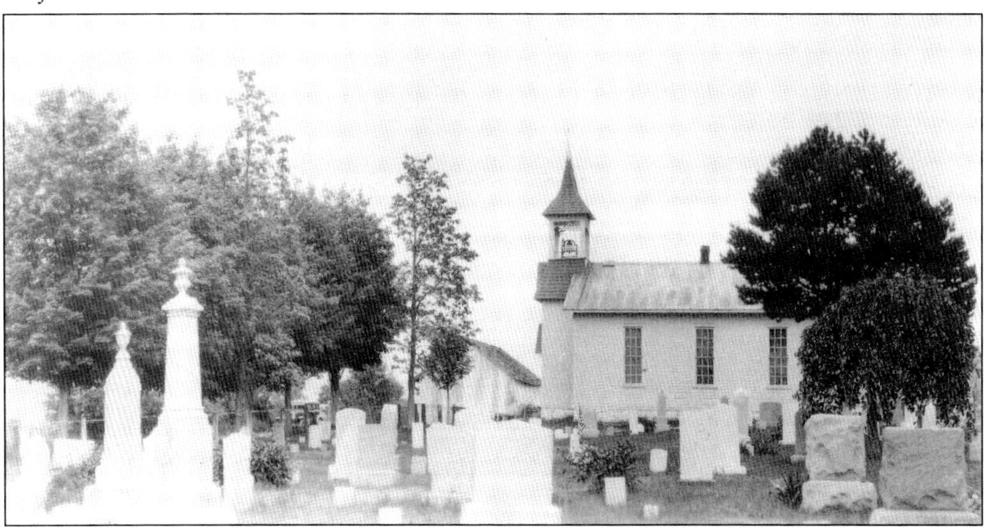

In this c. 1920s photograph is St. Paul's Evangelical Association Church on the winter road. It was erected in the late 1870s, replacing an earlier log church that was constructed around 1825. St. Paul's was also known as "Miller's Church" because a man named Miller sold 80 perches (0.5 acres) of land for the church site for $5. Regular services ended in 1964, but one service is still held each year.

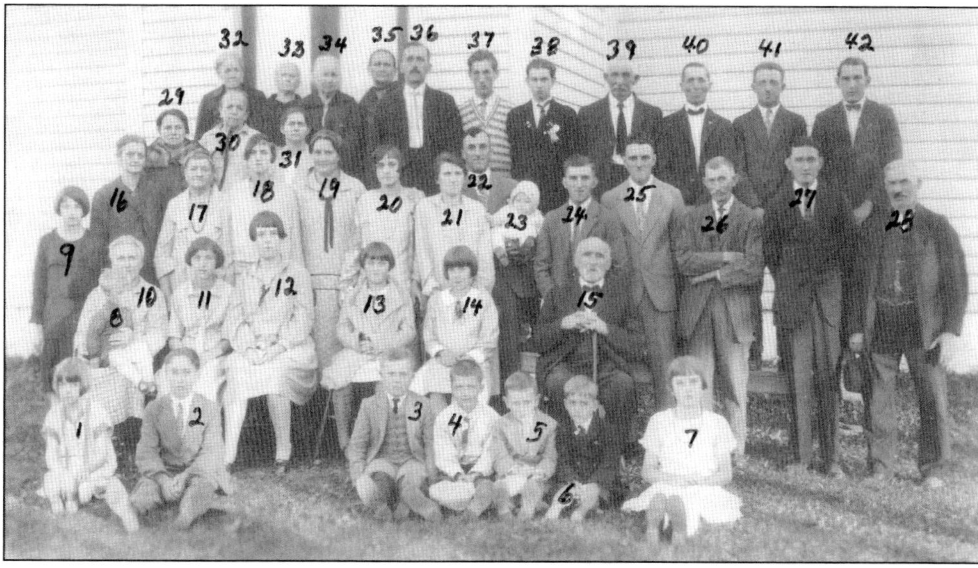

A group from Miller's Church is gathered in this c. 1926 photograph. Those included in this image are identified by number from lowest to highest and are as follows: F. Showers, H. Schreckengast, R. Brumgard, F. Lamey, W. Stecher, L. Schreckengast, M. Schade, D. Clark, Miriam Showers, E. Bartges, R. Schreckengast, T. Schade, M. Schefler, E. Bletz, ? Hunselman, T. Bowersox, H. Shaffer, S. Moyer, L. Schreckengast, Idella Moyer, Iva Moyer, D. Moyer, D. Bartges, C. Moyer, J. Moyer, D. Glantz, L. Bartges, E. Emig, A. Emig, C. Glantz, B. Schrack, ? Stihah, H. Eiseman, Mary Showers, E. Lamey, H. Lamey, R. Schreckengast, J. Schrack, H. Showers, N. Schreckengast, A. Showers, and F. Emig.

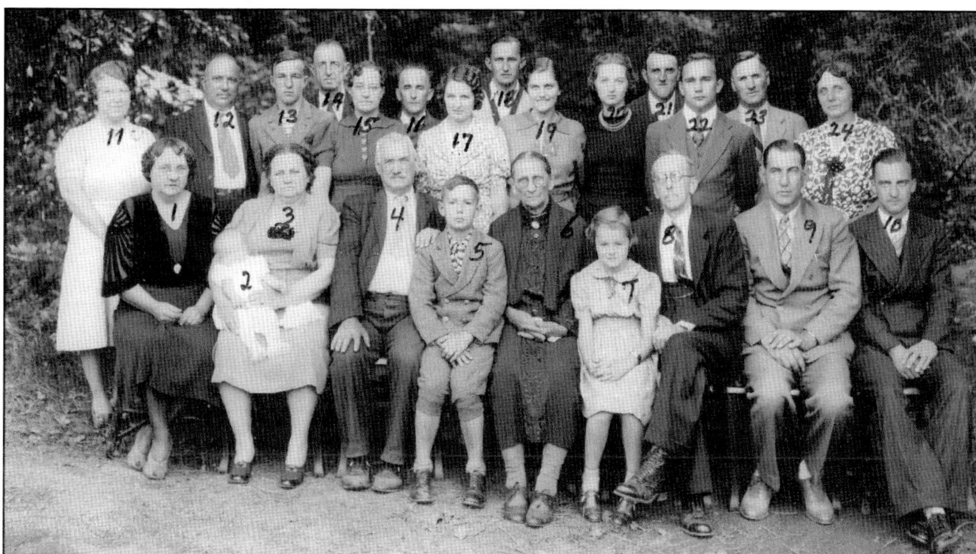

The Miller's Church members included in this 1939 photograph are, from left to right, the following: (seated) Jenna Welshans, Janice Geisewite, Anna Showers, Elmer Emig, Elwood Welshans, Etta Emig, Josephine Moyer, Harvey Lamey, Frank Emig, and Floyd Lamey; (standing) ? Showers, Ralph Welshans, Calvin Welshans, Ammon Showers, Idella Moyer, Ernest Geisewite, Miriam Geisewite, Hillaire Welshans, Hazel Welshans, Frances Kulhavy, Jerry Moyer, Lester Welshans, Lester Douty, and Elizabeth Douty.

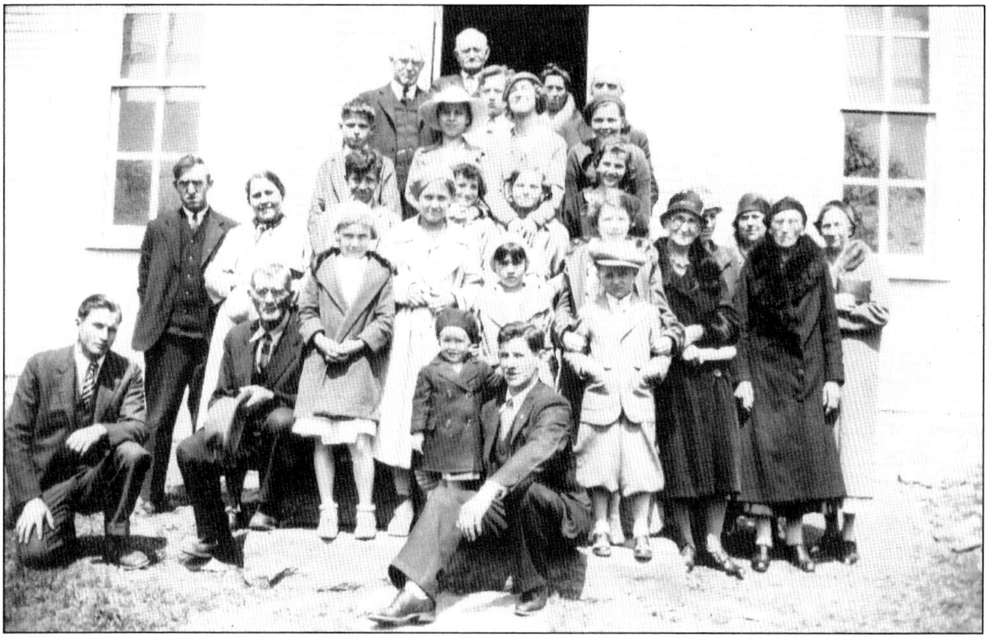

This c. 1933–1934 Carroll's United Evangelical Church group includes, from left to right, the following: (first row) C. Limbert and S. Limbert; (second row) H. Embich, E. Embich, G. Kohlberger, A. Johnson, A. Snook, and C. Bennett (boy with cap); (third row) C. Harbach, E. Harbach, R. Penticoff, G. Snook, G. Yarrison, J. Bletz, A. Harbach, Christine Embich, E. Limbert, I. Harbach, and Catherine Embich (the five women grouped together on the far right); (fourth row) B. Yarrison, I. Baker, D. Meixel, M. Fieter, and H. Harbach (directly in front of Fieter); (fifth row) Rev. Lester Fuhrman (served 1931–1935), O. Harbach, D. Embick, M. Wolford, and L. Wolford.

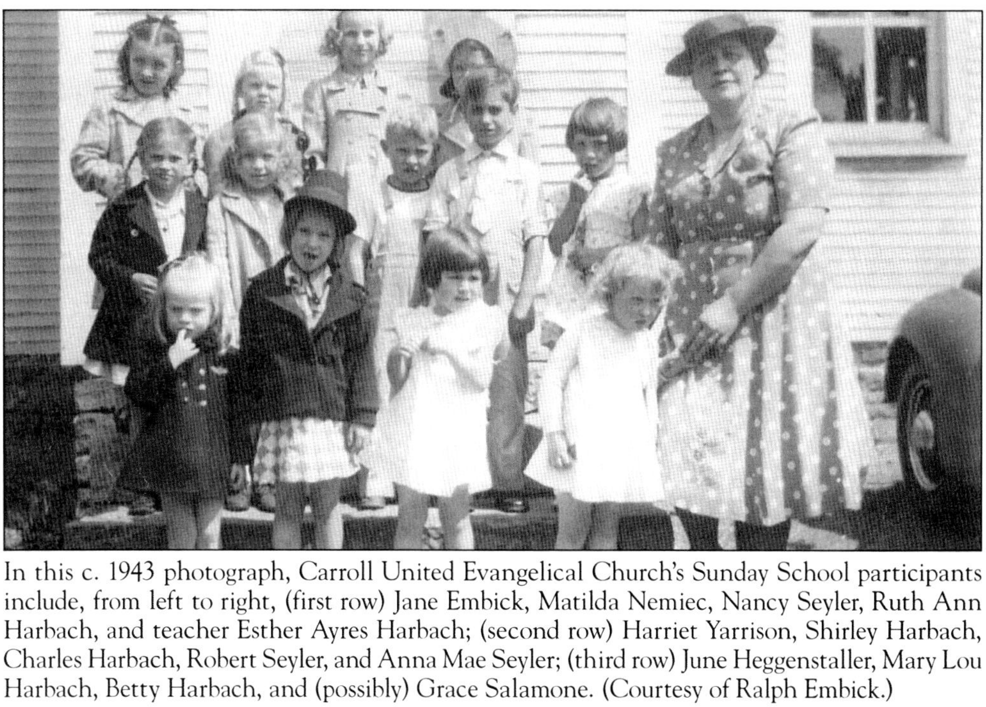

In this c. 1943 photograph, Carroll United Evangelical Church's Sunday School participants include, from left to right, (first row) Jane Embick, Matilda Nemiec, Nancy Seyler, Ruth Ann Harbach, and teacher Esther Ayres Harbach; (second row) Harriet Yarrison, Shirley Harbach, Charles Harbach, Robert Seyler, and Anna Mae Seyler; (third row) June Heggenstaller, Mary Lou Harbach, Betty Harbach, and (possibly) Grace Salamone. (Courtesy of Ralph Embick.)

The Booneville "Esher" Evangelical Association Church, shown in this c. 1922 photograph, was erected in 1862. It closed during the 1920s, most likely shortly after the 1922 merger of United Evangelical and Evangelical Association Churches. In 1929, the Greenburr Cornet Band purchased it for $135, dismantled it, then rebuilt it almost exactly as it had been—save the steeple—in Greenburr, where it functioned as their band hall. Grange hall meetings were also held there.

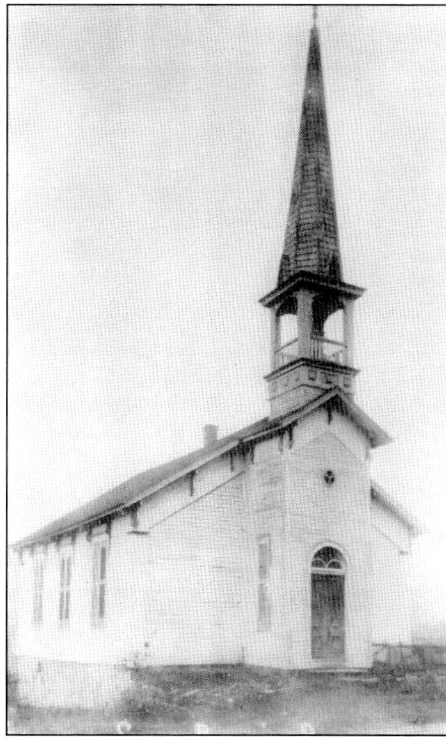

The brick St. John's Lutheran Church in Booneville was built in 1900. It replaced a wooden church on the same site that had been erected by the United Brethren in 1854, sold to the Lutherans a few years later, and razed in 1890. The church still holds services today. There is a burial ground behind the church. The dismantled Booneville Evangelical Association Church's cemetery is diagonally across the road from St. John's. (Courtesy of Ralph Embick.)

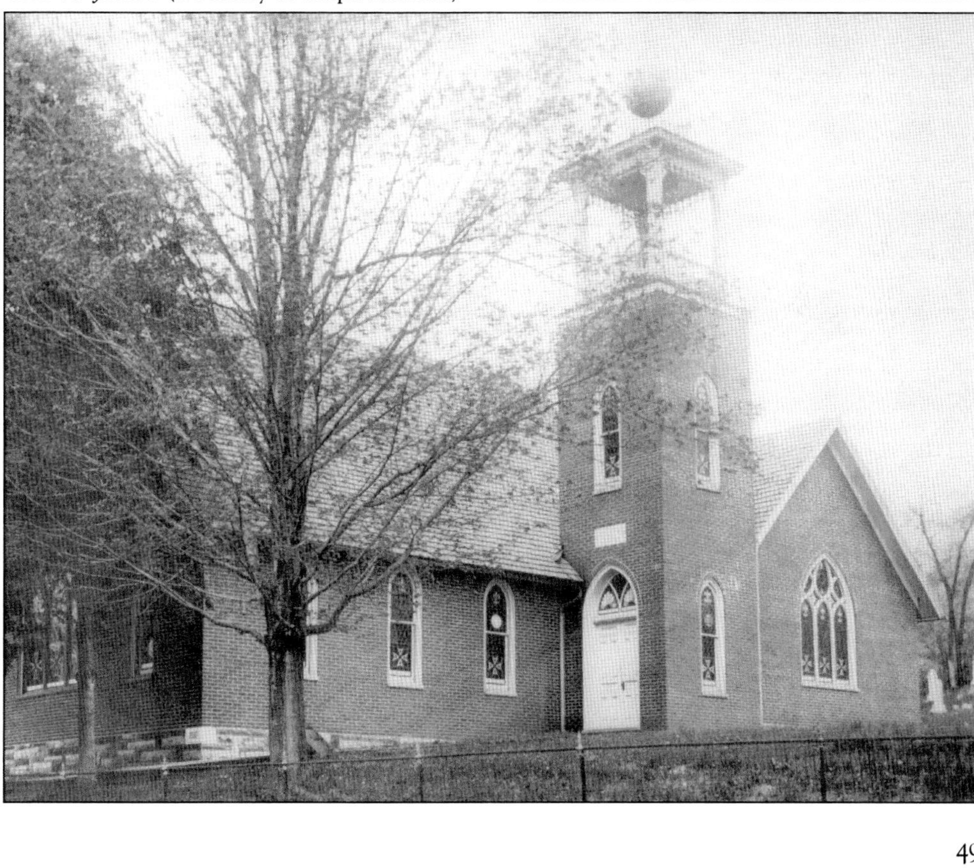

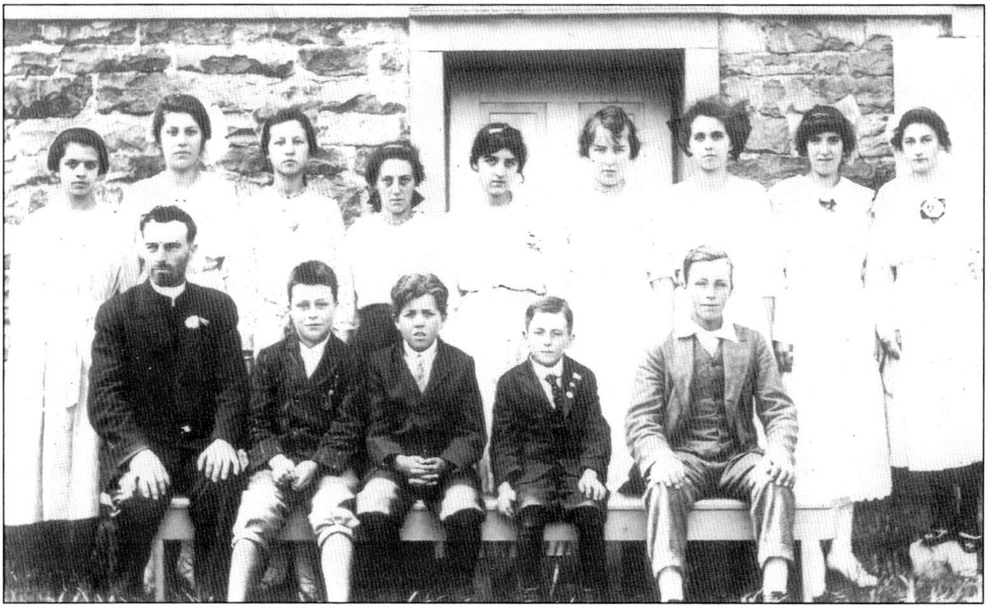

This c. 1910 Eastville Church of the Brethren Sunday School photograph includes, from left to right, (first row) Charles Schwenk (teacher and minister), Edmund Shively, Harvey Brungard, Ernest Geisewite, and Harry Boob; (second row) Jennie Geary, Flavia Martz, Mary Brunner, Susie Cashner, Florine Frank, Etta Long, Mary Brungard, Martha Geisewite, and Jennie Schwenk.

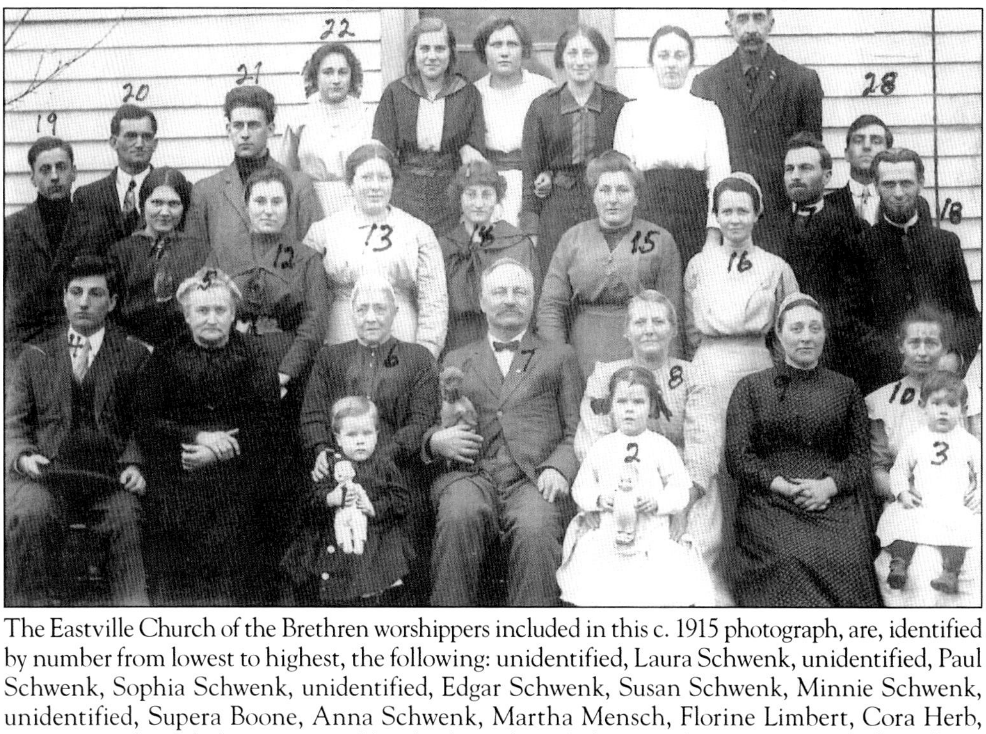

The Eastville Church of the Brethren worshippers included in this c. 1915 photograph, are, identified by number from lowest to highest, the following: unidentified, Laura Schwenk, unidentified, Paul Schwenk, Sophia Schwenk, unidentified, Edgar Schwenk, Susan Schwenk, Minnie Schwenk, unidentified, Supera Boone, Anna Schwenk, Martha Mensch, Florine Limbert, Cora Herb, Margaret Schwenk (minister's wife), Charles Schwenk (minister), two unidentified, William Schwenk, Milford Martz, Jennie Schwenk, Flavia Martz, Mary Brunner, unidentified, Mary Norris, unidentified, and Russell Schwenk.

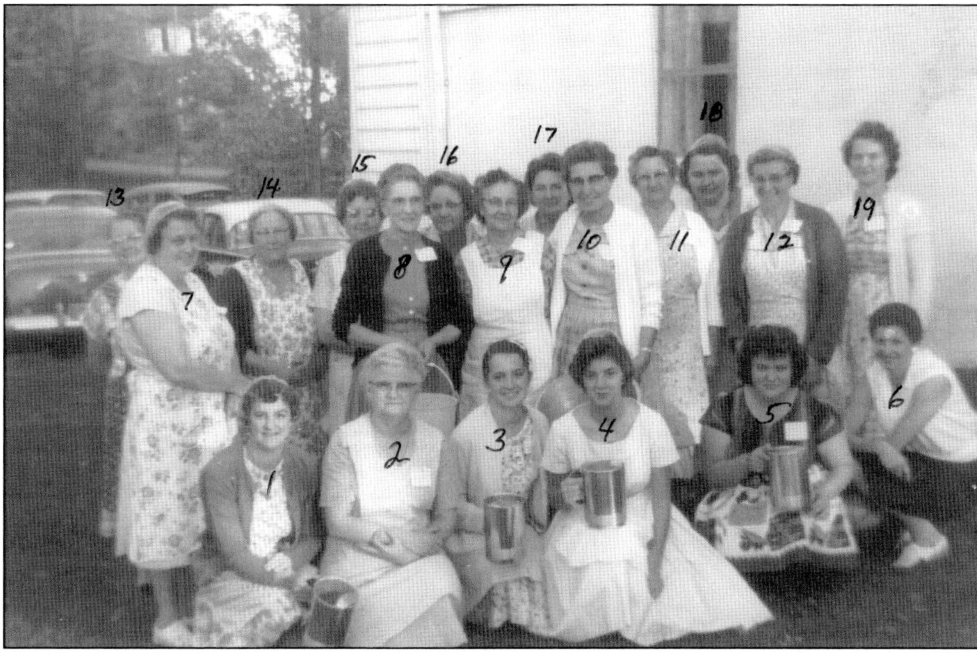

Included in this c. 1950 photograph of an Eastville Church of the Brethren group are, numbered and from left to right, (first row) LelaBell Miller, Ada Brungard, Jane Renninger, Peggy Barner, Doris Nicholas, and Lucille Libbey; (second row) Mabel Bressler, Aurelia Lupold, Helen Prescar, Hilda Jefferies, Margaret Holdren, and Thelma Confer; (third row) Thema Walizer, Myrtle Fogleman, Hester Bartges, Liella Philips, Miriam Geisewite, Betty Dickey, and Theora Smith.

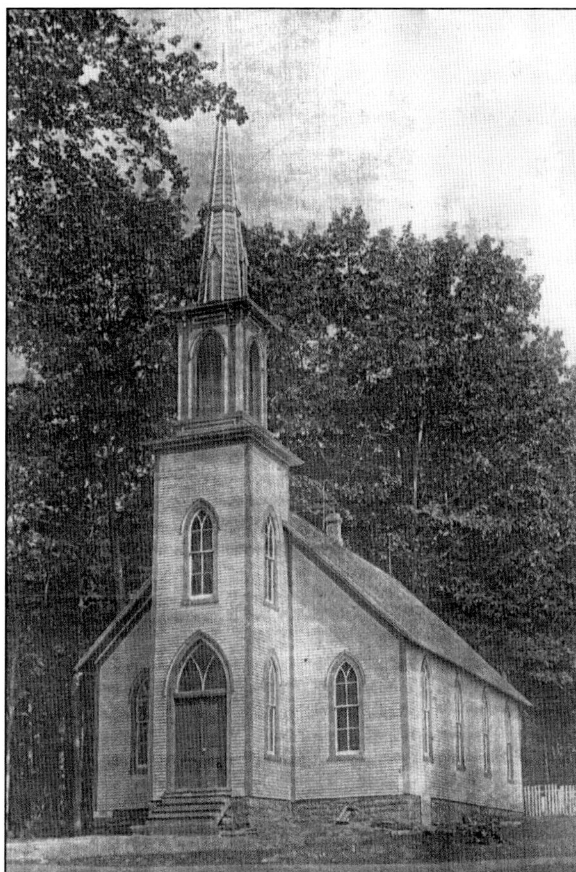

The Brungard Lutheran Church, located about two miles east of Loganton, was dedicated on October 19, 1890. Early members included the Esterline, Gramley, Geisewite, Kreamer, Engle, Frankenberger, Brungard, Reuther, Barner, and Yarrison families. The church closed in 1937, was sold in 1943, and was razed shortly afterward. (Courtesy of Ralph Embick.)

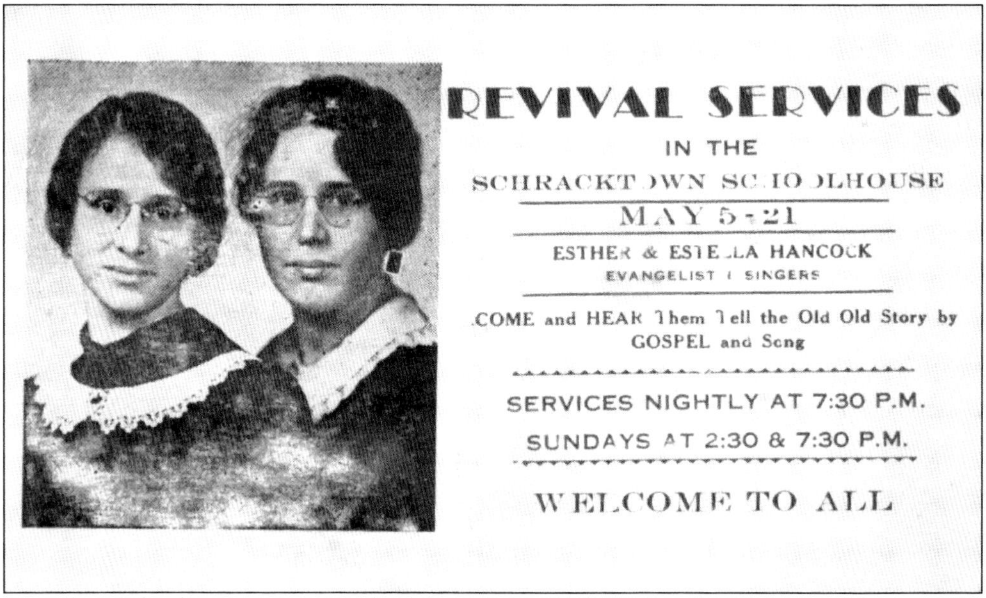

The Pilgrim of Holiness congregation held this c. 1939–1940 revival at the Schracktown (Centerville) schoolhouse, just west of Loganton. These two sisters, Esther (left) and Estella Hancock, were noted gospel singers. The congregation originated in 1937 and built the church in 1941 in Rosecrans.

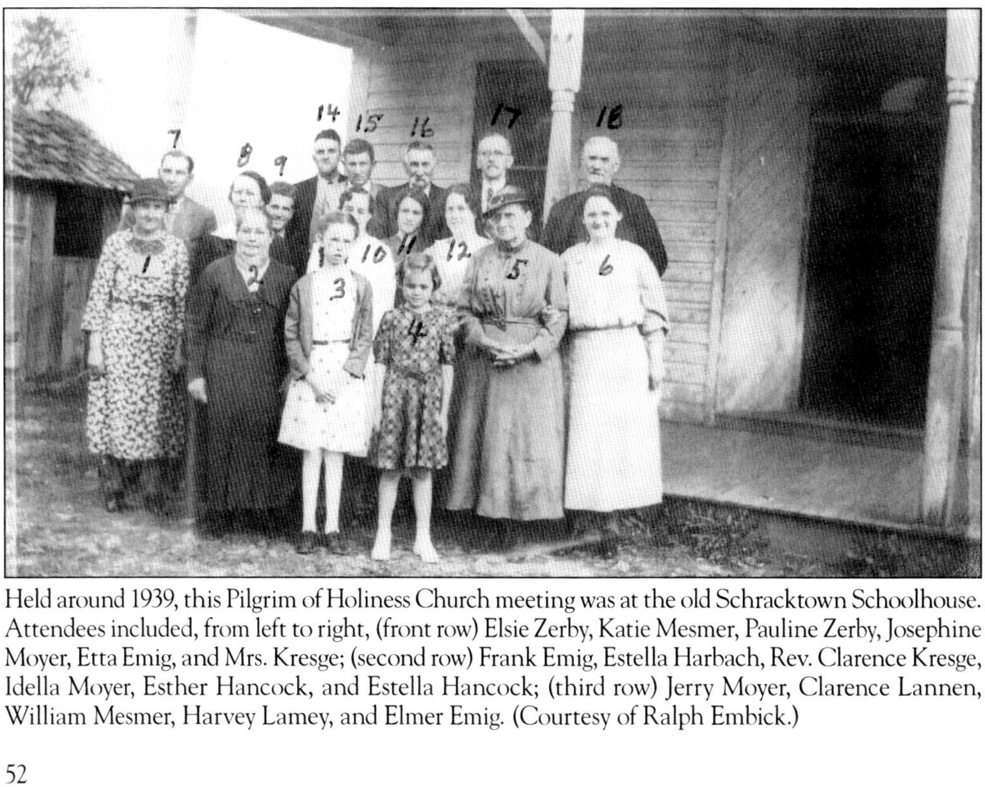

Held around 1939, this Pilgrim of Holiness Church meeting was at the old Schracktown Schoolhouse. Attendees included, from left to right, (front row) Elsie Zerby, Katie Mesmer, Pauline Zerby, Josephine Moyer, Etta Emig, and Mrs. Kresge; (second row) Frank Emig, Estella Harbach, Rev. Clarence Kresge, Idella Moyer, Esther Hancock, and Estella Hancock; (third row) Jerry Moyer, Clarence Lannen, William Mesmer, Harvey Lamey, and Elmer Emig. (Courtesy of Ralph Embick.)

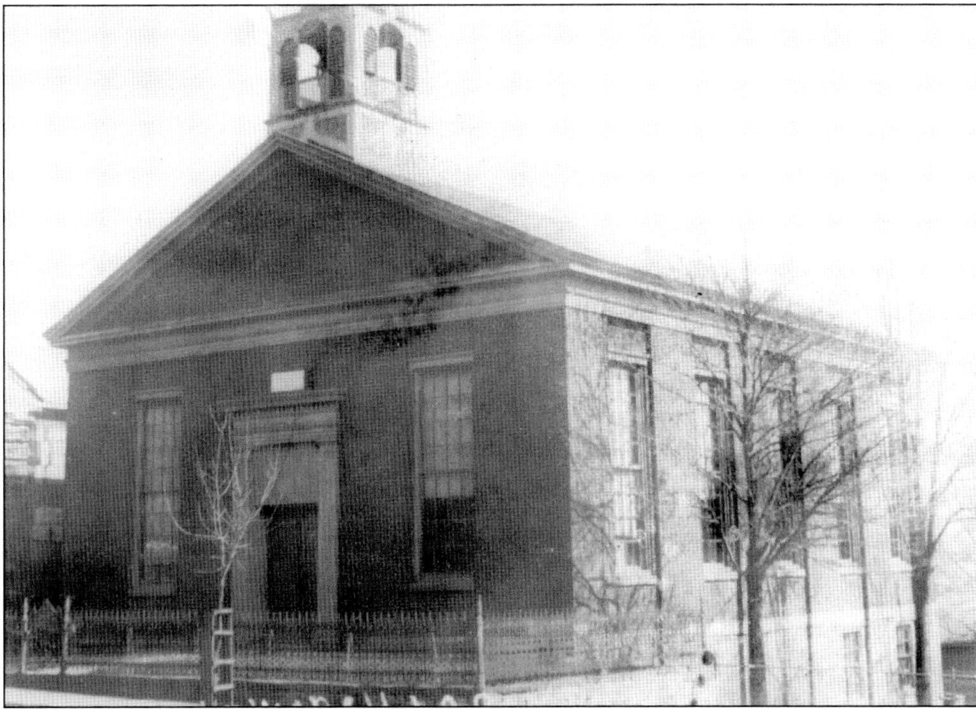

Built in 1851, with Jacob Zehring serving as the first pastor, St. Paul's Evangelical Lutheran and High German Reformed Church of Loganton was remodeled and improved in 1882. It was destroyed by the great fire of 1918, but by 1921, the congregation erected a replacement edifice where the Logan House (also a victim of the fire) had stood. St. Paul's continues to serve the community today.

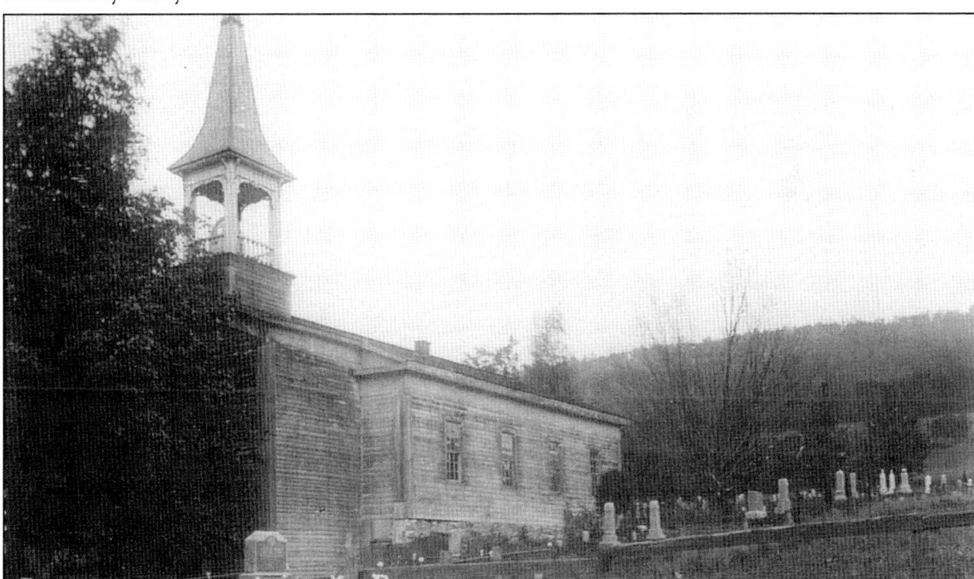

The Salem Evangelical Church of Loganton (shown in 1915) was built in 1852, eight years after the congregation was organized under Pastor John Sindlinger. The church was added to in 1874, closed in 1922, and razed in 1927. It was next to Fairview Cemetery, at the east end of the community.

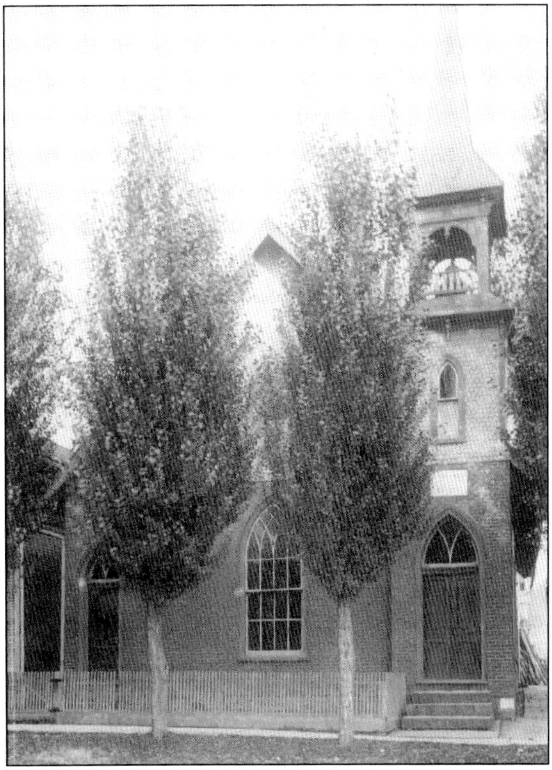

In 1895, the Albright United Evangelical Church was erected in Loganton on the site of an old woodworking shop. Prominent families who attended the church included Frankenberger, Schrack, Yarrison, Douty, Morris, Myers, Held, Lupold, and Lamey. The church was lost in the fire of 1918, but a new church and parsonage were built at the same site in 1919.

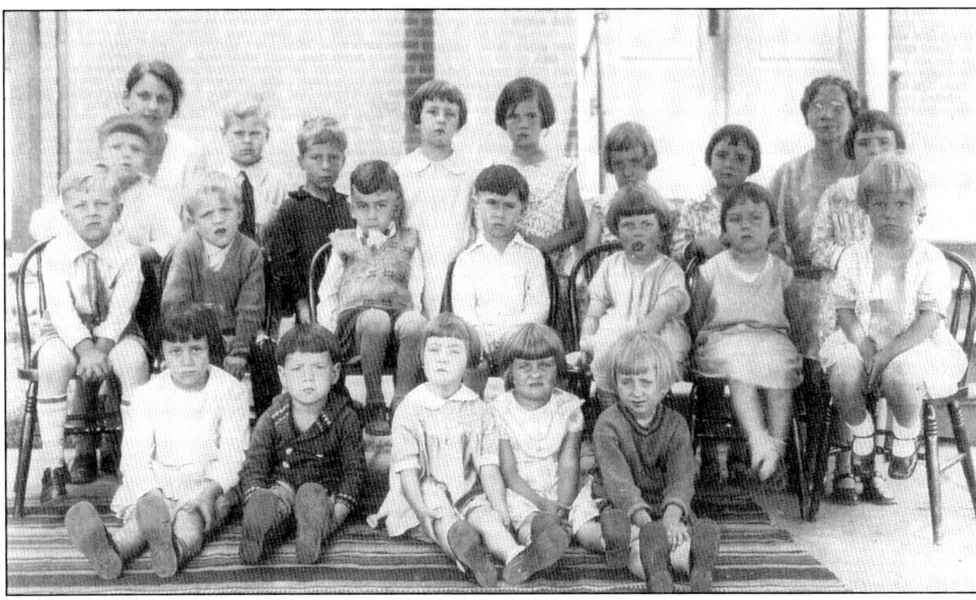

This c. 1932 Loganton Albright United Evangelical Church Bible School photograph includes, from left to right, (first row) Mary Lamey, Gordon Confer Jr., Mary Ilgen, Ruth Washburn, and Lois Kohlberger; (second row) Charles Bennett, Leo Held, Jack Rockey, Nevin Lamey, Ruth Mingle, Verna Renninger, and Betty Bierly; (third row) Gene Harbach, Grace Welshans (teacher), Lynn Mark, Henry Wren, June Raudabaugh, Lucille Rockey, Eleanor Duck, Lois Kleckner, Catherine Morris (teacher), and Doris Kleckner.

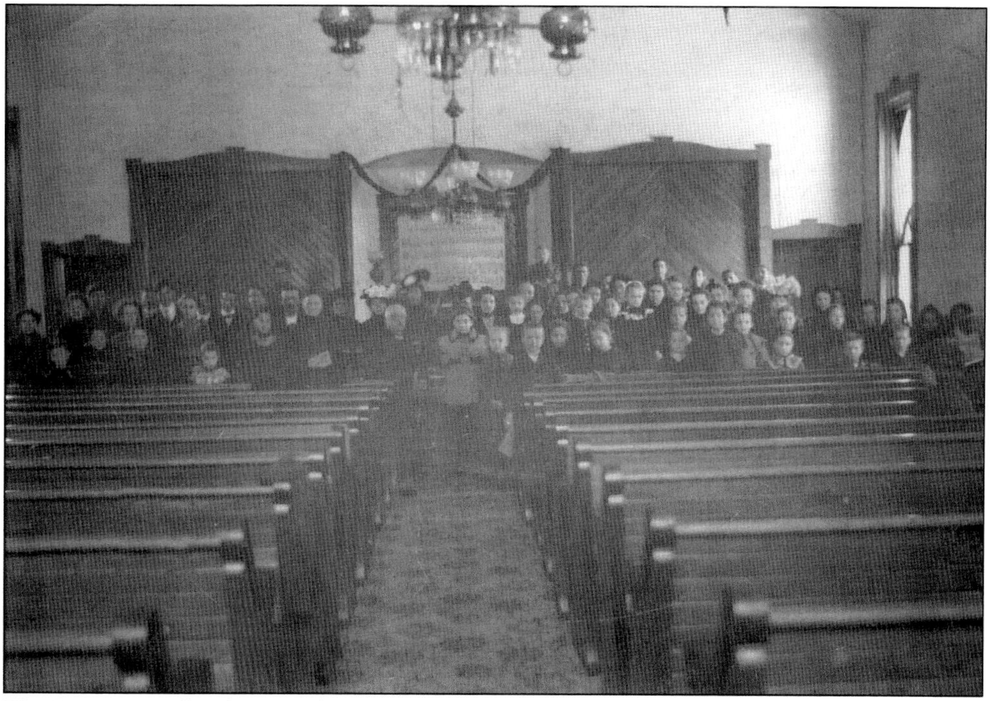

This Loganton Albright United Evangelical Church Singing School of 1900 photograph includes seven Karstetters, five Morrises, four Berrys, four Wises, four Dices (including the Reverend Lyman Dice's wife, Alice), three Lameys, three Whites, two Stamms, two Bierlys, two Gramleys, two Helds, two Hellers, two Knepps, and Tama Thompson, among others.

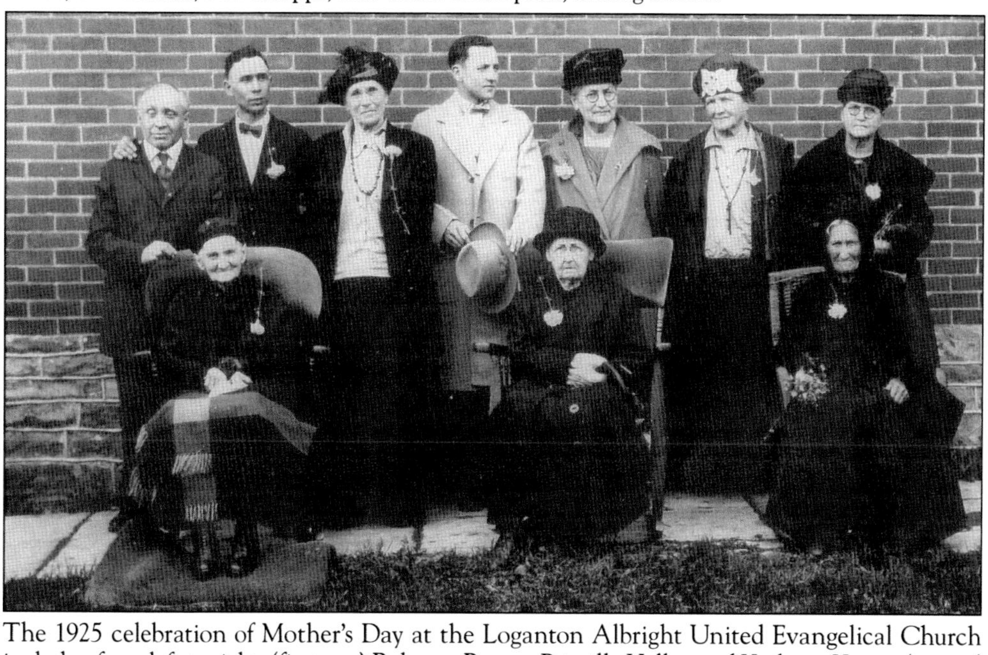

The 1925 celebration of Mother's Day at the Loganton Albright United Evangelical Church includes, from left to right, (first row) Rebecca Boone, Priscilla Heller, and Kathryn Knarr; (second row) Harry Boone (blind), Ellis Lamey, Leah Kleckner, John Heller, Jane "Jennie" Frankenberger, Ida Karstetter, and Kathryn Mark.

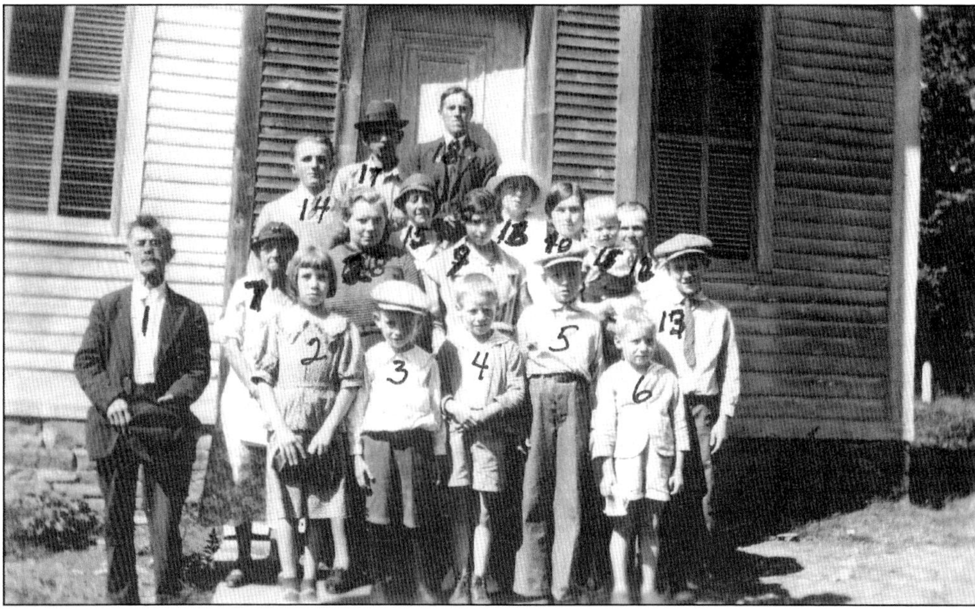

Members of this c. 1933–1934 Mount Zion Church group, are, from left to right, (first row) James Sheasley, Evelyn Rich, Russell Jamison, Warren Rich, Allen Jamison, and Frank Rich; (second row) Myrtle Eyer, Elvina Rich, Mildred Sheasley, Helen Sheasley (holding son Robert Sheasley), Styles Shaffer, and William Jamison; (third row) Robert Shaffer, Margaret Weaver, and Laura Eck; (fourth row) Elmer Weaver and an unidentified preacher. The Mount Zion Church was erected in 1865 and dismantled in 1963.

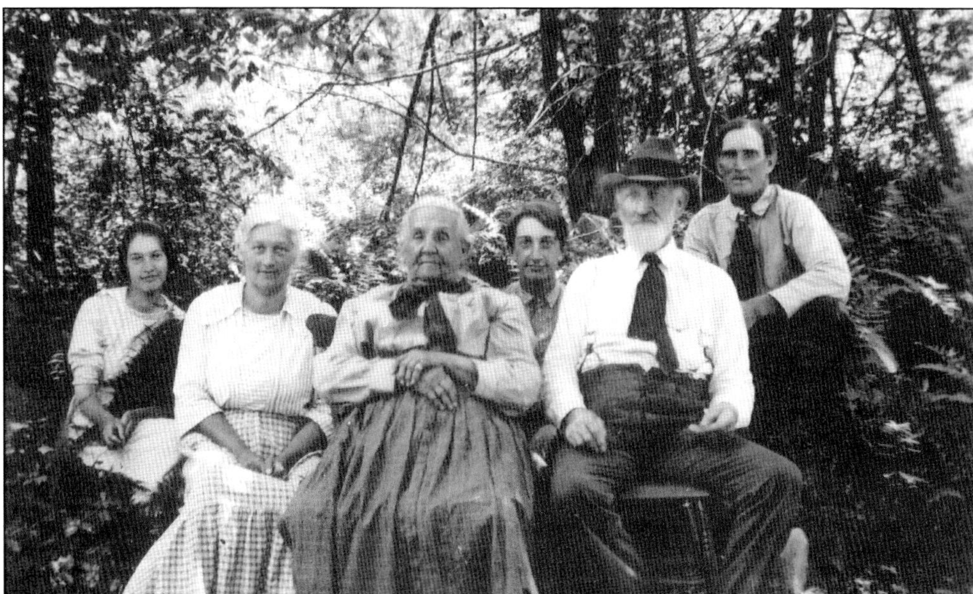

This Mount Union Lutheran Church family photograph from before 1934 includes, from left to right, Viola Lehman (1903–1963), Wilimina Lehman (1880–1952), Margaret Miller Lehman (1861–1928), William Lehman (1906–1962), Alexander Lehman (1855–1934), and Harvey Lehman (1873–1941). By the 1960s, Mount Union Lutheran Church (on Carroll Mountain) was taken over by God's Missionary Church.

Four

TRAVERSING THE LAND

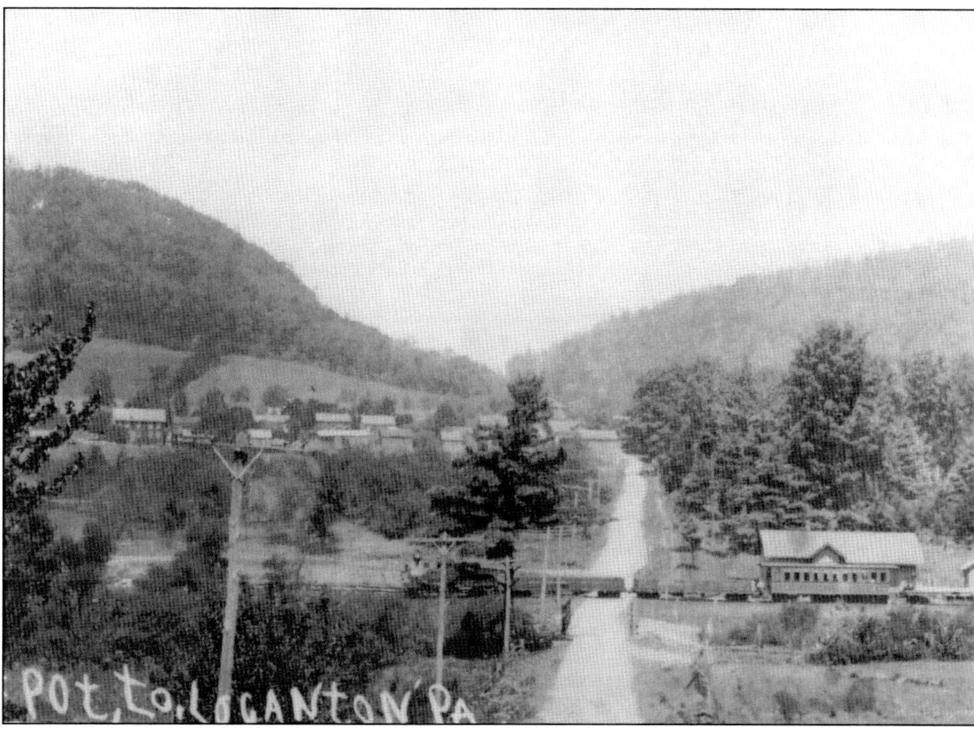

Some time between 1907 and 1916, a Climax locomotive pulls a White Deer & Loganton Railway train past the Loganton Depot and across present-day Route 477. Two men, at first John Duncan and later William Whitmer, were responsible for the creation of the railroad. This view looks north to the borough of Loganton, with the mountain pass that is visible leading to the village of Rosecrans and present-day Interstate 80.

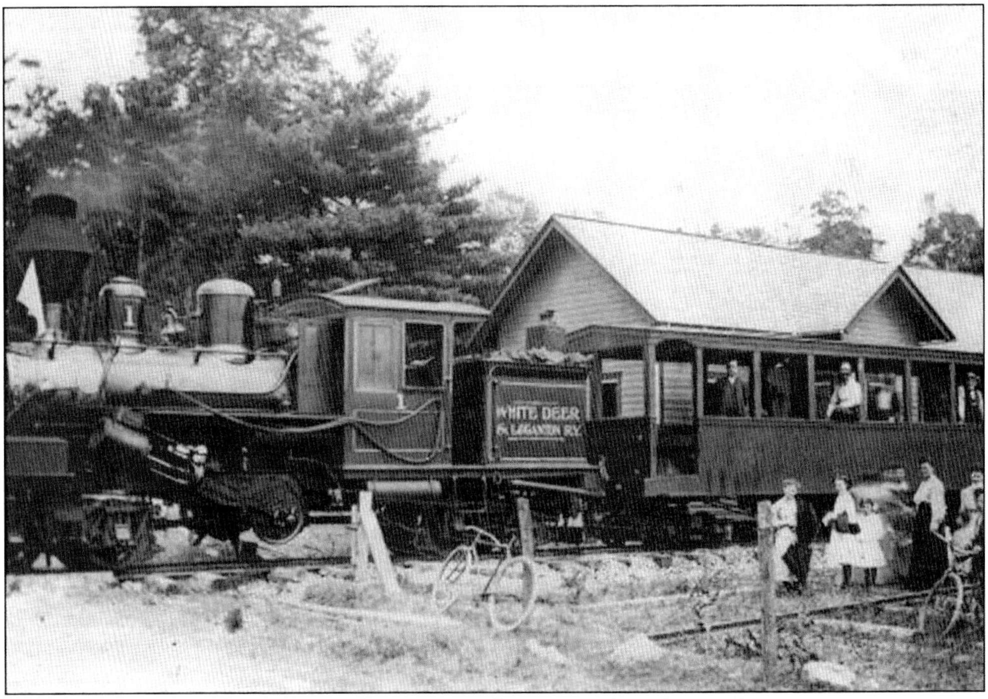

These passengers at the Loganton Depot around 1914 are aboard one of the two open excursion cars built by local carpenters for the White Deer & Loganton Railway. Climax locomotive No. 1 (one of four to serve the railroad) offered air brakes and steam heat. In 1916, No. 1 was sold to the South River Lumber Company of Cornwall, Virginia, and subsequently to the W.M. Ritter Lumber Company in 1941 for $850.

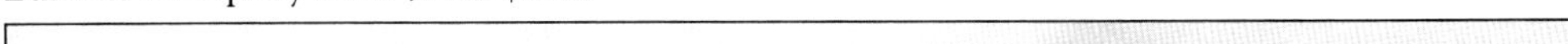

This 1908 noon train stopped at the Loganton Depot. Shown is ticket agent William Rhoads, with his foot on the engine. The White Deer & Loganton Railway was incorporated on April 17, 1906. It transported passengers, mail, lumber, coal, fertilizer, and various types of merchandise. With the depletion of timber in the valley, the railway lost its profitability, and service ended on May 31, 1916.

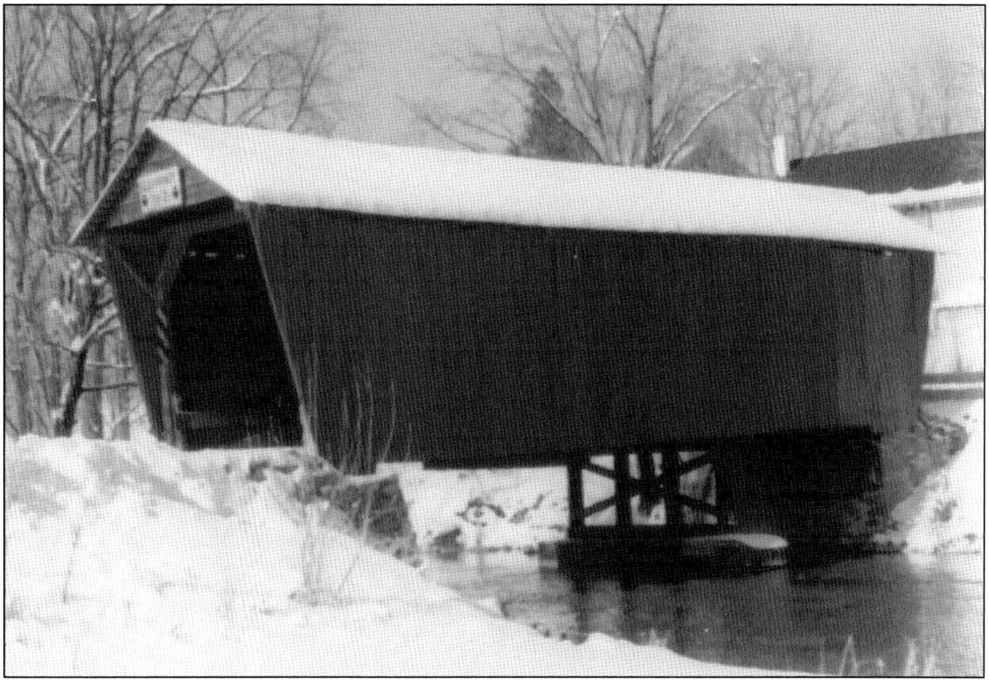

Across Fishing Creek at Logan Mills is Clinton County's only remaining covered bridge. Constructed in 1874, the bridge is 63 feet long and uses a queen-post truss. Maintained by the state since the 1930s, the red, wooden span was placed on the National Register of Historic Places on August 6, 1979. It was refurbished in 1993. (Courtesy of Allen Weaver.)

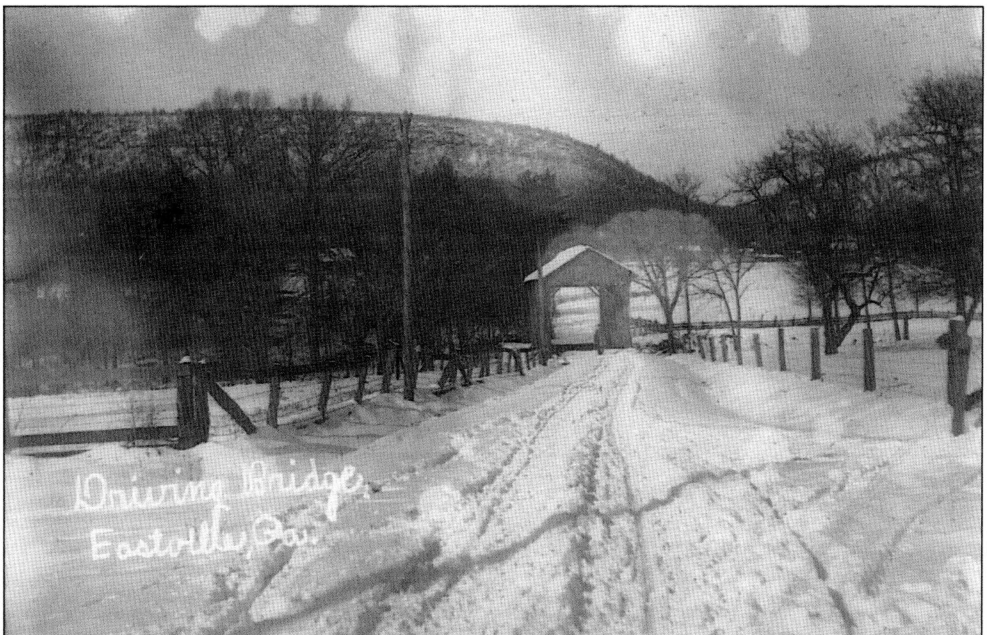

The covered bridge across Fishing Creek between Carroll and Eastville was dismantled in 1937. Today, its concrete replacement is part of the east end of the winter road that still connects the two communities.

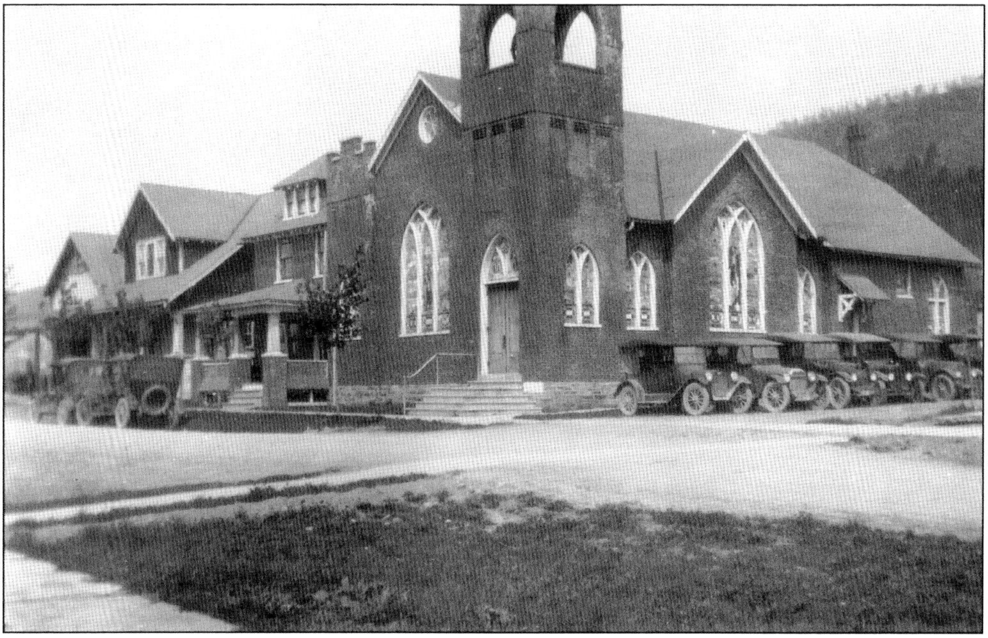

In 1922, these eight automobiles were parked beside and in front of the Albright United Evangelical Church in Loganton. The house of worship was dedicated on November 2, 1919, replacing the church that burned in the fire of 1918. It still serves the community as the Albright United Methodist Church.

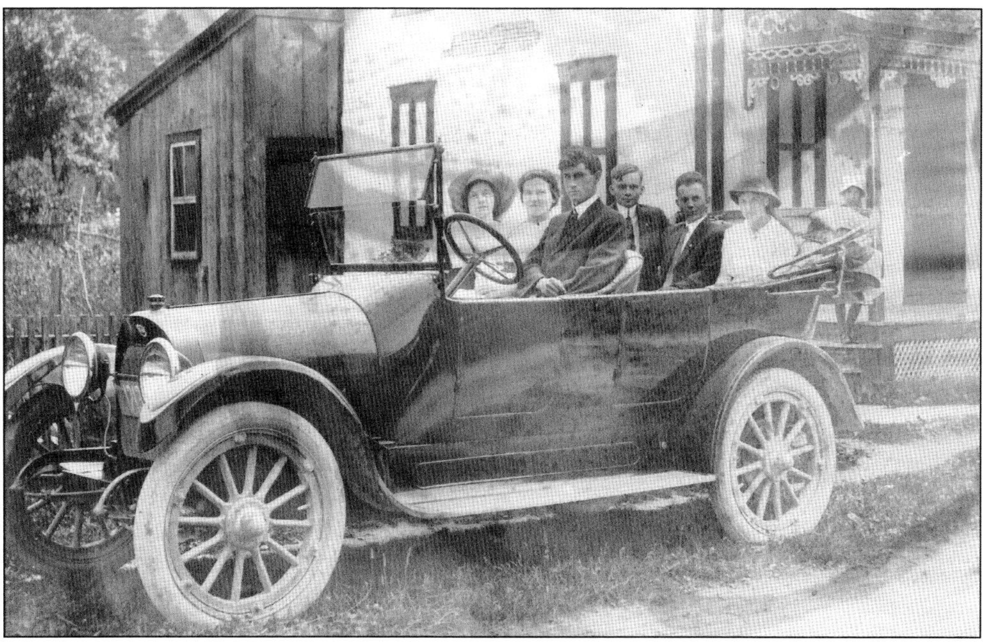

The young people posing in a Dodge touring automobile in front of a house in Tylersville, probably between 1915 and 1919, are, from left to right, (front seat) Cora Hubler (1892–1977), Zelda Greninger (1895–1919), and Lester McCaleb (1896–1941); (back seat) Oscar Gilmore (1892–1972), Roy Weaver (1891–1955), who became a well-known teacher, and Mary Barner (1898–1994).

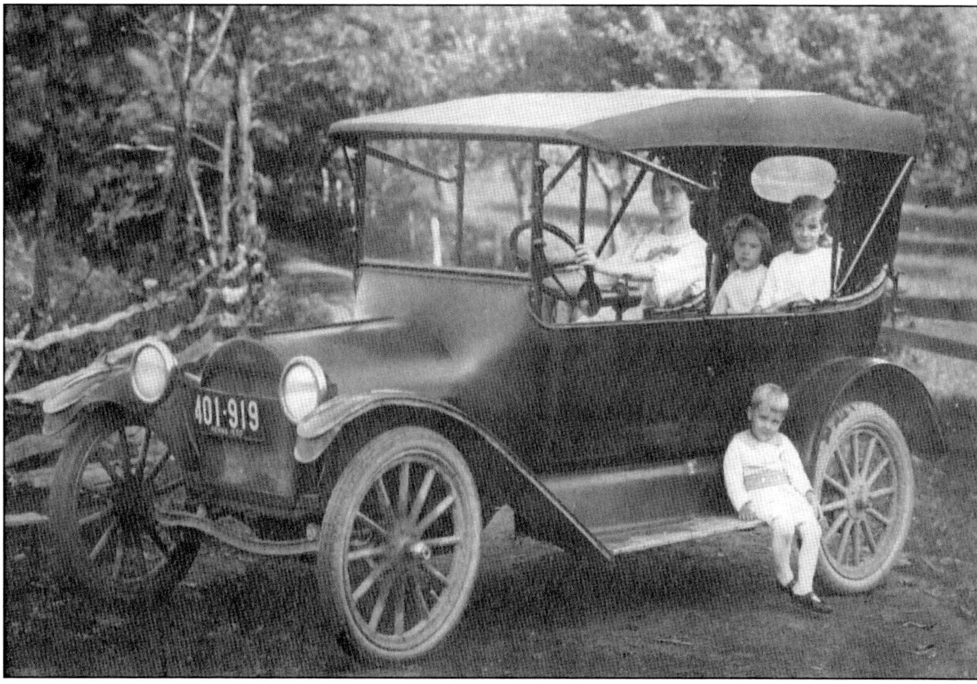

Nellie Eckel Glover Snyder (1886–1970) is in the driver's seat of this Chevrolet, plated in 1920. Starting a teaching career at age 16 in 1902, she later attended Central State Normal School, now Lock Haven University. She retired in 1930, having taught both in the Sugar Valley area and northern Clinton County schools. She was the mother of Myra Glover Grieb and Stanley and Byron Glover. The children pictured are unidentified. (Courtesy of Kenneth and Peggy Karstetter.)

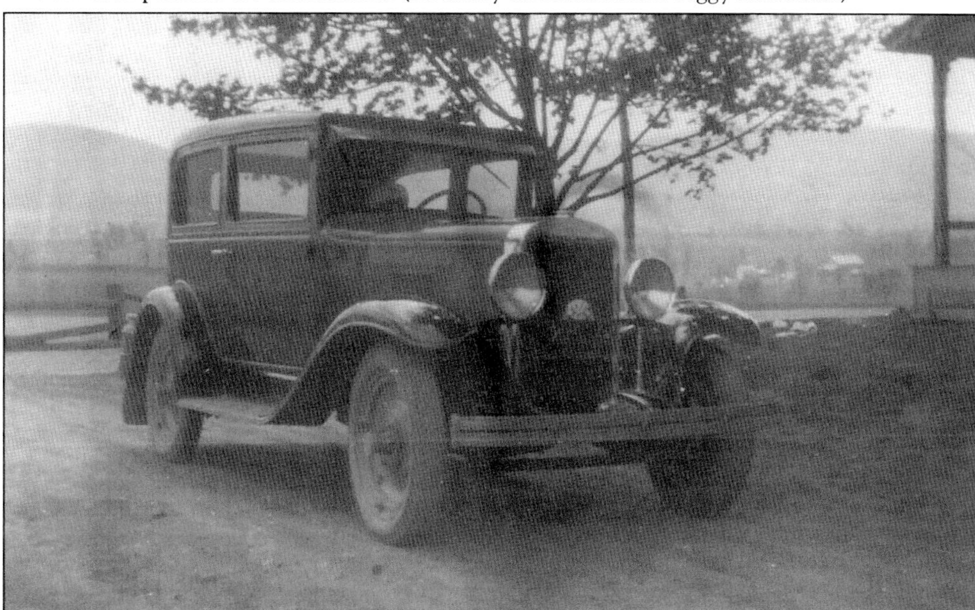

Maurice Wolfe (1908–1971) of Booneville, son of William and May Klepper Wolfe, owned this 1929 Chevrolet. He married Sara Schreckengast in 1932 and later moved to Woolrich, where he worked in the woolen mills for 27 years.

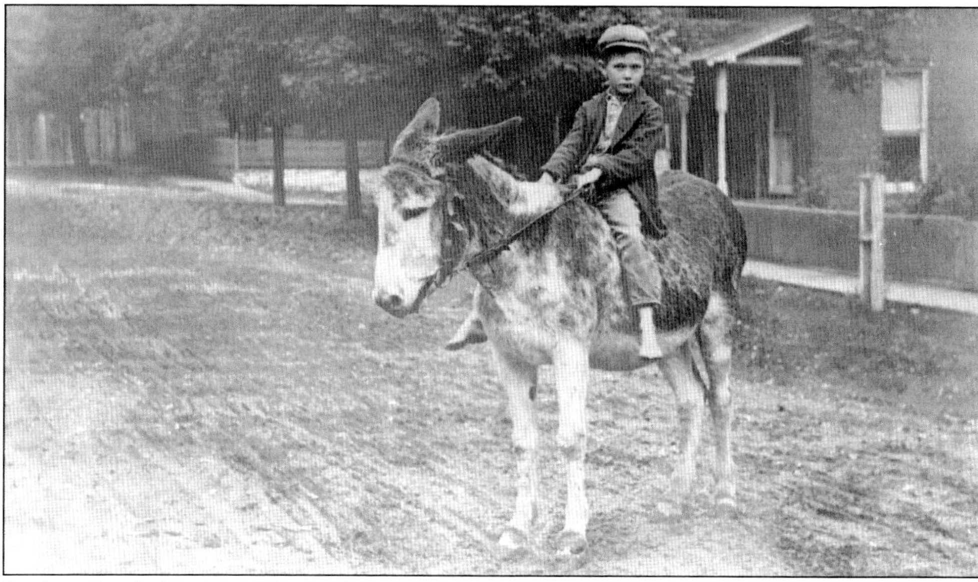

Reuben Duck (1894–1976) was the youngest of the 13 children of Isaac Duck (1844–1910), a Civil War veteran and blacksmith in Loganton. Reuben became a butcher. This photograph was probably taken in Loganton, possibly by an itinerant photographer traveling with the donkey for the express purpose of photographing children for a fee.

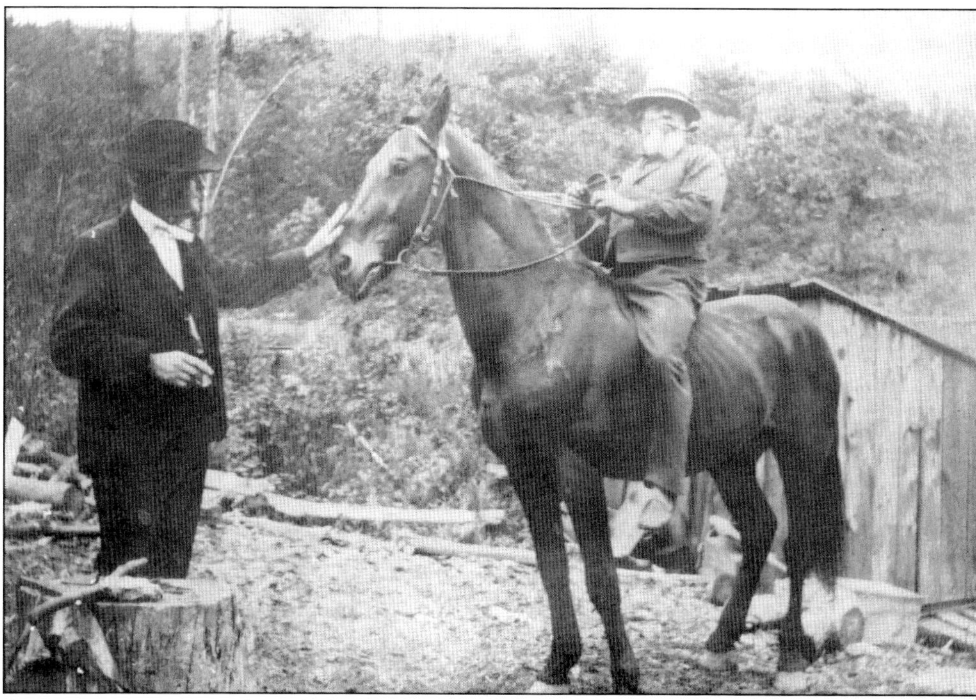

As a young man, Daniel Mark (1835–1922), shown astride his horse in 1900, hauled goods from Lewistown to John Brown's Loganton store, the first in the valley. After his first marriage to Susanna Englehart, who died in childbirth in 1865, Mark married Rebecca Heller in 1869. During his long life, Mark also went into the lumber business (running a steam sawmill), hauled railroad ties, ran a boardinghouse at a lumber camp, and farmed.

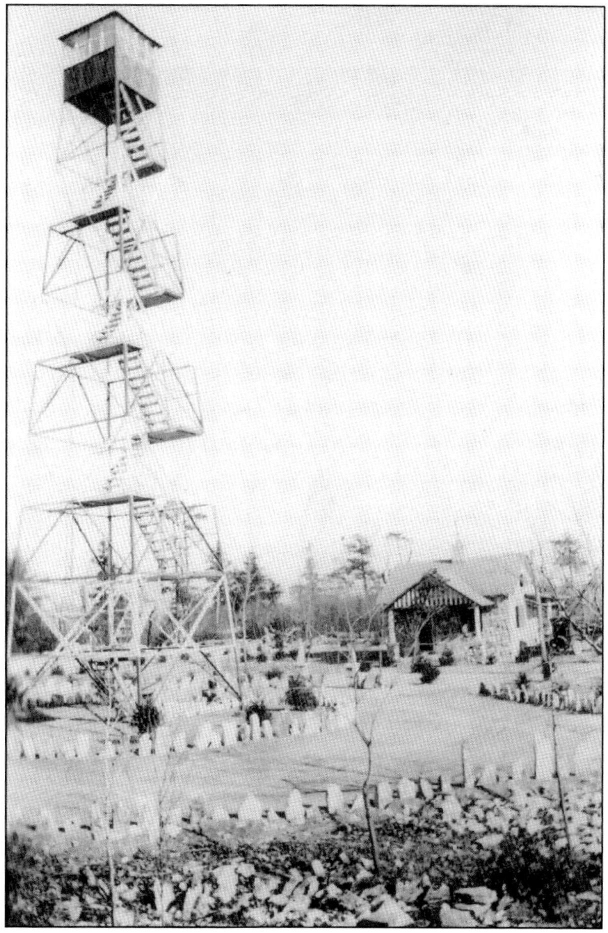

On top of Mount Riansares, about 2,300 feet above sea level and the highest peak in the area, was this fire tower and ranger cabin, shown in 1934. The name Riansares reputedly came from the Spanish queen Maria Christina, who married Augustin Munoz in 1833 after the death of her husband, King Ferdinand VII. She bestowed to Munoz the title Duke di Riansares y di Montmorat. Christina had obtained the title to this piece of land when King Ferdinand died.

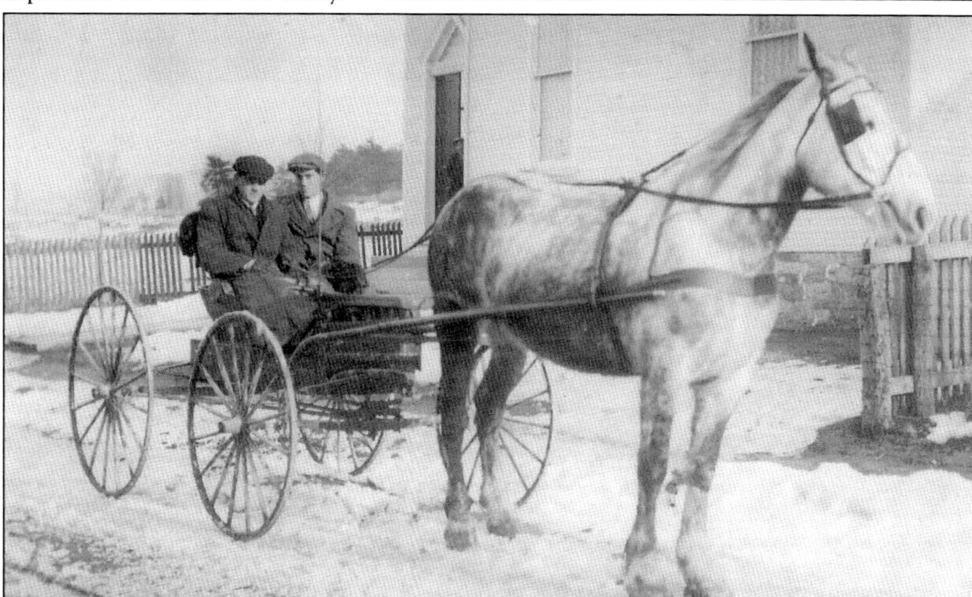

In their horse-drawn carriage by the St. Paul's Evangelical Association (Miller's) Church near Logan Mills are Robert Gilmore (left) and Lester McCaleb. Their fathers were both Sugar Valley farmers, but Robert and Lester ended up leaving to experience life outside the valley.

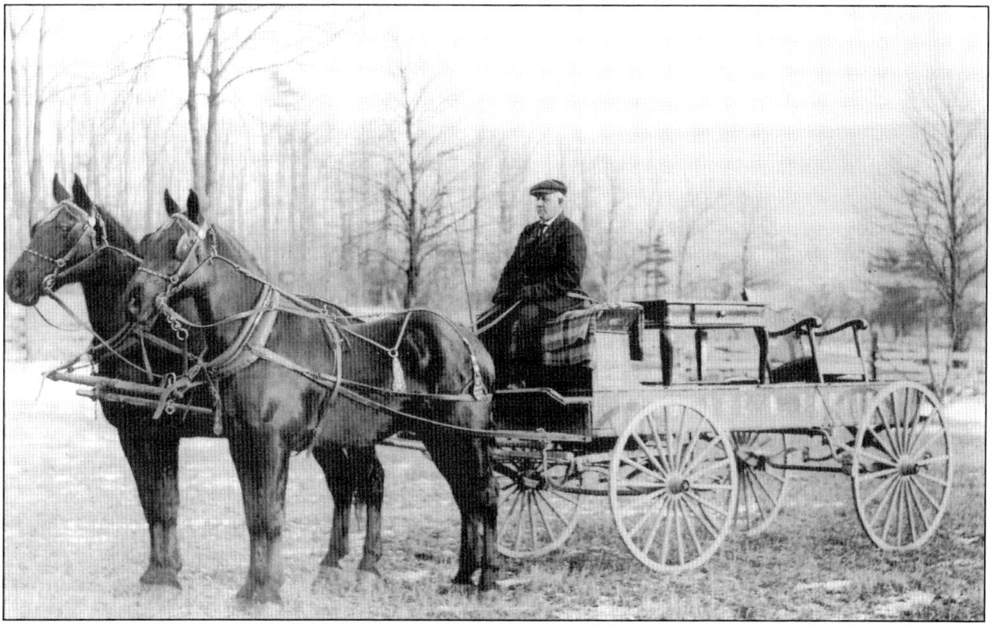

Elmer Morris (1861–1923) is pictured delivering furniture around 1910. His hardware, farm implements, and furniture store was in Loganton. Also an undertaker (along with his brother W. Morris), Morris even had a special child's hearse that was built in 1880. Elmer's father, Daniel Morris, had been an undertaker before his sons. Elmer's son Lee Morris became an undertaker in 1908.

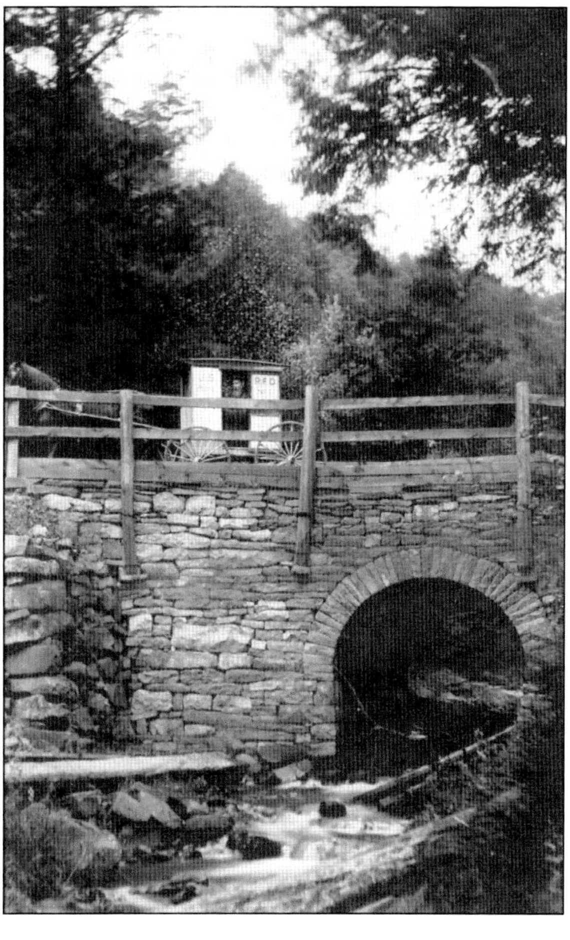

RFD service out of Loganton began on November 16, 1906. Samuel C. Frankenberger, Loganton's first RFD driver, served from 1906 to 1910. He paused along his route on this bridge near Sulphur Spring, just above Loganton.

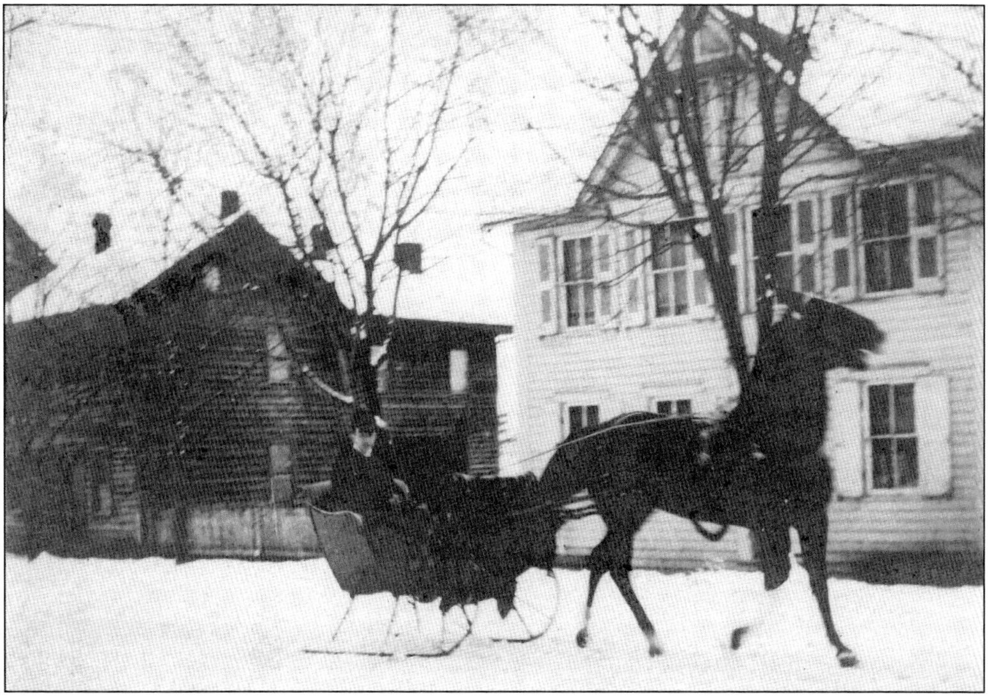

On a snowy day in 1907, Guy Boone (1881–1940), in his horse-drawn sleigh, passed by the Keister and Henry Karstetter homes, believed to be in Loganton. This image was sent on a postcard addressed to Miss Tama Boob of Loganton. Boone ran a general store in Loganton, and he also owned two stone quarries. He was president of the Loganton National Bank from 1938 to 1940.

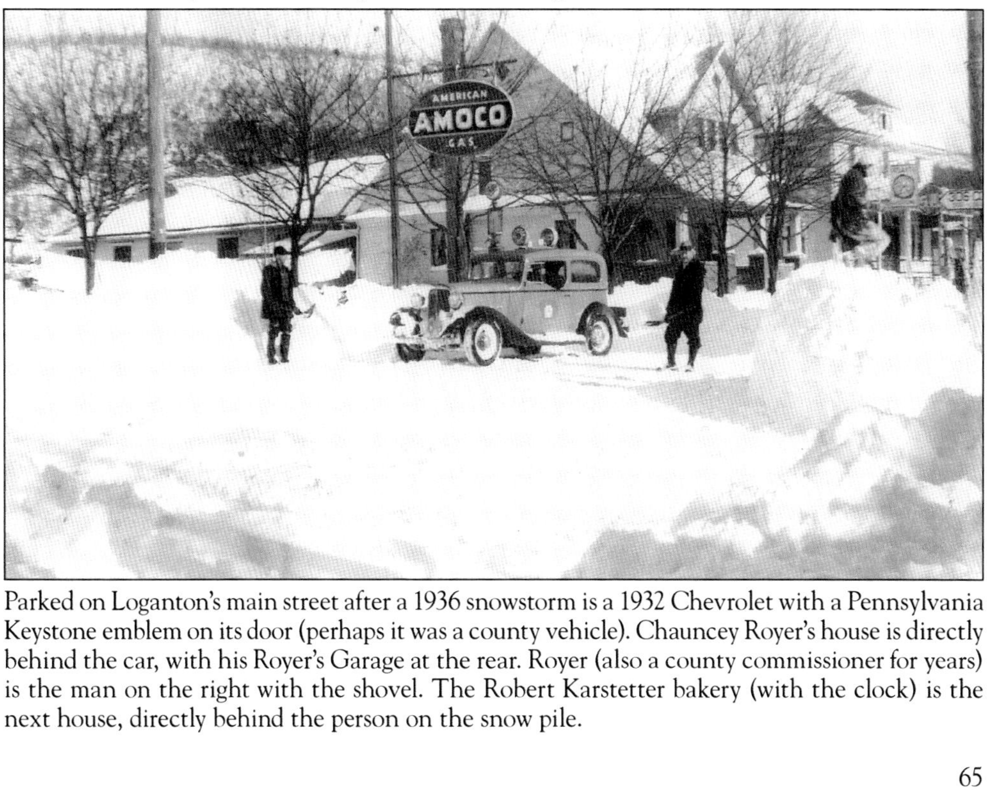

Parked on Loganton's main street after a 1936 snowstorm is a 1932 Chevrolet with a Pennsylvania Keystone emblem on its door (perhaps it was a county vehicle). Chauncey Royer's house is directly behind the car, with his Royer's Garage at the rear. Royer (also a county commissioner for years) is the man on the right with the shovel. The Robert Karstetter bakery (with the clock) is the next house, directly behind the person on the snow pile.

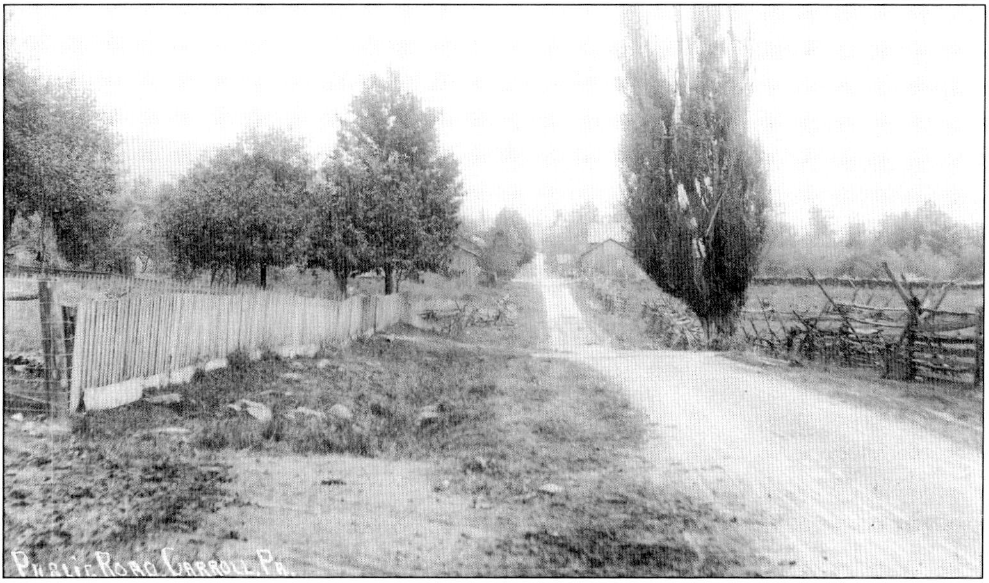

Around the year 1900, picket and rail fences (typical of Sugar Valley farms) lined this section of the highway running west to east to the village of Carroll. The steeple, seen in the distance at the northeast corner of the intersection of present-day Route 880 and Valley Road, is that of the St. John's United Evangelical Church, built in 1896. It closed in 1961 and was sold in 1964 to Charles Klobe, who subsequently dismantled it.

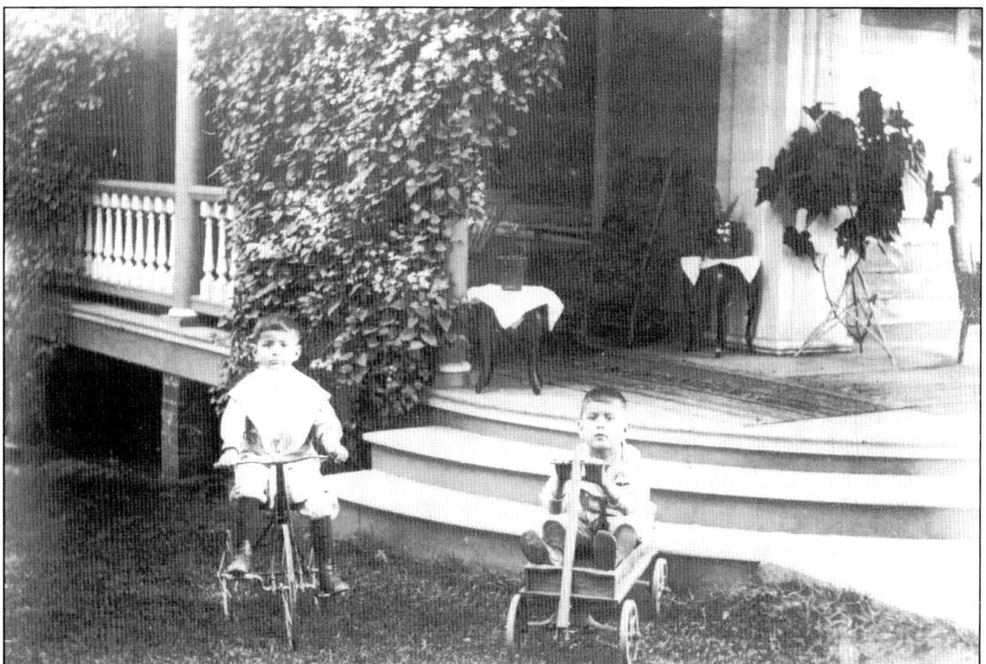

In the early 1910s, Maurice Wolfe (1908–1971) and his brother Hugh Wolfe (1907–1976) travel, respectively, by tricycle and wagon in front of their Booneville home. Their parents were William Luther Wolfe (1872–1925) and Clara Klepper Wolfe (1871–1955). Both brothers went on to raise families and live in Woolrich, where they had long, successful careers working in the Woolrich Woolen Mills.

Five

RECEIVING AN EDUCATION

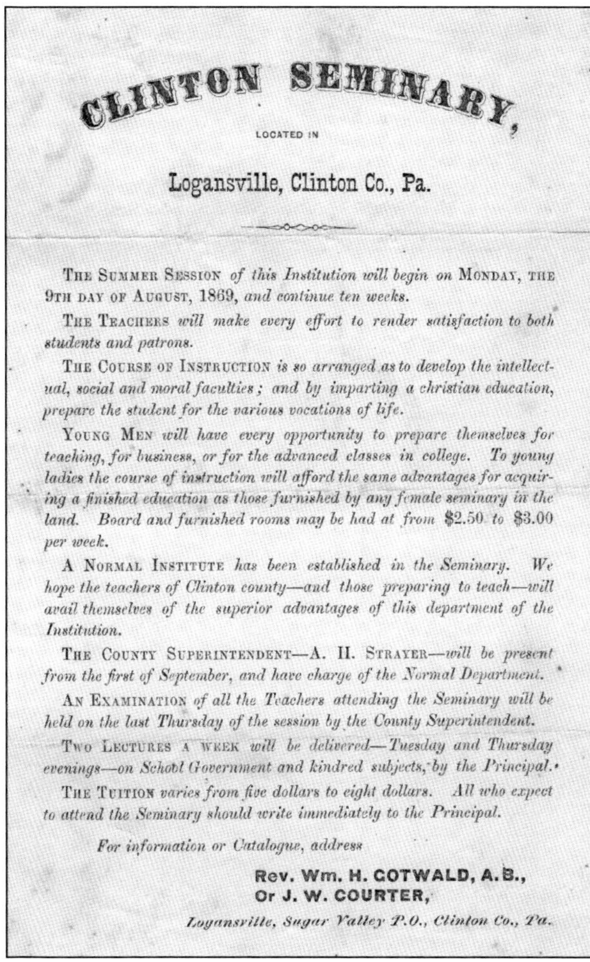

CLINTON SEMINARY,

LOCATED IN

Logansville, Clinton Co., Pa.

THE SUMMER SESSION *of this Institution will begin on* MONDAY, THE 9TH DAY OF AUGUST, 1869, *and continue ten weeks.*

THE TEACHERS *will make every effort to render satisfaction to both students and patrons.*

THE COURSE OF INSTRUCTION *is so arranged as to develop the intellectual, social and moral faculties; and by imparting a christian education, prepare the student for the various vocations of life.*

YOUNG MEN *will have every opportunity to prepare themselves for teaching, for business, or for the advanced classes in college. To young ladies the course of instruction will afford the same advantages for acquiring a finished education as those furnished by any female seminary in the land. Board and furnished rooms may be had at from* $2.50 *to* $3.00 *per week.*

A NORMAL INSTITUTE *has been established in the Seminary. We hope the teachers of Clinton county—and those preparing to teach—will avail themselves of the superior advantages of this department of the Institution.*

THE COUNTY SUPERINTENDENT—A. H. STRAYER—*will be present from the first of September, and have charge of the Normal Department.*

AN EXAMINATION *of all the Teachers attending the Seminary will be held on the last Thursday of the session by the County Superintendent.*

TWO LECTURES A WEEK *will be delivered—Tuesday and Thursday evenings—on School Government and kindred subjects, by the Principal.*

THE TUITION *varies from five dollars to eight dollars. All who expect to attend the Seminary should write immediately to the Principal.*

For information or Catalogue, address

Rev. Wm. H. GOTWALD, A.B.,
Or J. W. COURTER,

Logansville, Sugar Valley P.O., Clinton Co., Pa.

Some time between 1860 and 1863, the Clinton Seminary was established under Professor Biddle at what was then Logansville. Biddle, who came from Mifflinburg, was succeeded by the Lutheran reverend Dr. William Gotwald. Under Gotwald's direction, a normal institute for teacher education was added to the seminary, as this 1869 flyer advertised. Clinton Seminary only lasted a few years after that date.

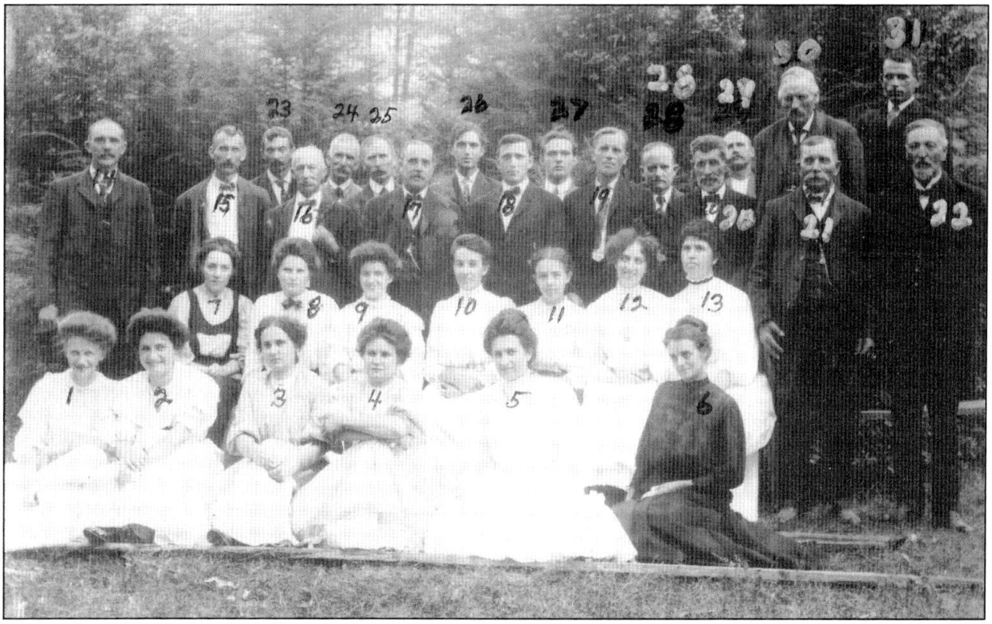

The Sugar Valley teachers' reunion of 1908 at the Booneville Campground included, from left to right, (first row) unidentified, M. Briggs, A. Kahl, L. Kahl, S. Meyer, and L. Ilgen; (second row) unidentified, M. Douty, unidentified, A. Bartges, L. Shaffer, P. Boone, and H. Heller; (third row) P. Caris, P. Greninger, P. Wycoff, I. McCloskey, N. Bartges, two unidentified, J. Herb, and unidentified; (fourth row) D. Tyson, A. Greninger, unidentified, C. Strohecker, F. Greninger, D. Karstetter, W. Mark, H. Graffius, and G. Meyer.

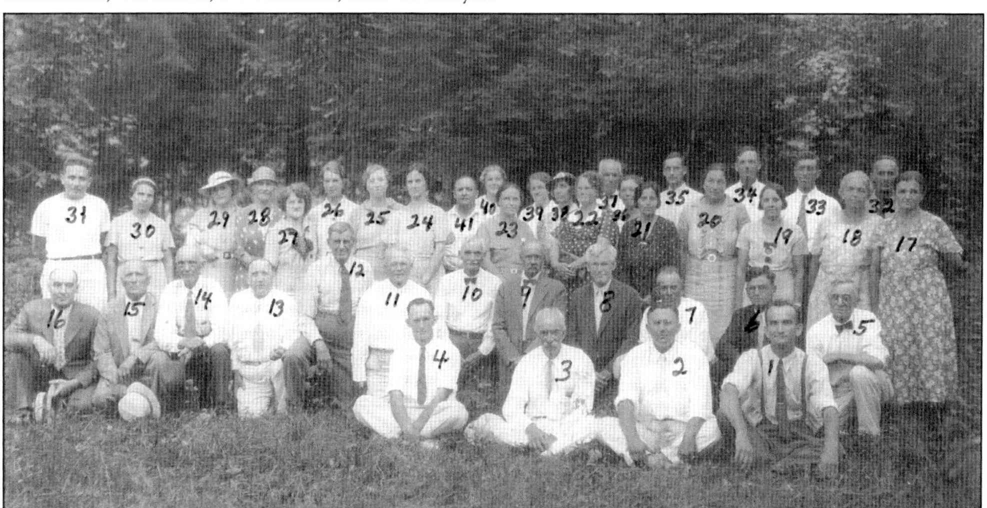

Sugar Valley teachers were photographed at the Booneville Campground around 1935. Those included in this image are identified by number from lowest to highest and are as follows: S. Schreckengast, T. Smith, D. Tyson, W. Frankenberger, E. Emig, E. Ilgen, R. Weaver, Rev. F. Fuhrman, W. Mark, A. Greninger, Rev. C. Wolfe, L. Bierly, N. Bartges, J. Schreckengast, J. Smith, A. Eckel, N. Yarrison, E. Shaffer, M. Imes, E. Mark, C. Simcox, M. Douty, L. Bierly, G. Waite, J. Renninger, K. Klaer, R. Barner, S. Meyers, M. Briggs, R. Currin, S. Schrack, H. Wren, H. Wise, A. Lamey, R. Douty, S. Lannen, G. Meyer, M. Ilgen, B. Klinefelter, M. Bauman, and J. Mark.

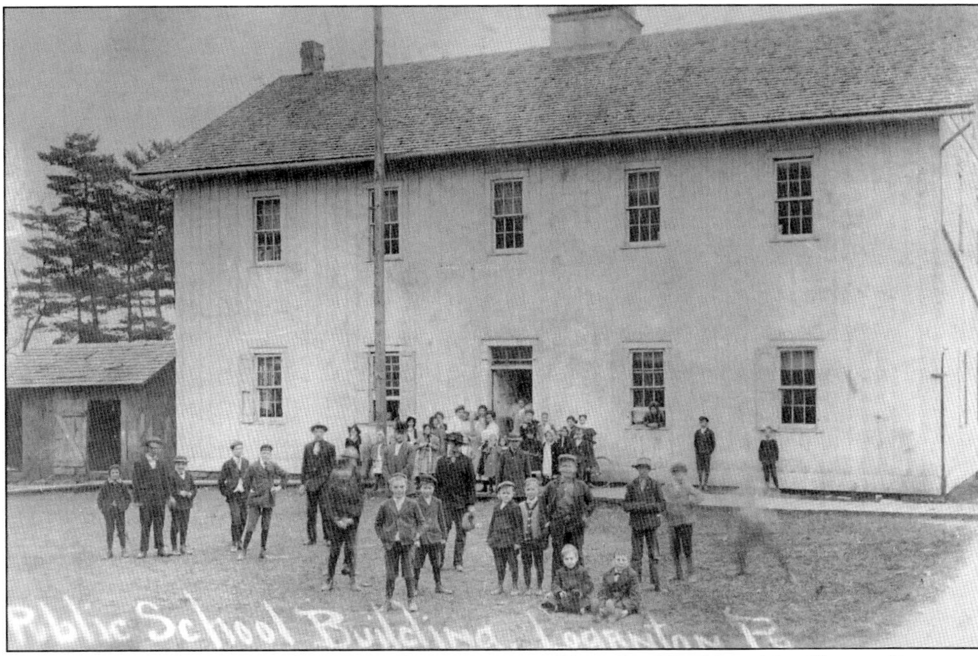

Believed to have been erected in 1864, the Loganton public school building (the Clinton Seminary also held classes there) was divided into primary and grammar schools in 1880. It was reorganized in 1891 and a ninth grade was added; a tenth grade was added in 1908. The building was destroyed by a mysterious fire at 2:30 a.m. on September 18, 1909.

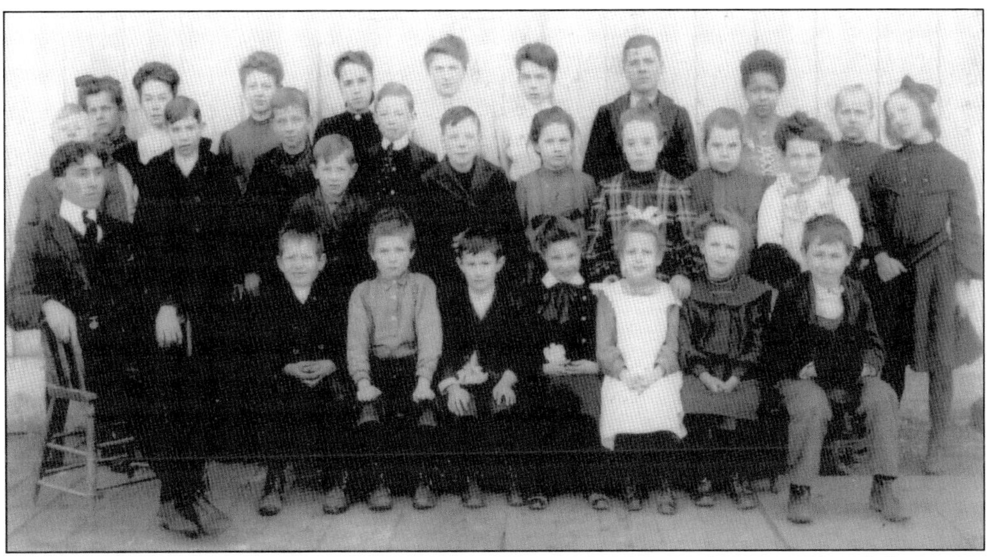

The members and teacher of the Loganton Elementary School class of 1906 are, from left to right, (first row) teacher George Gramley, Richard Wise, Howard Wren, Carl Herlocker, Martha Morris, Mittie Mark, Esther Snyder, and Torrence Womeldorf; (second row) Chiner Haun, Russell Berry, Robert Wise, Gilse Kissell, Paul Harter, Harvey Milnor, Hilda Herlacher, Bernice Karstetter, Esther Berry, Hazel Kissell, and Sarah Haas; (third row) Emma Raudabaugh, Tama Boob, Marge Harter, Elsie Wren, Ella Engle, Ada Keller, Edward Wirth, Eveline Barnum, and Florence Held.

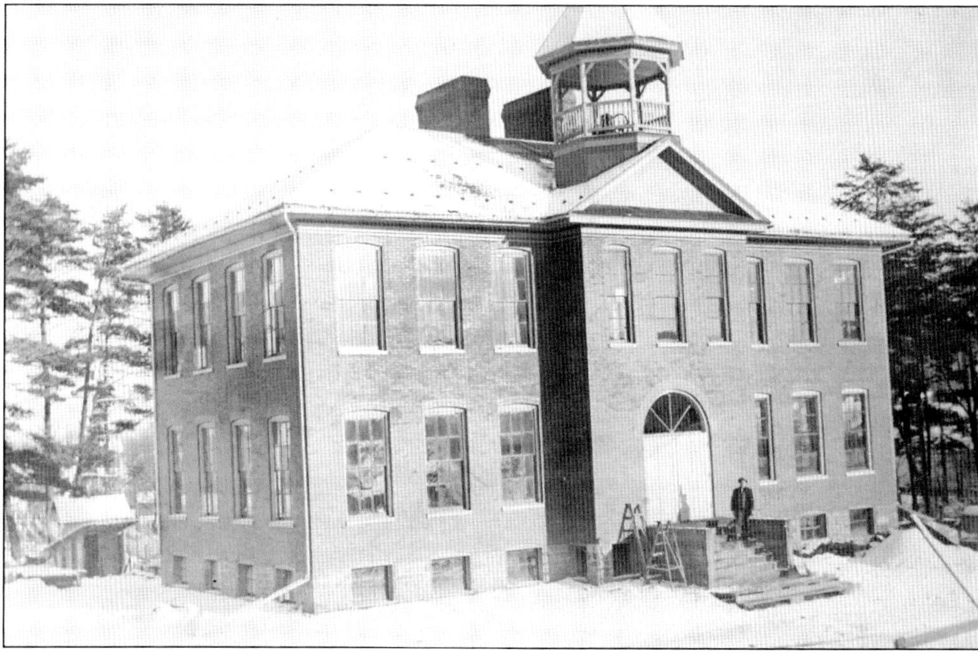

This two-story brick school building in Loganton was erected in 1910 to replace the structure destroyed by fire in 1909. Additions were made to the building in 1939 (a high school level was incorporated, which was a Work Projects Administration effort), in 1955 (to accommodate the consolidation that ended all one-room schools in the valley), and in 1965. This image was on a penny postcard postmarked in Logan Mills on March 3, 1911, and sent to Miss Lizzie Emig of Logan Mills. (Courtesy of Clinton County Historical Society.)

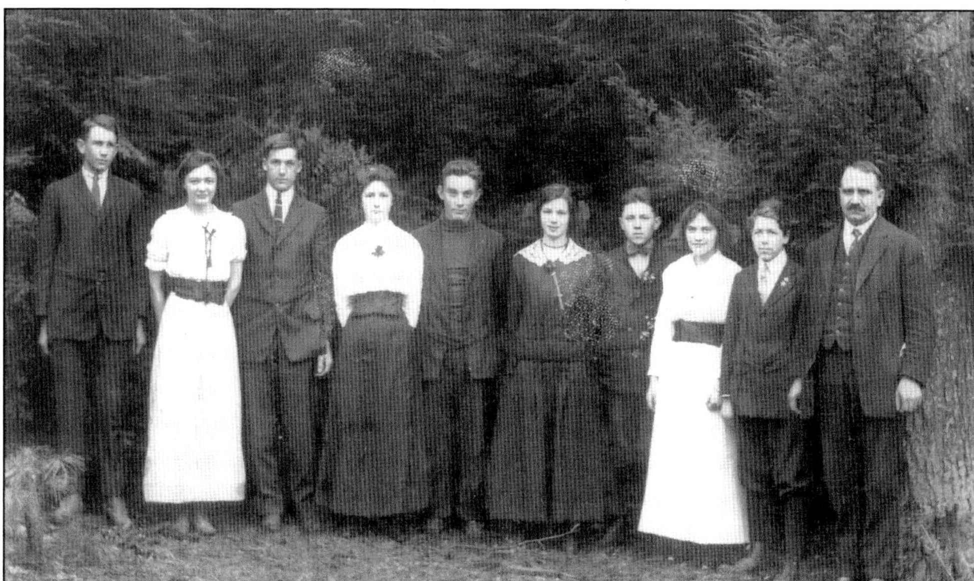

The members of the Loganton High School class of 1917 are, from left to right, Thomas Heckel, Helen Harter, Russell Douty, Mildred Wolfe, Neil Kleckner, Mildred Morris, Charles Jackman, Margaret Held, Walter Stover, and the principal, Prof. Joseph Rothrock Hanawalt (1871–1944). The class flower was the white rose, and the class colors were black and orange.

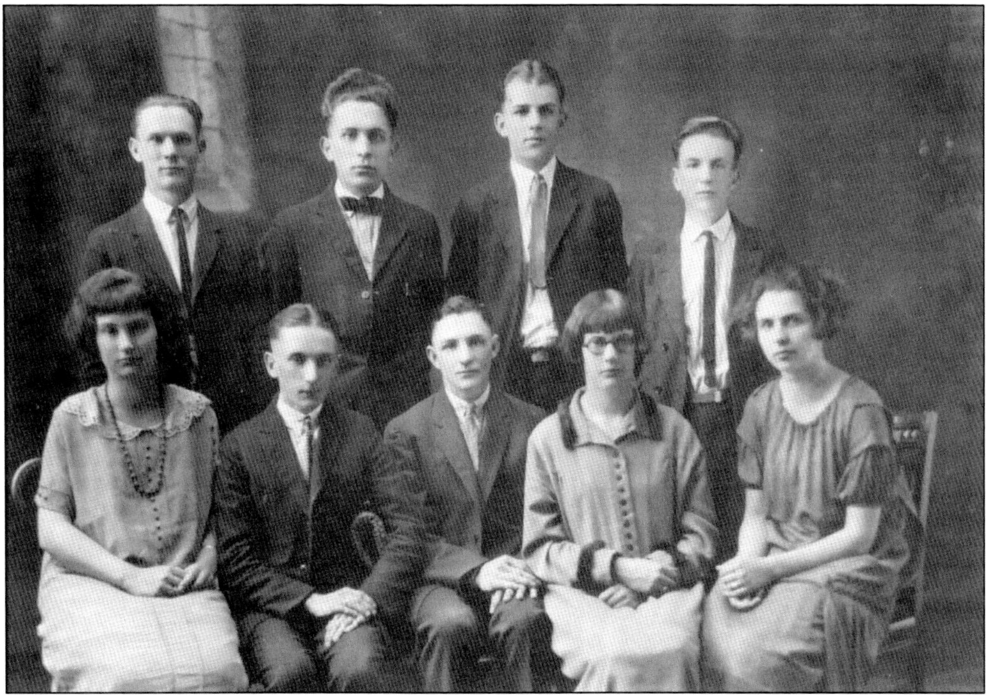

In 1926, the first four-year Loganton High School class graduated. The members of this class are, from left to right, (first row) Floretta Martz, Ernest Geisewite, Lester Heller, Mary Greninger, and Rhea Miller; (second row) Howard Lamey, Stewart Schrack, Gordon Adams, and Hector Eckel. All nine enrolled in college and became teachers, which was not common in 1926.

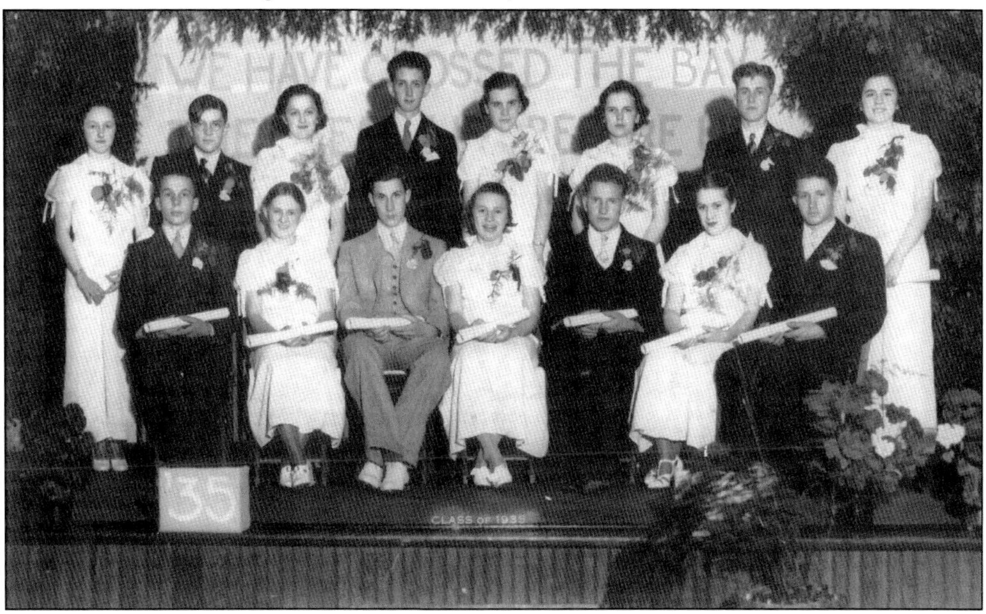

The 1935 graduates of Sugar Valley High School are, from left to right, (first row) Paul Miller, Sylvia Wilt, James Rockey, Cecelia Lamey, Harold Weaver, Vida Fiedler, and Kermit Karstetter; (second row) Mary Brungard, Norman Bressler, Beatrice Bressler, Glenn Lupold, Miriam Schade, Irene Meyer, John Washburn, and Ruth Adams.

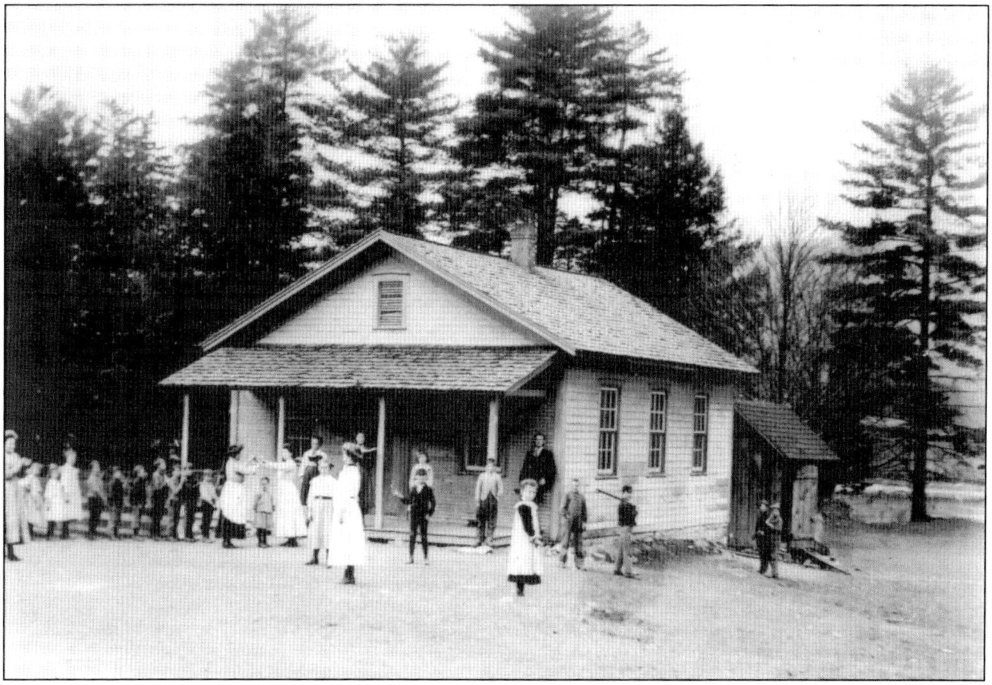

Logan Mills had a one-room school, also known as the "Bartges School," back in the 1820s. In this image, children play outside the school around 1910. Their teacher, Frederick Greninger, looks on from the porch. Later, the building was used as a workshop for an Amish farm and still serves in that capacity.

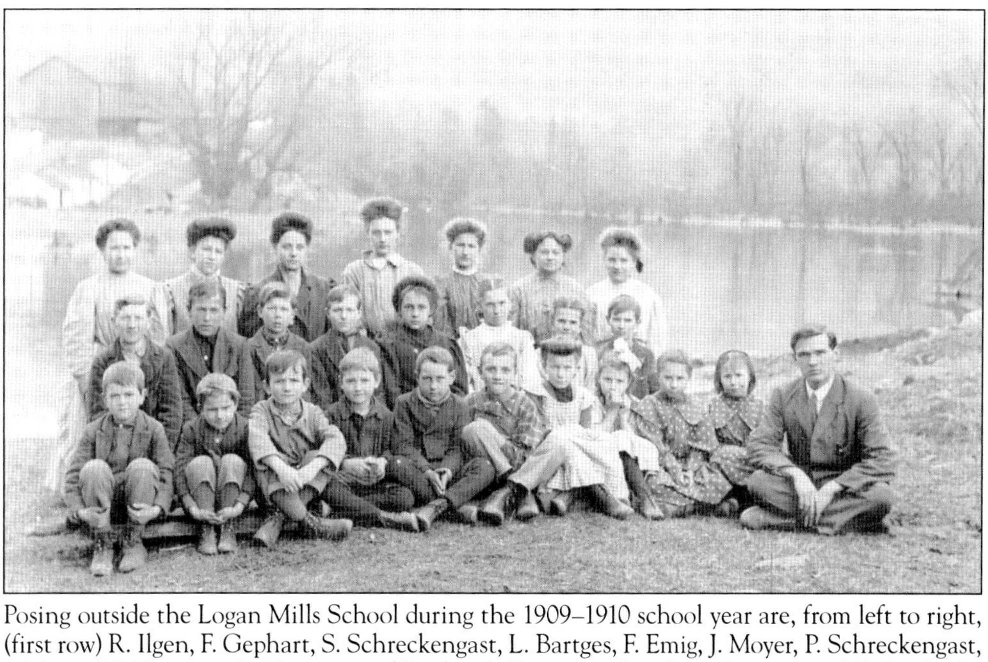

Posing outside the Logan Mills School during the 1909–1910 school year are, from left to right, (first row) R. Ilgen, F. Gephart, S. Schreckengast, L. Bartges, F. Emig, J. Moyer, P. Schreckengast, I. Moyer, M. Herman, C. Herman, and Frederick Greninger (teacher); (second row) F. Snyder, L. Schultz, L. Bower, A. Herman, J. Emig, A. Bierly, E. Bierly, and C. Lamey; (third row) F. Weaver, M. Schultz, E. Emig, M. Snyder, E. Thomas, A. Emig, and M. Frank.

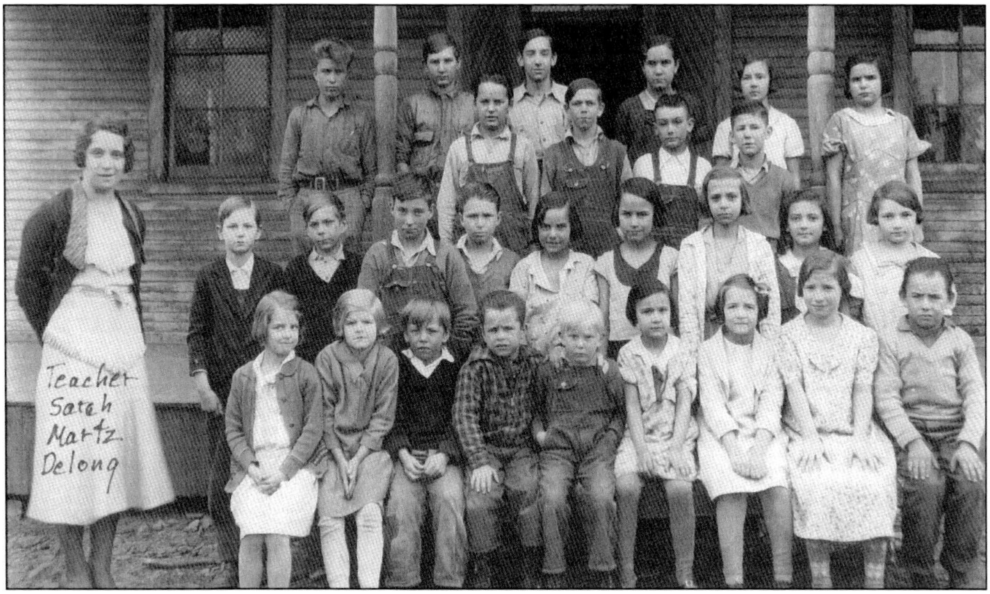

Sarah Martz Delong's 1934 Bull Run School class consisted of, from left to right, (first row) Lela Bell Bartges, Mary Brungard, Lynn Geyer, William Rishel, Robert Shaffer, Mary Douty, Betty Lamey, Betty Varner, and James Rishel; (second row) Harold Brungard, Arnold Geyer, Dale Rudy, Lawton Davis, Bertha Douty, Gladys Rishel, Irene Geyer, Bernice Heltman, and Phyllis Day; (third row) Allen Douty, Floyd Geyer, Joseph Heltman, and Bernard Day; (fourth row) Albert Rudy, Lynn Brungard, Harry Meyer, Ethel Mitcheltree, Inez Mark, and Kathryn Rishel.

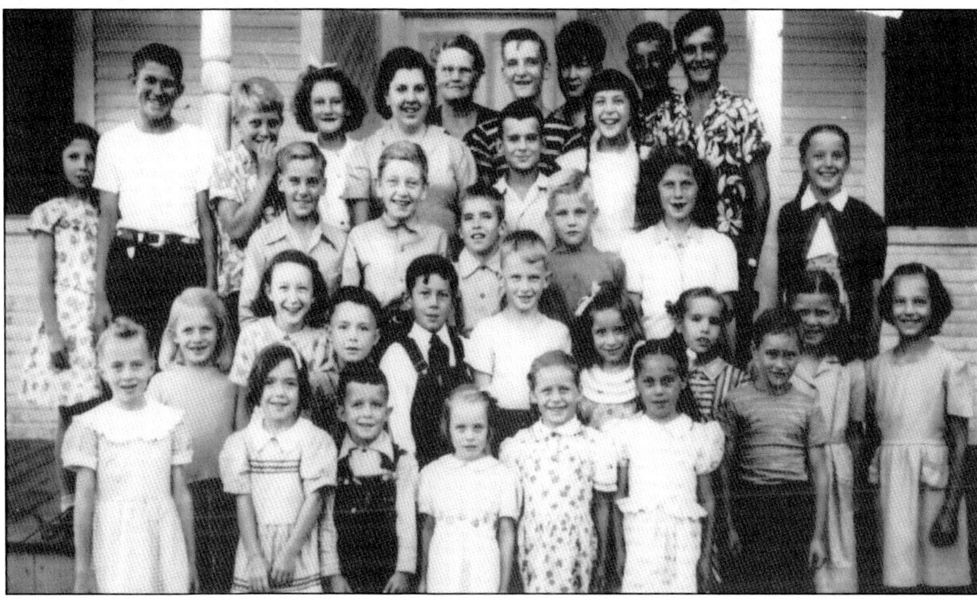

The 1948–1949 Bull Run School class members and teacher are, from left to right, (first row) J. Embick, F. Rishel, W. Walizer, I. Lamey, B. Courter, K. Lamey, and L. Lamey; (second row) L. Walizer, D. Rishel, R. Rishel, F. Lamey, G. Duck, V. Meyer, S. Rishel, J. Courter, and J. Lamey; (third row) W. Miller, G. Herlocher, J. Rishel, R. Duck, N. Lamey, and L. Truckenmiller; (fourth row) C. Powers (with fingers to mouth), P. Rossman, G. Walizer, and A. Bressler; (fifth row) E. Lamey, R. Mingle (against post), R. Heltman, Mayme Douty (teacher), D. Miller, G. Gentzel, R. Raudabaugh, and B. Raudabaugh.

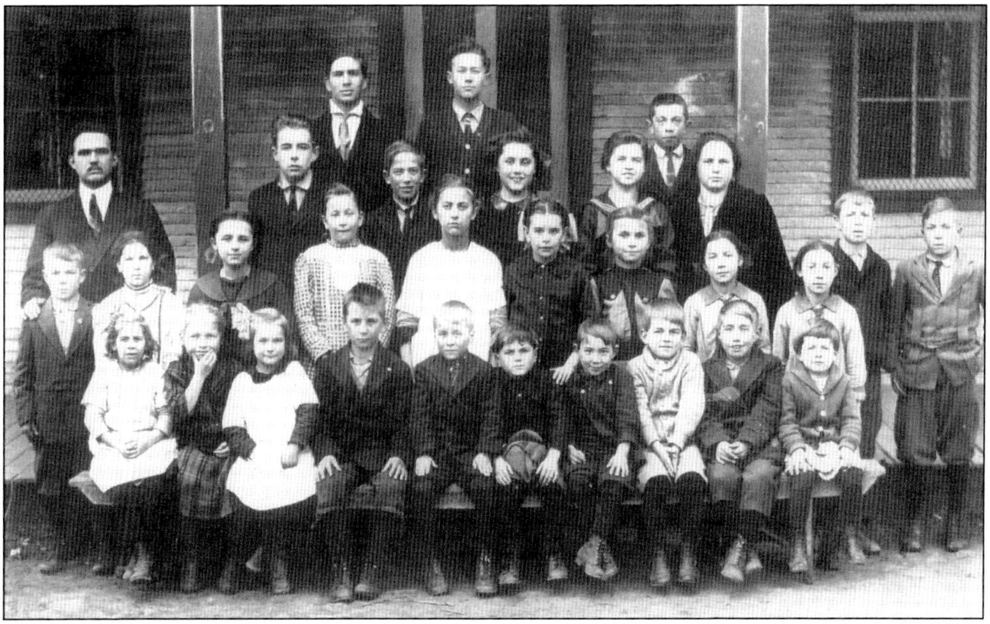

In this photograph from the Greenburr School in 1914 are, from left to right, (first row) Margaret Snyder, Fleda Walizer, Rhea Fiedler, Ralph Schade, Clifford Walizer, unidentified, Howard Lebo, Gordon Adams, Walter Lebo, and Glenn Adams; (second row) George Fiedler, Carrie Confer, Edna Stamm, two unidentified, Ethel Schade, Jennie Walizer, Martha Lebo, Mary Lebo, Bruce Miller, and Edwin Fiedler; (third row) unidentified teacher, Guy Schade, unidentified, Marian Schreckengast, Lillian Walizer, and unidentified: (fourth row) unidentified, Thomas Smith, and Edward Tyson.

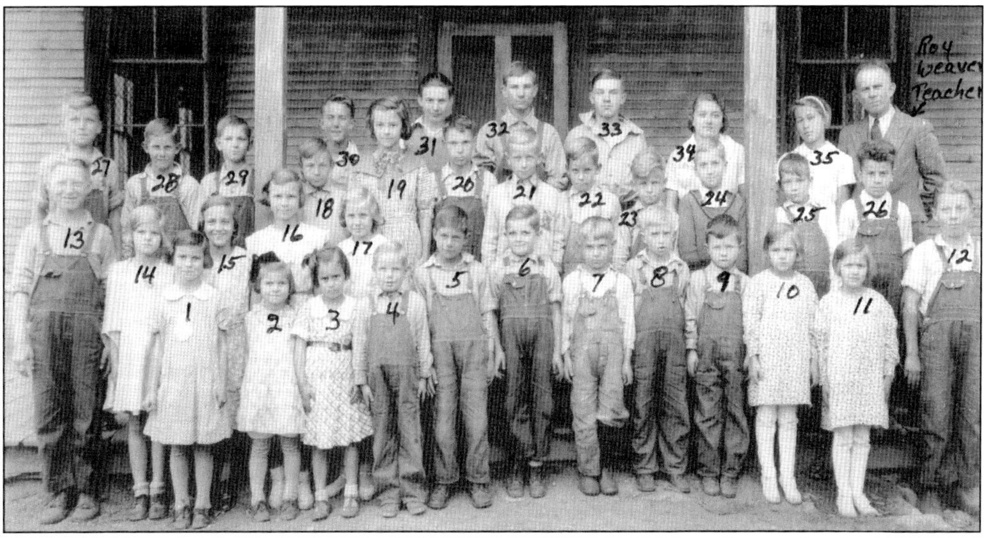

Pictured in this 1934 Greenburr School class photograph are, identified by number from lowest to highest, L. Schreckengast, A. Schreckengast, H. Miller, B. Sheats, J. Miller, L. Bressler, L. Lamey, C. Brungard, R. Karstetter, Ilene Lesher, Irene Lesher, A. Bletz, M. Bletz, M. Brungard, J. Lamey, R. Schreckengast, R. Miller, C. Welshans, J. Adams, L. Kramer, G. Sheats, S. Miller, D. Sheats, N. Fiedler, L. Fiedler, H. Adams, L. Sheats, A. Miller, H. Brungard, D. Miller, G. Karstetter, L. Brungard, Glenn Lesher, R. Bressler, B. Yarrison, and Roy Weaver (teacher).

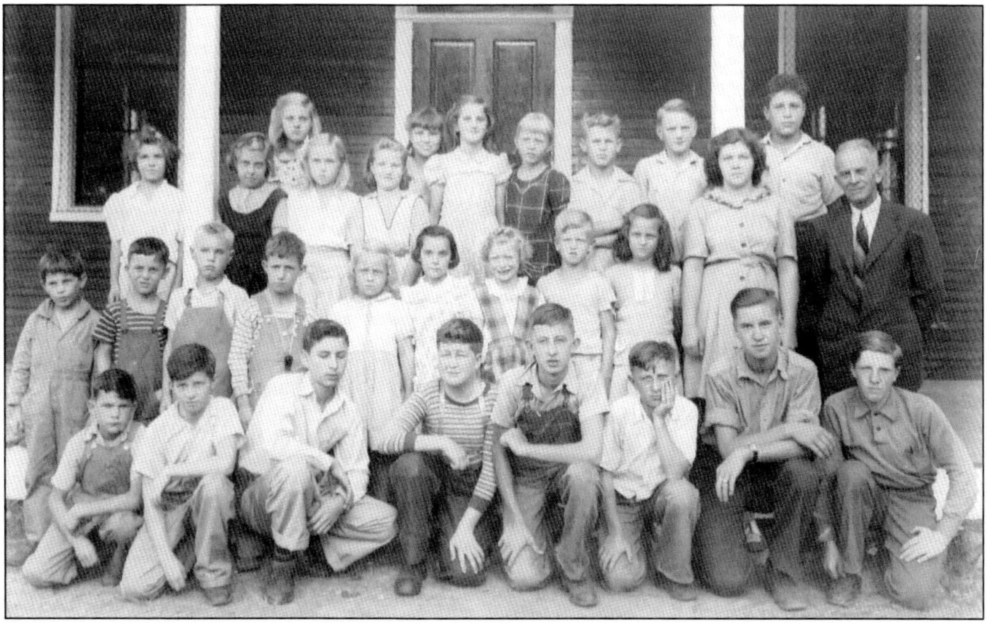

In this photograph of the Greenburr School class of 1946 are, from left to right, (first row) W. Douty, F. Lamey, J. Goodman, G. Gentzel, F. Slegle, E. Slegle, D. Tressler, and J. Lamey; (second row) D. Douty, K. Karstetter, J. Beck, D. Bowers, H. Summers, S. Douty, C. Weaver, T. Sheats, J. Summers, J. Karstetter, and Roy Weaver (teacher); (third row) J. Douty, J. Greninger, C. Beck, K. Lamey, Doris Brungard, J. Shaffer, D. Karstetter, C. Ruhl, and J. Summers; (fourth row) Dorothy Brungard and A. Lesher.

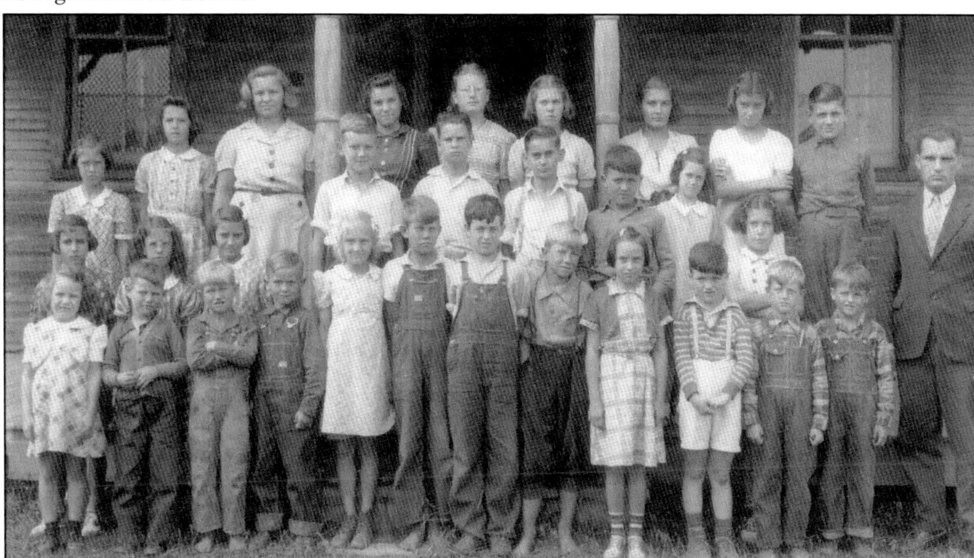

Standing in front of the Eastville (or Franklin) School in 1940 are, from left to right, (first row) G. Salamone, P. Frank, R. Mingle, D. Nicholas, L. Boone, S. Mingle Jr., R. Bower, L. Mingle, M. Miller, L. Heggenstaller, R. Raudabaugh, B. Raudabaugh, and Harold Douty (teacher); (second row) H. Slaterbeck, E. Raudabaugh, A. Slaterbeck, D. Boone, N. Matter, H. Martz, P. Heggenstaller, F. Bower, and R. Bletz; (third row) P. Frank, F. Raudabaugh, B. Hammersley, E. Meixel, A. Heggenstaller, R. Mingle, I. Martz, L. Slaterbeck, and J. Heggenstaller.

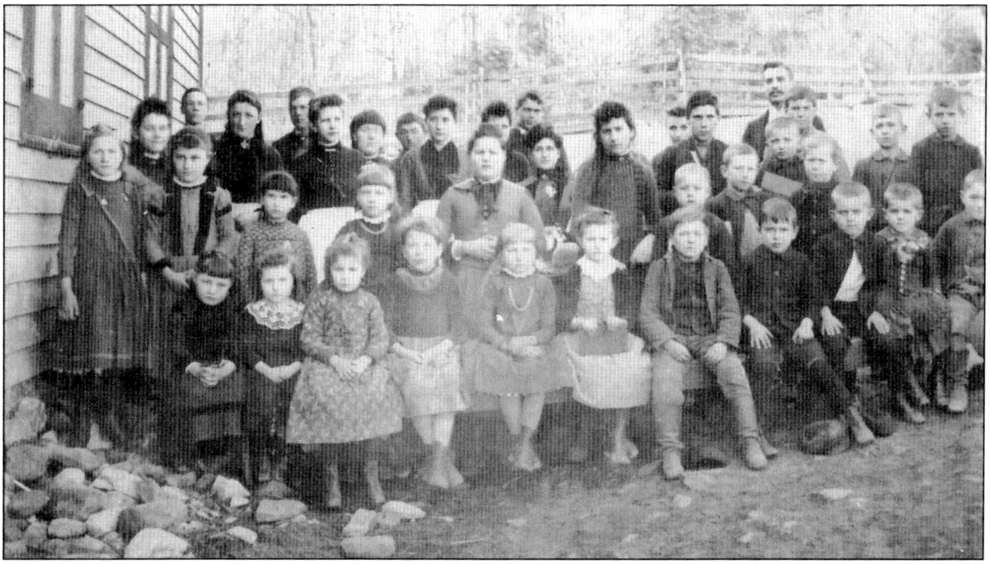

Included in this Booneville School photograph from 1889 are, from left to right, (first row) L. Bierly, M. Meyer, R. Sheats, B. Currin, N. Wolf, L. Wert, O. Lamey, R. Meyer, G. Schrack, R. Schrack, and R. Gharet; (second row) I. Wolfe, M. Bierly, M. Kahl, J. Karstetter, A. Wolf, S. Meyer, L. Miller, G. Boone, S. Gharet (holding a book), T. Delong, H. Meyer, and G. Meyer; (third row) L. Wolfe, A. Bartges, L. Boone, S. Karstetter, B. Herb, G. Boone (partially visible), M. Klepper, E. Sheats, A. Bierly, Edward Emig (teacher), and V. Wolfe (in front of Emig); (fourth row) D. Delong, R. Overdorf, J. Bartges, and H. Karstetter.

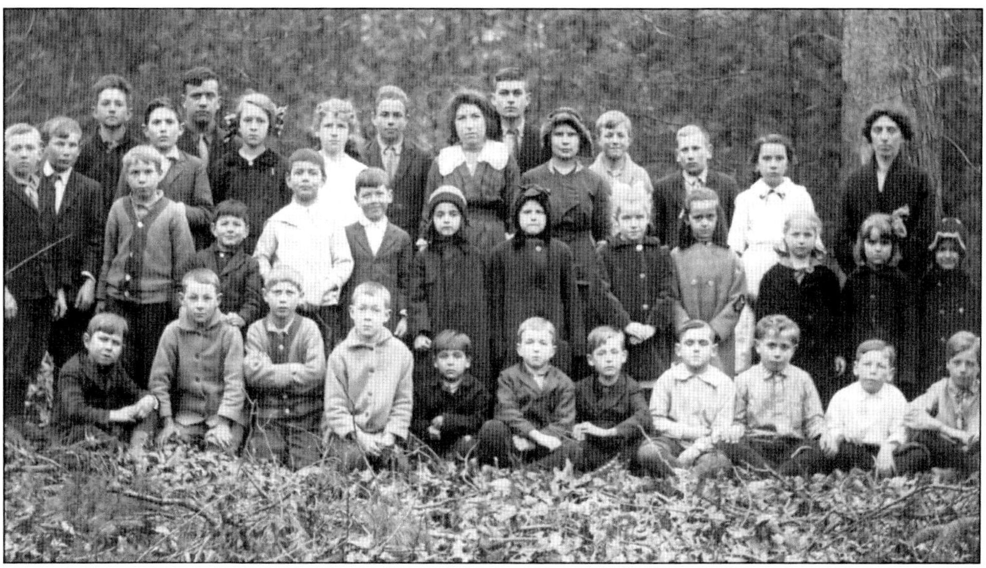

In this c. 1915–1916 class photograph at the Booneville School are, from left to right, (first row) J. Pick, E. Douty, C. Karstetter, C. Douty, S. Pick, H. Eckel, P. Bartges, B. Schrack, S. Schrack, T. Greninger, and I. Bartges; (second row) E. Karstetter, R. Kleckner, T. Karstetter, unidentified, M. Wolfe, H. Wolfe, Vella Schrack, T. Fidler, B. Pick, E. Overdorf, L. Schrack, L. Fidler, and J. Schrack; (third row) R. Shaffer, R. Schrack, C. Welshans, A. Shaffer, E. Klepper, R. Overdorf, Velma Schrack, J. Goodman, R. Kleckner, ? Gilbert, C. Smith, T. Welshans, and Mabel Shoemaker (teacher).

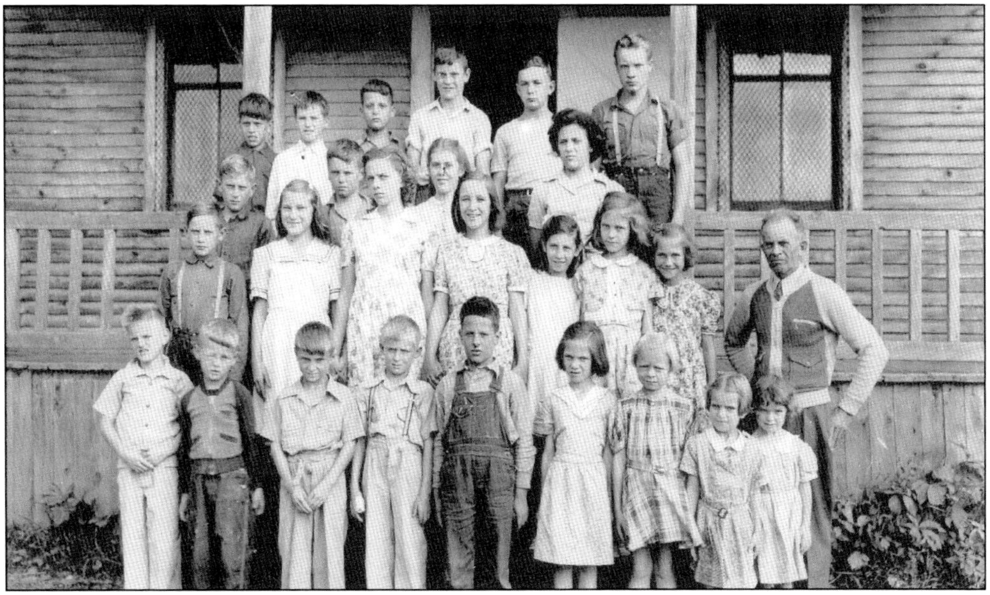

Included in this Booneville School photograph from the year 1942–1943 are, from left to right, (first row) C. Ruhl, D. Karstetter, J. Schreckengast, W. Schreckengast, J. Summers, R. Karchner, J. Shaffer, B. Karstetter, and M. Karstetter; (second row) L. Kleckner, M. Bierly, B. Ruhl, D. Wolfe, A. Slegle, S. Karchner, P. Wolfe, and Roy Weaver (teacher); (third row) J. Welshans, W. Karstetter, S. Ilgen and M. Summers; (fourth row) W. Karchner, D. Tressler, S. Summers Jr., E. Tressler, E. Welshans, and R. Kleckner.

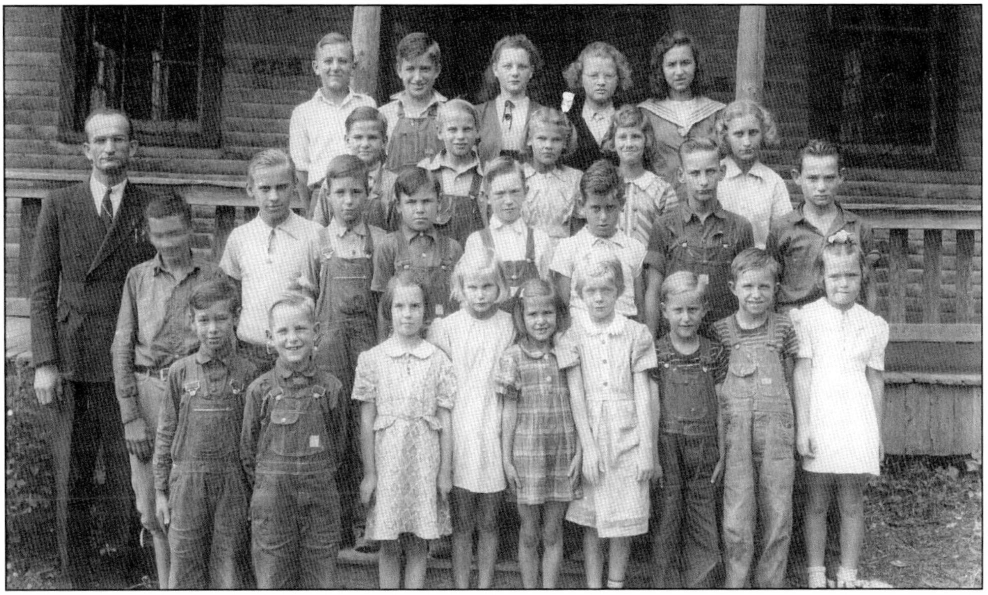

This Rock Grove (or Carroll) School photograph of the 1940–1941 school year includes, from left to right, (first row) G. Heggenstaller, C. Klobe Jr., D. Geary, M. Yarrison, R. Yarrison, J. Royer, H. Klobe, Donnell Jeffries, and A. Matthews; (second row) Snowden Schreckengast (teacher), H. George, R. Harbach, C. Heggenstaller, D. Harbach, J. Geary, P. Snyder, L. Klobe, and H. Snook Jr.; (third row) F. Yarrison, H. Harbach Sr., K. Yarrison, T. Klobe, and M. Klobe; (fourth row) C. Bennett, David Jeffries, T. Embick, V. Kelly, and M. Heggenstaller.

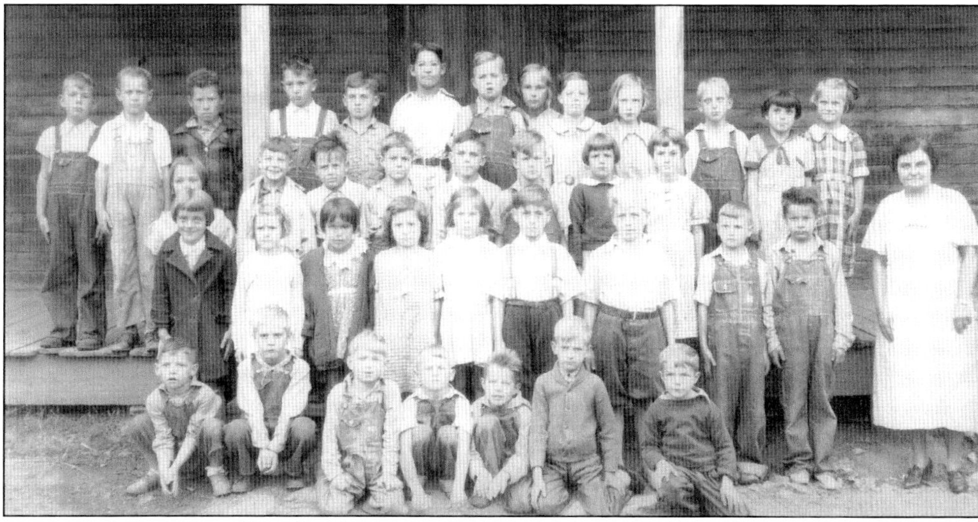

In front of the Tylersville School in 1937 are, from left to right, (first row) V. Miller, H. Boone, C. Sweeley, P. Ilgen, R. Simcox, W. Miller, and D. Slaterbeck; (second row) S. McCaleb, S. Schreckengast, B. Gummo, M. Vance, A. Greninger, O. Herlocher, H. Herlocher, E. Grieb, P. Simcox, and Lulu Kerstetter (teacher); (third row) E. Gummo, R. Sweeley Jr., W. Frantz, T. Nicholas, A. Schrack, D. Karstetter, D. Slaterbeck, and G. McCaleb; (fourth row) G. Overdorf, A. Gunsallus, G. Vance, W. Overdorf, K. Miller, R. Gummo, E. Moyer, I. Fiedler, B. Karstetter, M. Boone, R. Musick, M. Frank, and B. Bierly.

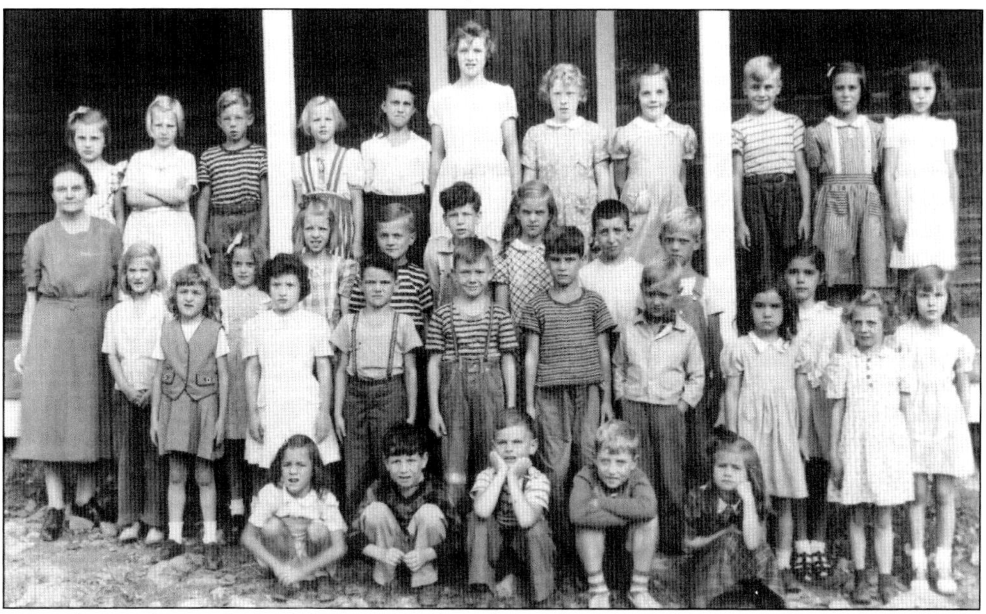

Attendees and a teacher of the Tylersville School in 1945 are, from left to right, (first row) Ellen Moyer, R. Beck, K. Miller, G. Gephart, and M. Burnell; (second row) P. Grieb, A. Vance, R. McCaleb, D. Overdorf, F. Houtz, I. Schreckengast, J. Miller, and L. Grieb; (third row) Lulu Kerstetter (teacher), L. Schreckengast, B. Wagner, C. Styers, P. McCaleb, C. Beck, C. Stover, Blaine Geise, F. Stover, J. McCaleb, and J. Toner; (fourth row) B. Mayes, T. Slaterbeck, E. Grieb, K. Kerstetter, Eunice Moyer, P. Vance, G. Vance, C. McCaleb, R. Miller, G. Monk, and J. Wagner. (Courtesy of Kenneth and Peggy Karstetter.)

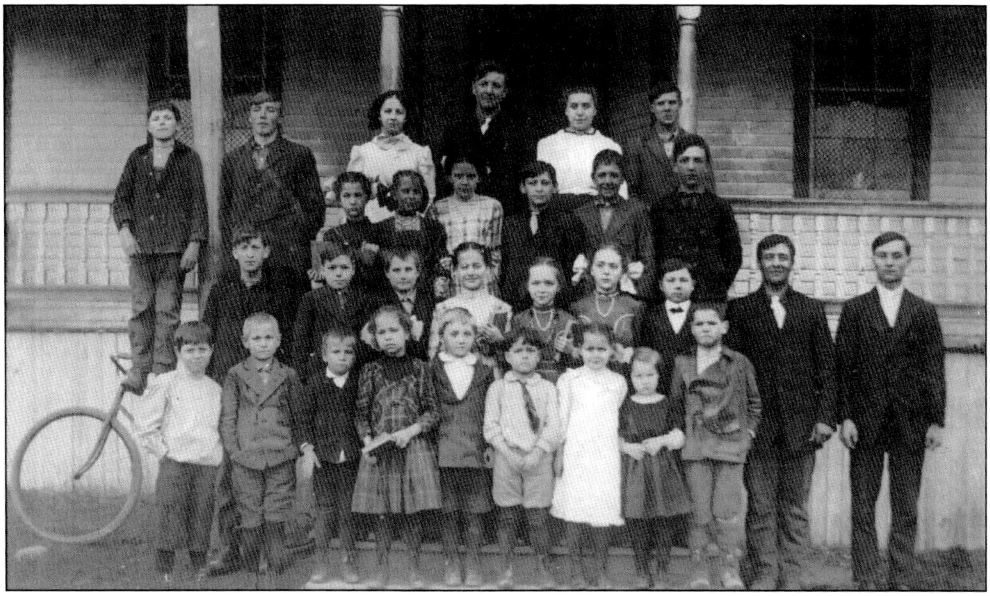

The Second Womeldorf (or Price) School 1912 class members and their teacher are, from left to right, (first row) S. Confer, A. Womeldorf, unidentified, Martha Bicksler, two unidentified, H. Confer, S. Confer, and W. Houtz; (second row) unidentified, I. Eckel, R. Womeldorf, R. Confer, G. Long, D. Royer, A. Glantz, C. Heggenstaller, and Guy Yarrison (teacher); (third row) Mildred Bicksler, E. Doerr, L. Confer, unidentified, J. Mark, and L. Heggenstaller; (fourth row) C. Eckel, G. Eckel, M. Mark, E. Heggenstaller, E. Eckel, and F. Mark.

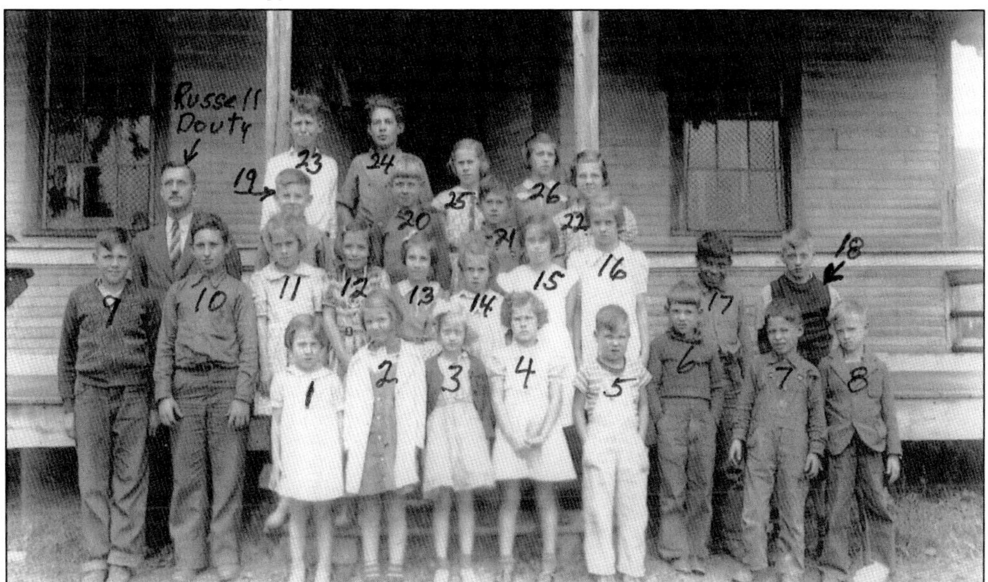

Posing at the First Womeldorf (or Wise) School during the 1940–1941 school year are, from left to right, (first row) J. Lamey, M. Kreamer, M. Frankenberger, E. Mark, P. Embick, J. Schrack, M. Snook, and D. Frankenberger; (second row) J. Harbach, C. Truckenmiller, V. Lamey, C. Snook, A. Slegle, S. Lamey, W. Embick, Z. Truckenmiller, L. Snook, and G. Frankenberger; (third row) Russell Douty (teacher), E. Bartges, D. Schrack, R. Lamey, and A. Burnell; (fourth row) A. Kreamer, E. Snook, L. Lamey, and E. Slegle.

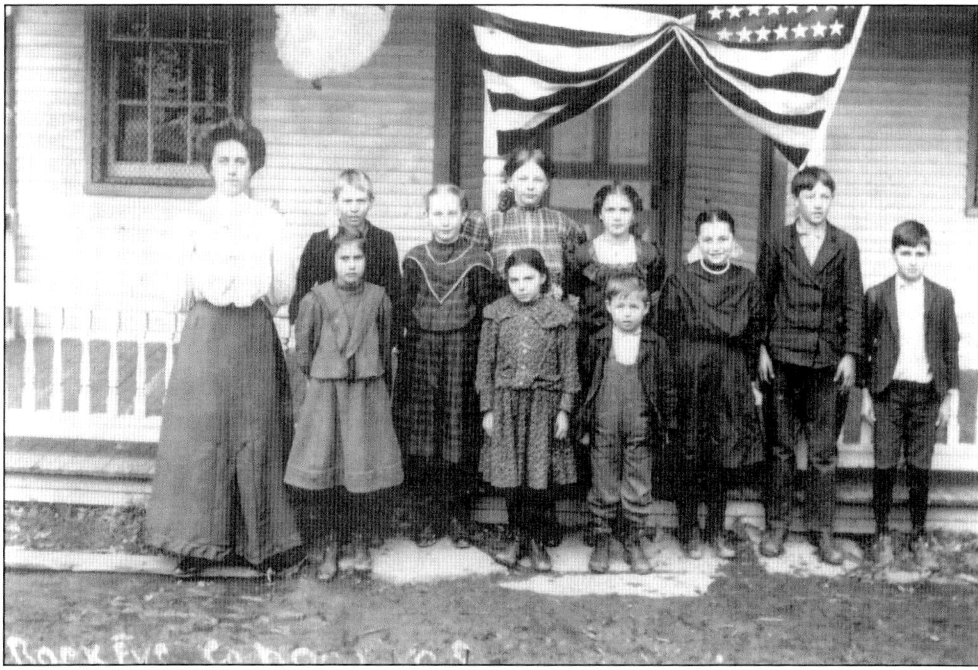

Included in this 1908–1909 photograph of the students and teacher at the Rockey (or Green Grove) School are, from left to right, (first row) Mabel Shoemaker (teacher), Irene Daugherty, Violet Zellers, and Clyde Bower; (second row, all with feet against the porch) George Zellers, Bessie Harbach, Mary Stark, May Daugherty, Edna Rockey, Guy Bower, and Charles Daugherty.

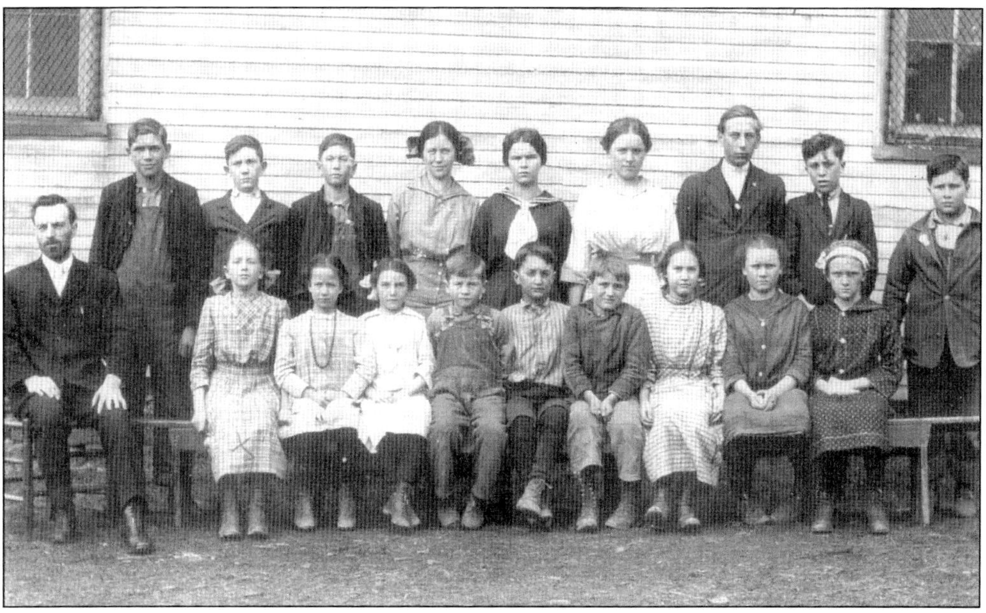

Teacher and students of the Hoffa-Yarrison (or Mount Union) School in the 1914–1915 school year are, from left to right, (first row) Charles Schwenk (teacher), Ruth Embick, Mabel Smith, Emma Embick, Henry Embick, Emerson Lehman, Lester Lehman, Elva Lehman, Erma Lehman, and Florence Embick; (second row) Albert Embick, Benjamin Embick, Elmer Embick, Helen Embick, Ernestine Bicksler, Julia Lehman, Harry Harbach, Orvis Yarrison, and Harold Bicksler.

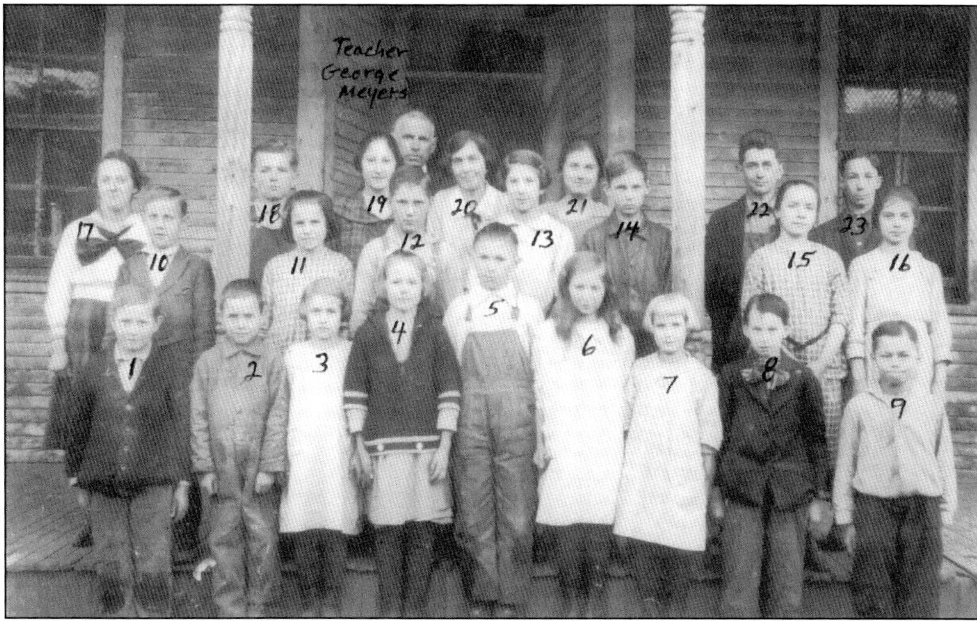

The Kemmerer School class members and teacher in this c. 1921 photograph are, from left to right, (first row) Richard Kemmerer, Hayes Rishel, Thelma Delong, Ruth Raudabaugh, George Fetter, Leah Douty, Helen Douty, Joy Schrack, and Jack Delong; (second row) Morris Womeldorf, Ida Rishel, Harold Douty, Grace Barner, Roy Douty, Nellie Rishel, and Hazel Heisley; (third row) Maude Beck, Floyd Wirts, Hazel Barner, George Meyers (teacher in back), Lydia Bartges, Dorothy Miller, Lynn Bartges, and Stewart Confer.

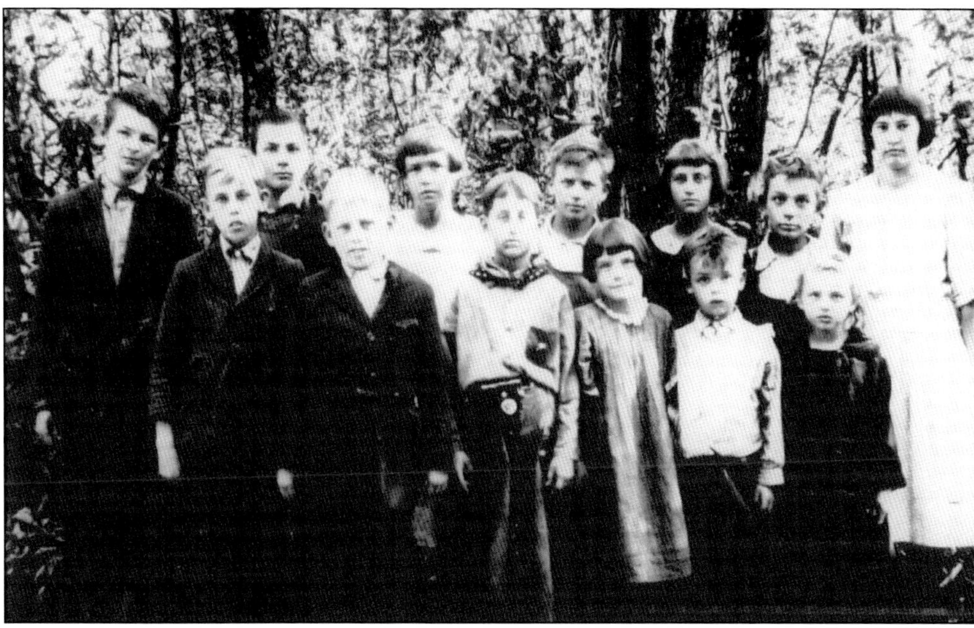

The 1924 class and teacher from the Mount Zion School are, from left to right, (first row) Richard Bixel, Glenn Rich, Alvin Eyer, Ethel Rich, David Bixel, and Bertha Miller; (second row) John Weaver, Delbert Eyer, Dorothy Bixel, John Miller, Dorothy Eyer, Charles Miller, and Viola Lehman (teacher).

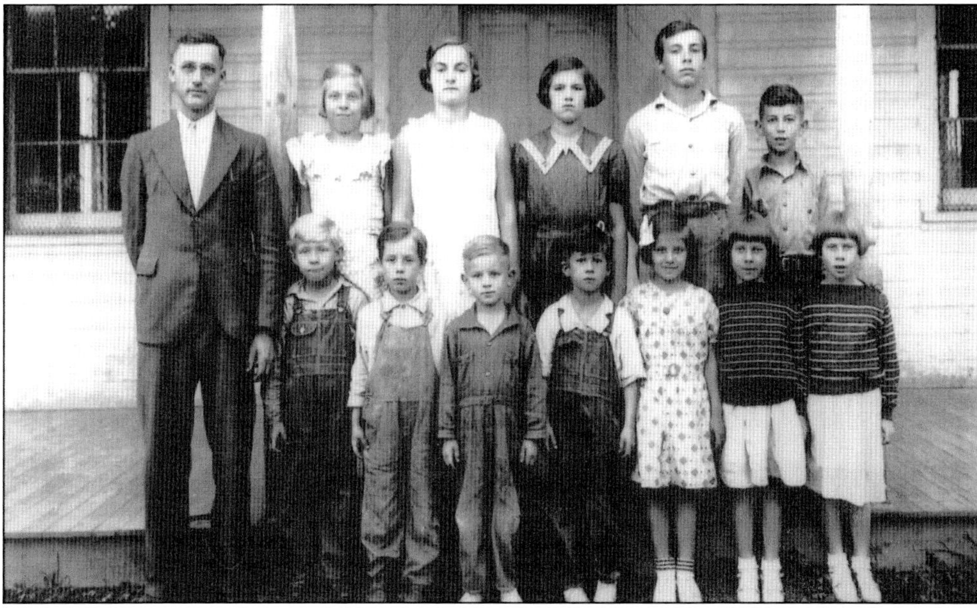

Posing in front of the Schracktown-Centerville School for the 1936–1937 school year photograph are, from left to right, (first row) Russell Douty (teacher), Daniel Schrack, Ralph Embick, Elwood Bartges, Robert Lamey, Eileen Slegle, Lois Lamey, and Louise Lamey; (second row) Lois Schrack, Martha Overdorf, Hazel Embick, Levi Embick, and Dean Bartges. This was the school's final year.

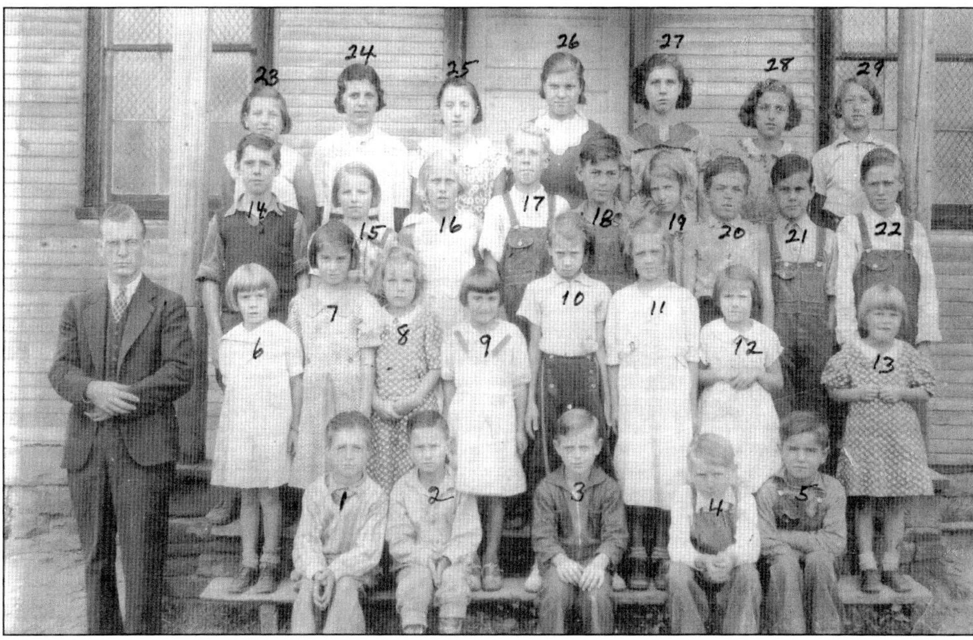

The Sheats (or Mount Pleasant) School class of 1936–1937 and its teacher are, from left to right, (first row) Paul Cooper (teacher), B. Cashner, G. Fleisher, D. Cooper, J. Seyler, and E. Wagner; (second row) M. Cashner, L. Slaterbeck, G. Wagner, A. Slaterbeck, B. Knarr, P. Cashner, M. Wagner, and J. Wagner; (third row) C. Cashner, A. Duck, M. Fleisher, C. Seyler, Russell Cooper, D. Seyler, R. Schwab, Raymond Cooper, and W. Seyler; (fourth row) B. Fleisher, H. Cooper, G. Schwab, G. Herman, H. Cashner, V. Fleisher, and E. Knarr. The school closed in 1952.

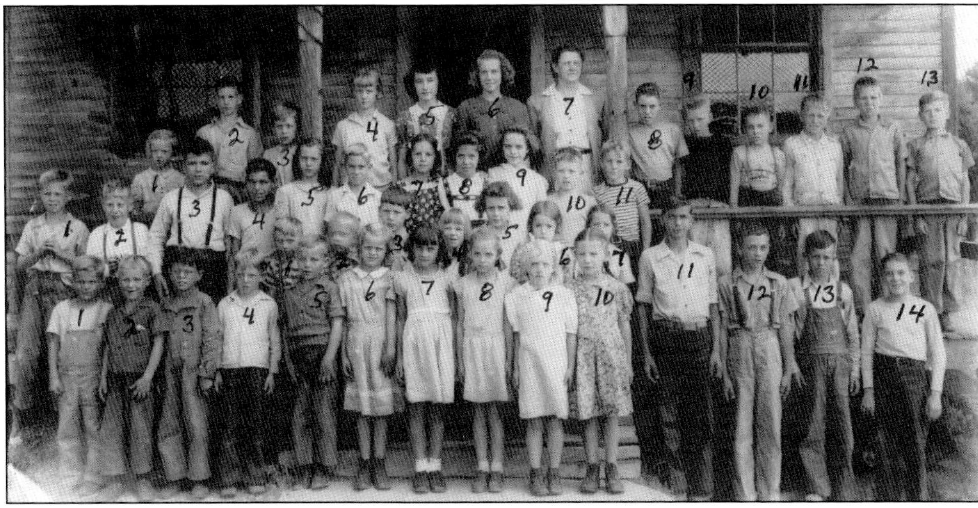

In front of the Knarr School in this c. 1946–1947 photograph are, from left to right, (first row) Roland Weaver, H. Herman Jr., E. Weaver, J. Quiggle, C. Geyer, S. Fegley, S. Reeder, M. Geyer, L. Snook, M. Confer, A. Weaver, A. Geyer, R. Baney Jr., and T. Herman; (second row) E. Mesmer, J. Matter, R. Cummings, A. Baney, M. Kulp, D. Matter, and M. Matter; (third row) R. Fegley, H. Confer, N. Geyer, Richard Weaver, S. Weaver, J. Snook, E. Matter, M. Brungard, J. Kulp, ? Kiefer, and C. Reeder; (fourth row) S. Kiefer, R. Kiefer, ? Kiefer, W. Kiefer, H. Kulp, A. Wagner, Mary Greninger (teacher), K. Snook, L. Kiefer, R. Herman, J. Baney, M. Geyer, and J. Cummings.

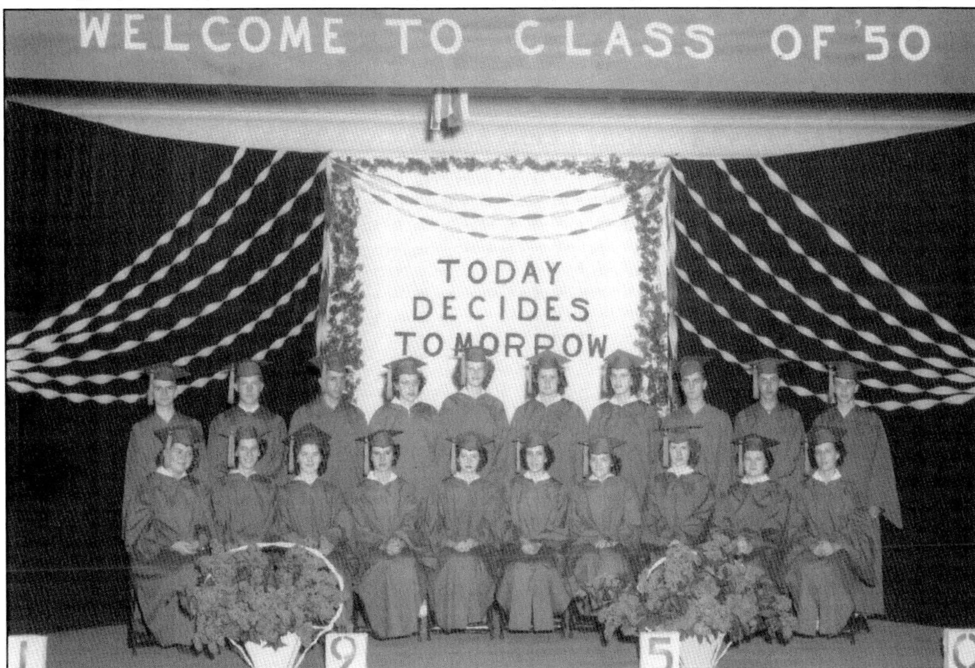

The members of the Sugar Valley High School class of 1950 are, from left to right, (first row) Betty Washburn, Anna Mae Slegle, Doris Rowe, Helen Slaterbeck, Janet Greninger, Barbara Imes, Vivian Douty, Betty Boone, Edna Ilgen, and Lois Bressler; (second row) Kenneth Meyers, William Rishel, Gerald Walizer, Grace McCaleb, Addalee Sheats, Zelda Truckenmiller, Beverly Sue Karchner, Ronald Douty, Frank Brungard, and William Vance.

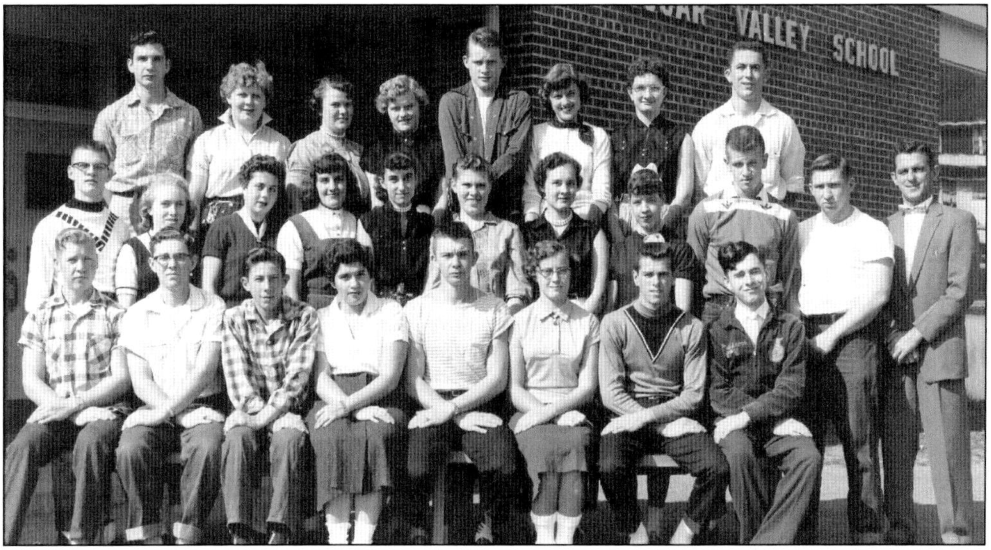

The Sugar Valley School 1957 graduating class members are, from left to right, (first row) W. Bailor, W. Brungart, F. Lamey, L. Ripka, D. Overdorf, L. Truckenmiller, E. Weaver, and D. Snook; (second row) R. Renninger, L. Snook, J. Barner, S. Reeder, D. Miller, M. Wagner, J. Lamey, M. Matter, T. Sheats, K. Roberts, and R. Weaver (class adviser); (third row) C. Geyer, J. Courter, D. Mingle, B. Frye, R. Duck, P. Grieb, J. Miller, and K. Karstetter. (Courtesy of Kenneth and Peggy Karstetter.)

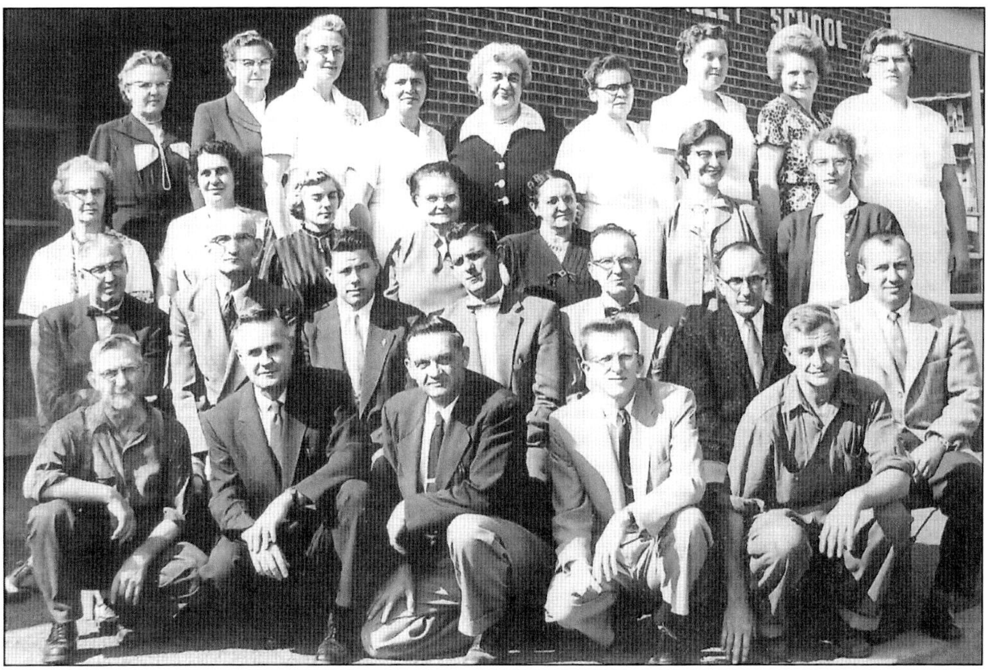

The Sugar Valley School faculty and staff in this 1956 photograph are, from left to right, (first row) E. Mesmer, C.S. Keister (supervising principal), A. Lamey, W. Harbach, and R. Bressler; (second row) G. Hancock, S. Schreckengast, A. Carey, R. Weaver, H. Eckel, E. Geisewite, and D. Dunn; (third row) G. Waite, A. Currin, E. Smith, L. Kerstetter, M. Imes, A. Thompson, and B. Freeze; (fourth row) H. Tussey, M. Greninger, O. Yarrison, C. Breon, E. Thompson, R. Lehman, L. Imes, M. Phillippi, and B. Brungard.

Six

Witnessing Historical Moments

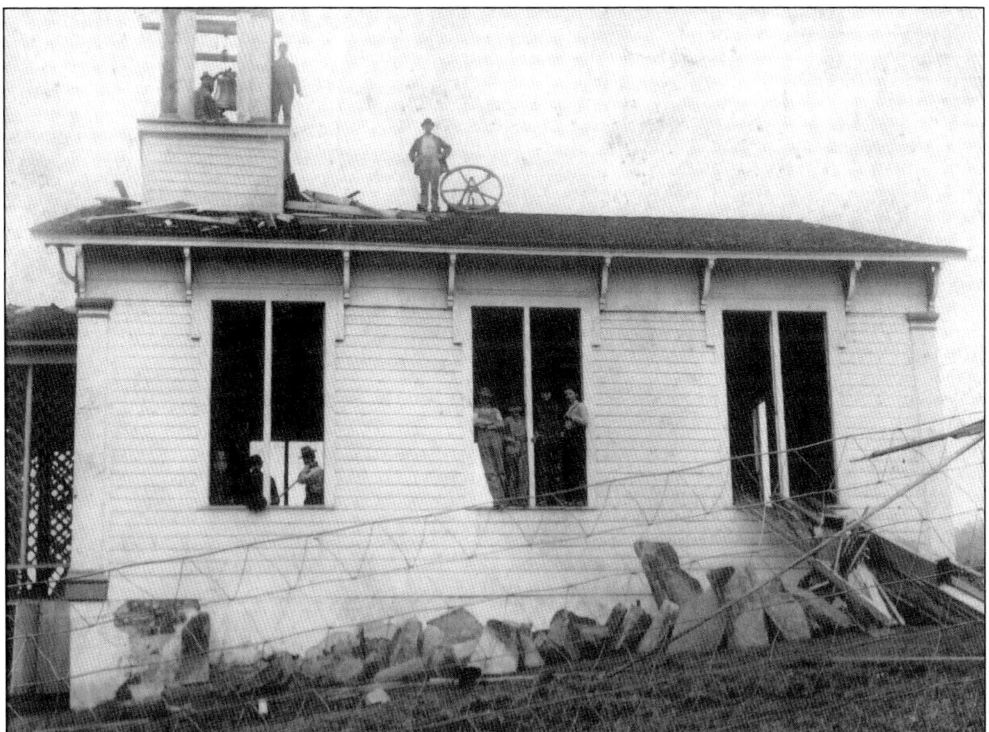

These men, photographed in 1890, are tearing down the wooden St. John's Lutheran Church in Booneville. Built in 1854, it was attended in its early years by the pioneer families of Boone, Strohecker, Schrack, and Klepper, among others. It was replaced in 1900 by a brick house of worship still serving the community today.

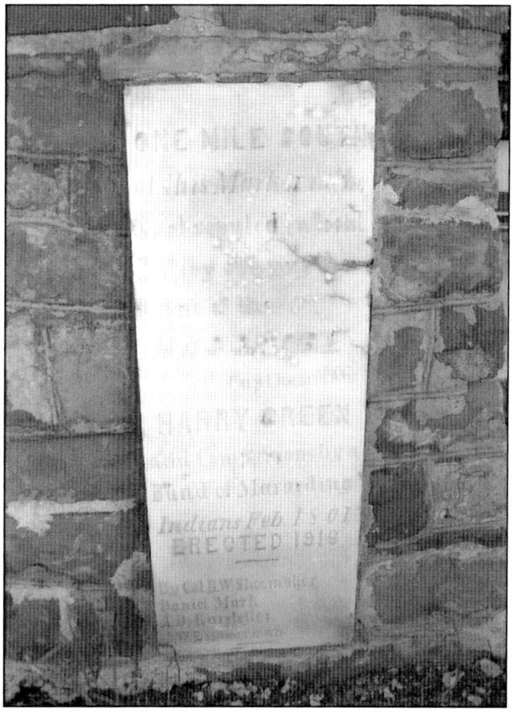

This historical marker, erected in 1916 by historian Col. Henry Shoemaker and three others, notes the reputed deaths of Capt. Harry Greene and his companions in February 1801. Greene (from Milton) and his six men had supposedly been pursuing a band of Indians who had been stealing cattle and burning buildings. While camped at what is now called Greene's Gap at the east end of the valley, the men were allegedly slain by the Indians. The marker stands off the south side of Valley Road, about two miles east of Carroll.

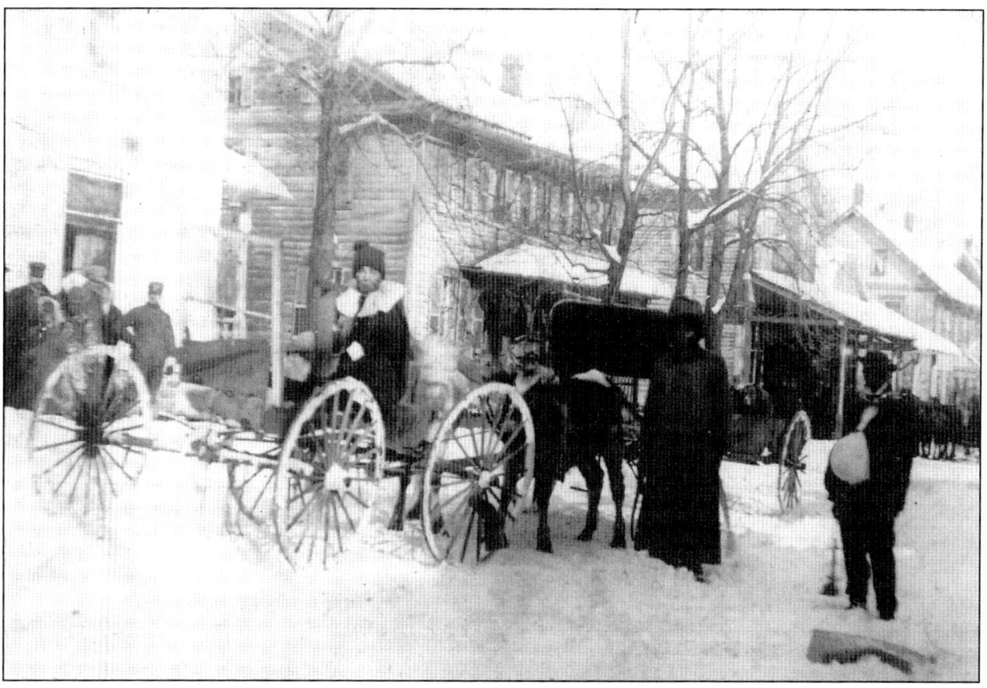

Loganton held this so-called Fantastics New Year's Day Parade, which featured burlesque costumes, around 1915. The "big belly man" on the right is Sterl Moyer, with Samuel Stamm's general store directly behind him. It is also believed that Harry Kemmerer is driving the horse and wagon. The Greenburr Cornet Band, in their "inconceivable and mirth-provoking garbs," according to the *Loganton Ledger*, played "lilting serenades" in front of local businesses.

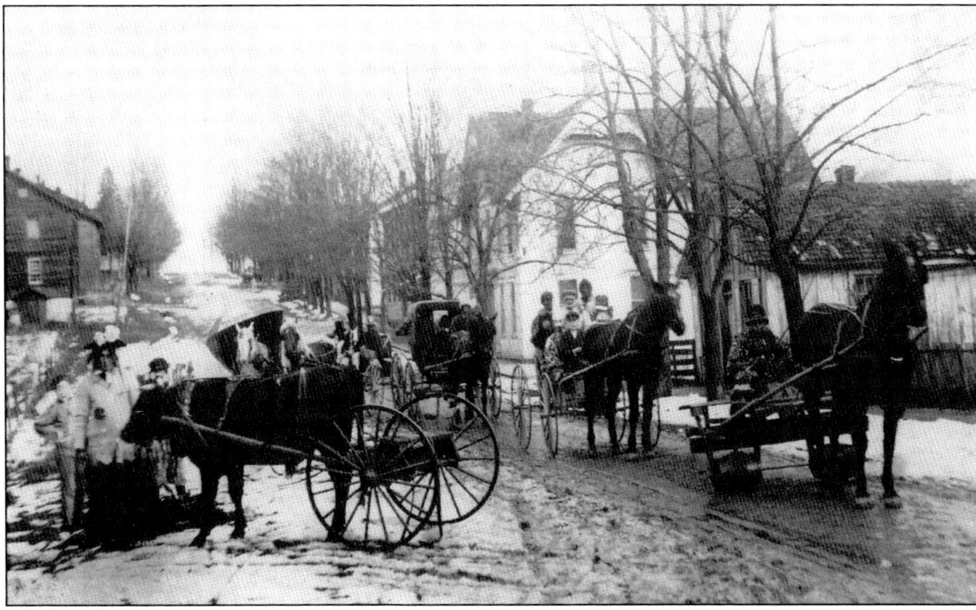

In an apparently different Loganton Fantastics New Year's Day Parade held in the 1910s, participants (again including Harry Kemmerer, standing at the head of the steer) are on Main Street looking east up Bunker Hill. The low building on the far right is the blacksmith's shop. Next to that is the large white David Price home, followed by the Emanuel Wirth residence. The fourth building up the hill is the Francis Gramley house. On the left are Mill Creek and an open field, followed by the David Mark home.

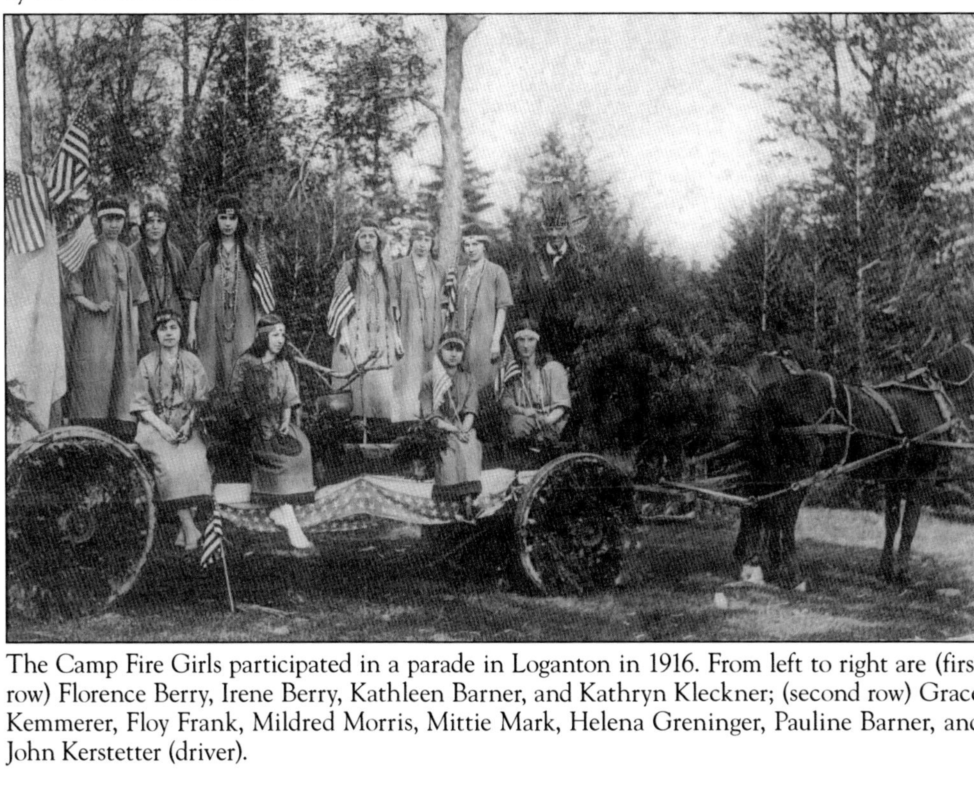

The Camp Fire Girls participated in a parade in Loganton in 1916. From left to right are (first row) Florence Berry, Irene Berry, Kathleen Barner, and Kathryn Kleckner; (second row) Grace Kemmerer, Floy Frank, Mildred Morris, Mittie Mark, Helena Greninger, Pauline Barner, and John Kerstetter (driver).

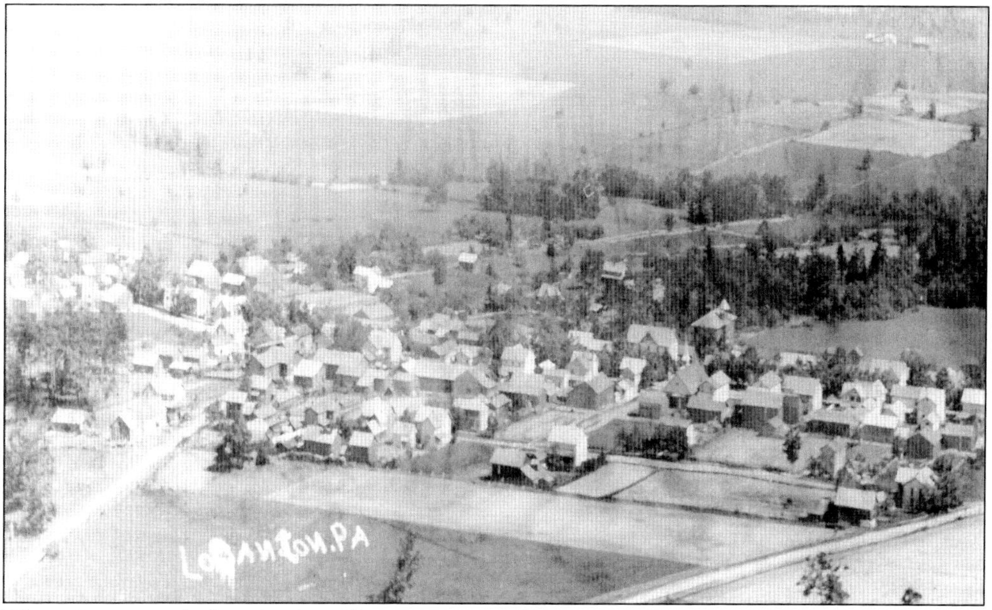

This is Loganton before the fire of June 19, 1918. The image is taken from the mountain, looking southeast across Sugar Valley and its rich farmlands. At right center, with its bell tower and the large open field to the right, is the Loganton High School (erected in 1910). Almost directly across the main street is the steepled Albright United Evangelical Church (erected in 1895). The church was destroyed in the fire, but the school survived. (Courtesy of Ralph Embick.)

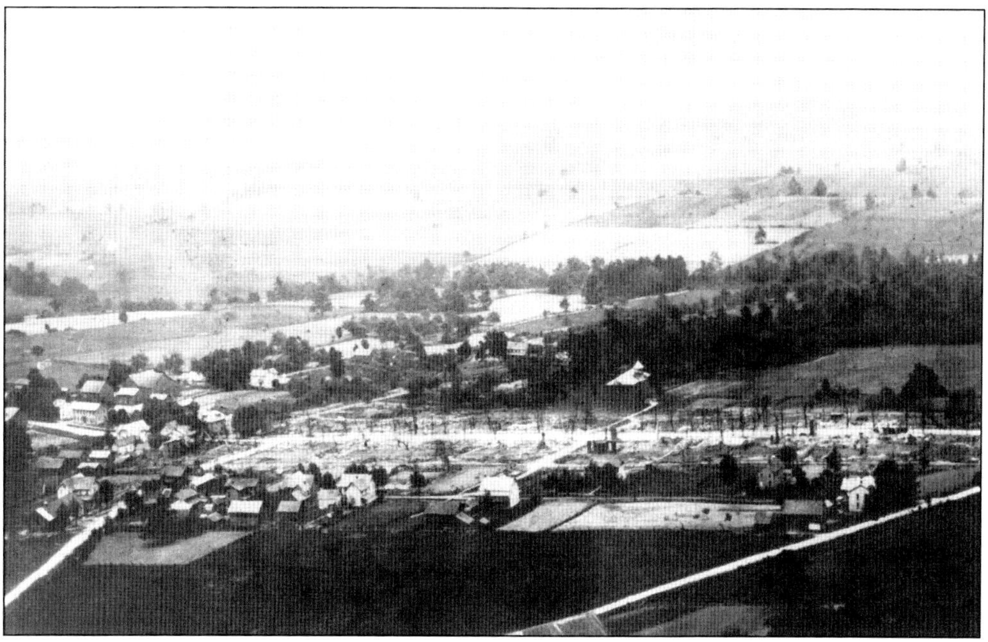

Not much of Loganton was left after the devastating 1918 fire. The school, with its bell tower, stands almost alone amid the destruction that claimed 39 homes and businesses, two churches, and 32 stables and barns. The conflagration rapidly swept eastward (from right to left in this image) for a half mile from its start at the borough's center. In three hours, it laid waste to the many buildings and beautiful shade trees of the community.

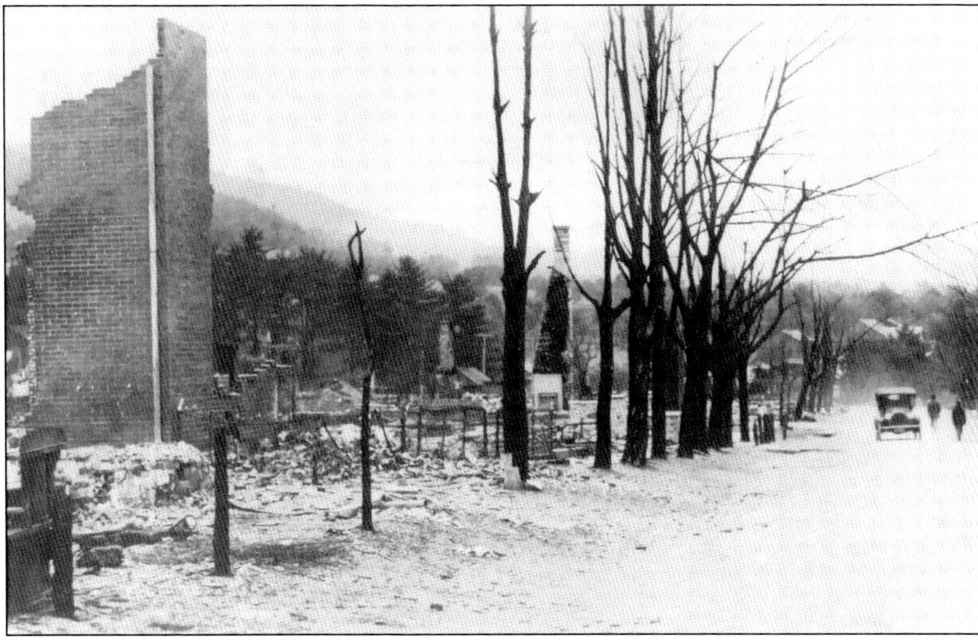

This view was shot looking east on Main Street in Loganton after the great fire of 1918. The iron fence and some of the brick wall of St. Paul's Evangelical Lutheran Church are visible on the left. Fortunately, no one died in the inferno that left 39 families homeless, many without any belongings. The estimate of the financial loss was as high as $300,000—a huge sum at that time.

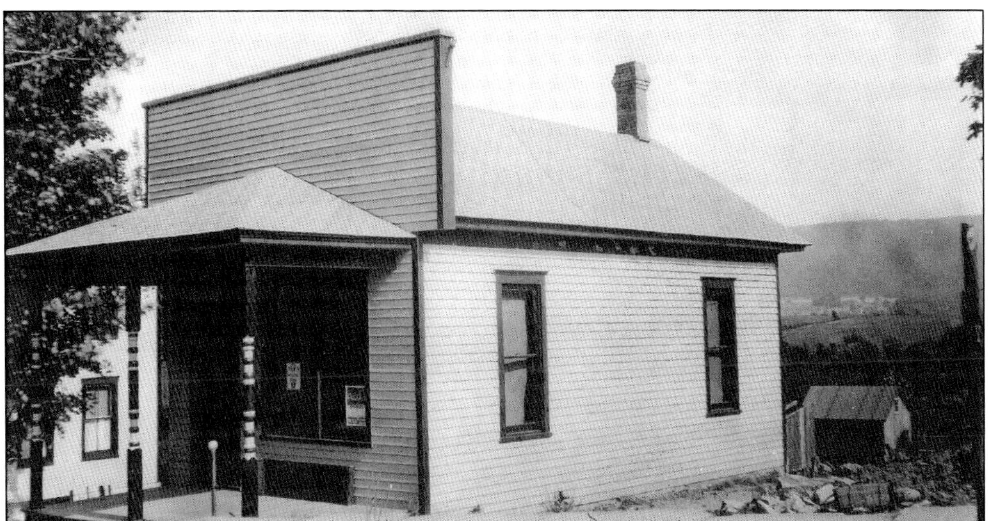

This Loganton Post Office was constructed on Main Street to replace the one destroyed in the 1918 fire, which had been located nearby in the Albert Karstetter building on the south side of Main Street. Karstetter was the postmaster at the time of the fire.

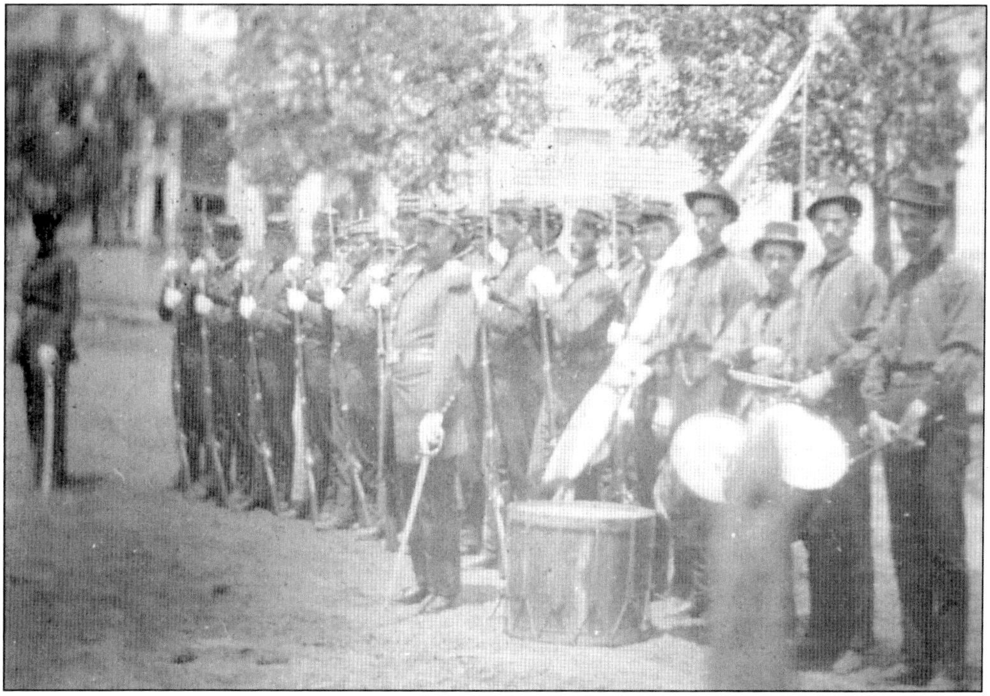

Charles Cyrus Harbach (1843–1927), pictured in the front with a sword, led a Grand Army of the Republic parade with men dressed in their Union Civil War uniforms. This parade was probably held in Loganton around 1900. Harbach was wounded on July 3, 1863, at the Battle of Gettysburg and later became a major of the 5th Regiment, Pennsylvania Civil War Reserves. During his long life living in Sugar Valley, Harbach worked as a millwright, farmer, butcher, blacksmith, and carpenter.

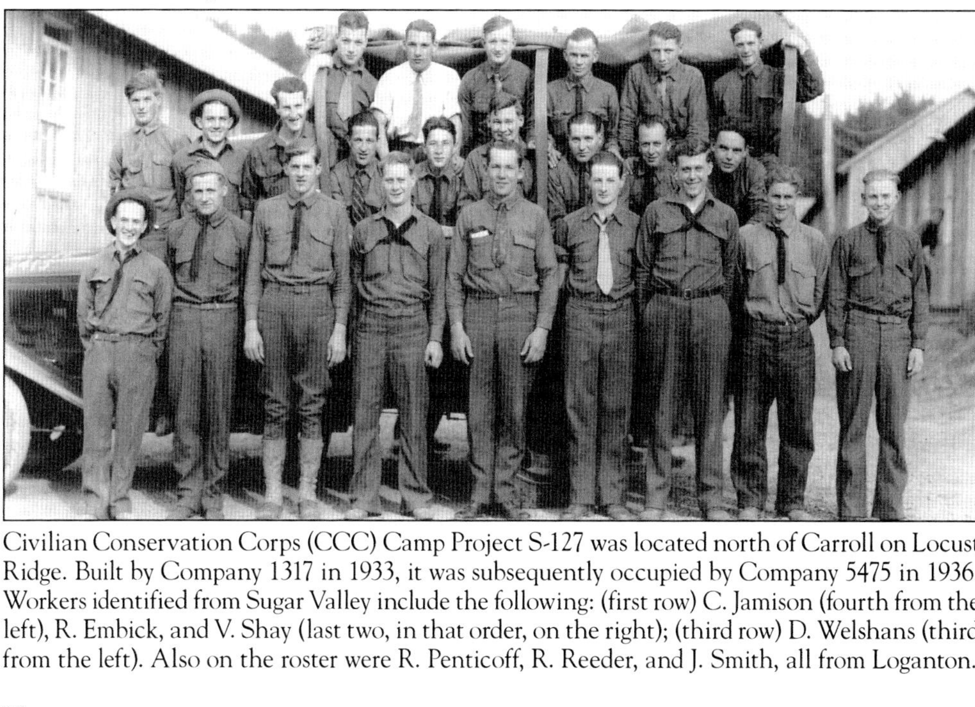

Civilian Conservation Corps (CCC) Camp Project S-127 was located north of Carroll on Locust Ridge. Built by Company 1317 in 1933, it was subsequently occupied by Company 5475 in 1936. Workers identified from Sugar Valley include the following: (first row) C. Jamison (fourth from the left), R. Embick, and V. Shay (last two, in that order, on the right); (third row) D. Welshans (third from the left). Also on the roster were R. Penticoff, R. Reeder, and J. Smith, all from Loganton.

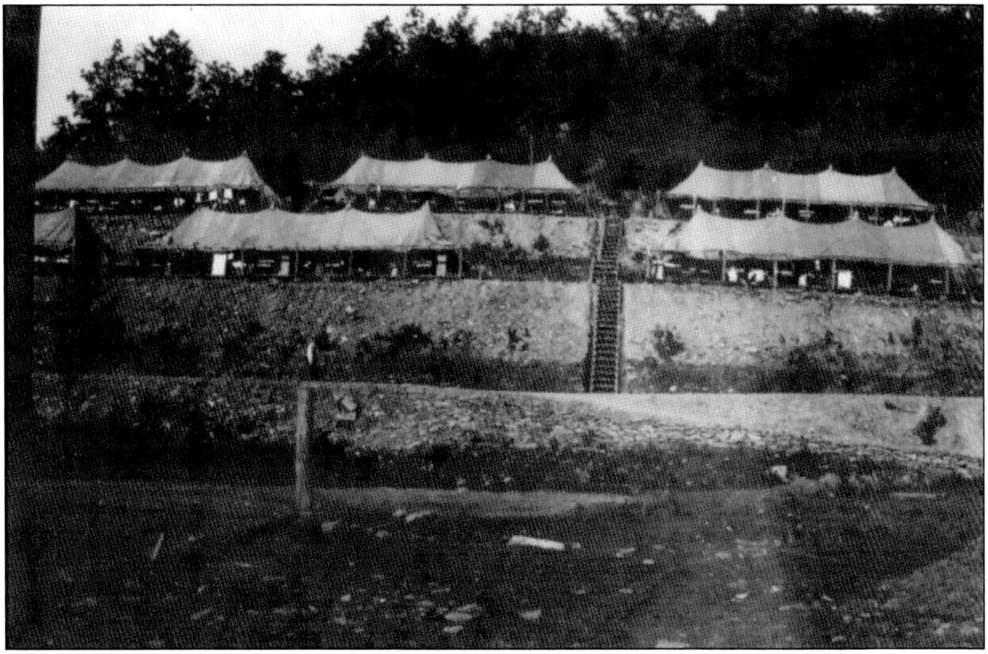

CCC Camp Project S-66, located on a mountainside by Long Run north of Loganton, opened in early May 1933. Company 306 lived at first in tents, then in barracks built later. These men were praised for their relief work in Lock Haven after the flood of March 1936. Those on the camp roster from Loganton included Samuel Jacob Frankenberger (camp superintendent), R. Klaer (a leader), and workers R. Limbert and J. Fegley.

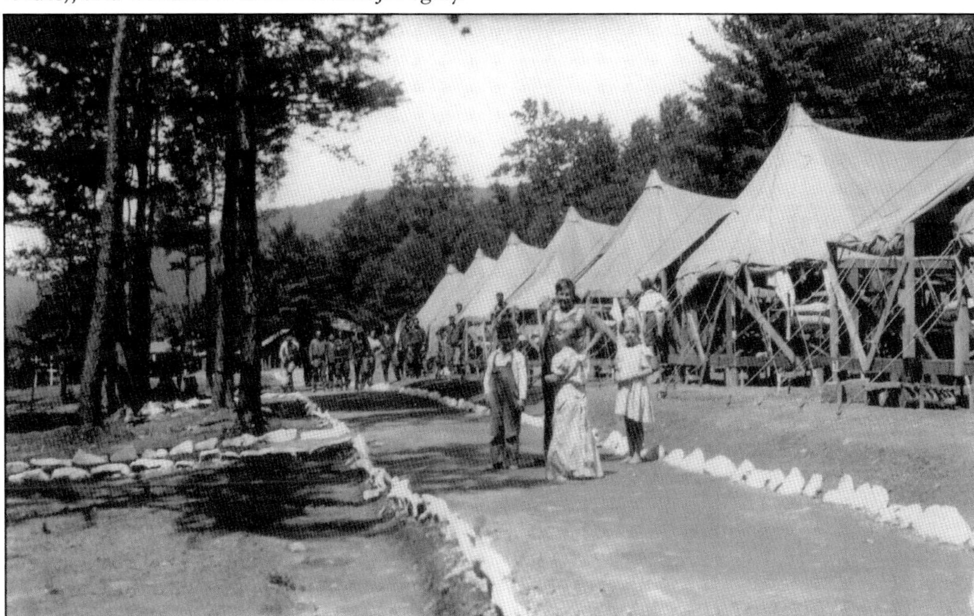

CCC Camp Project S-114 opened on May 30, 1933, and closed on October 31, 1935. Located at a place known as Tea Spring, two miles east of Carroll at the border of Clinton and Union Counties, this camp's Company 368 operated under Gen. Paul Malone. In this 1933 image, the boy visitors in the foreground are Lynn Mark (left) and Wilson Mark.

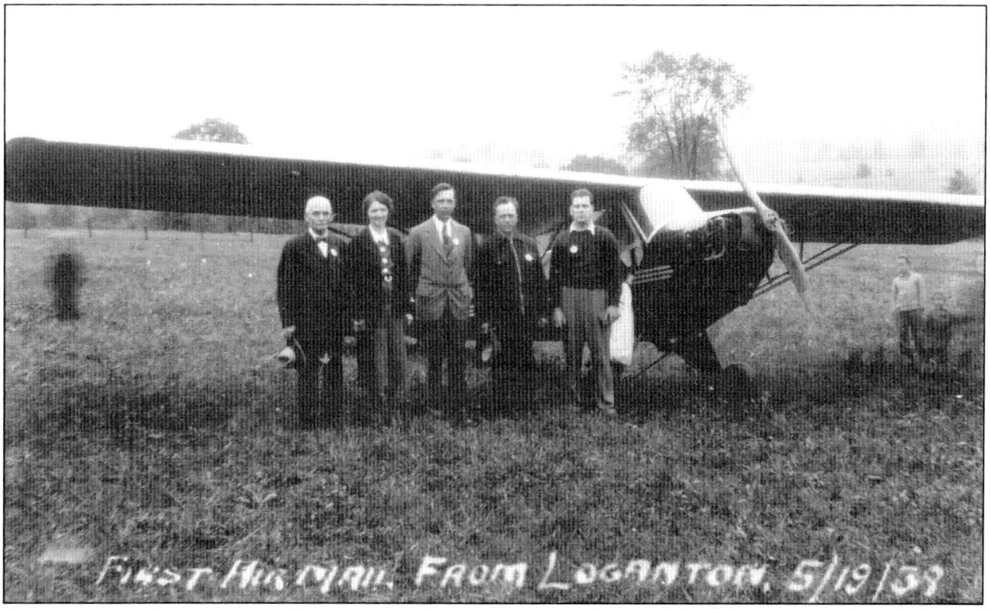

A celebration of the inauguration of airmail service out of Sugar Valley occurred on May 19, 1938, at a farm field just west of Loganton. Included in this photograph are, from left to right, Alexander Greninger (Tylersville postmaster), Catherine Held (longtime postal clerk at Loganton), Charles Held (Loganton postmaster), Clifford Held ("Star Route" mail driver between Mill Hall and Loganton), and the Piper pilot, "Scorchy" Monroe.

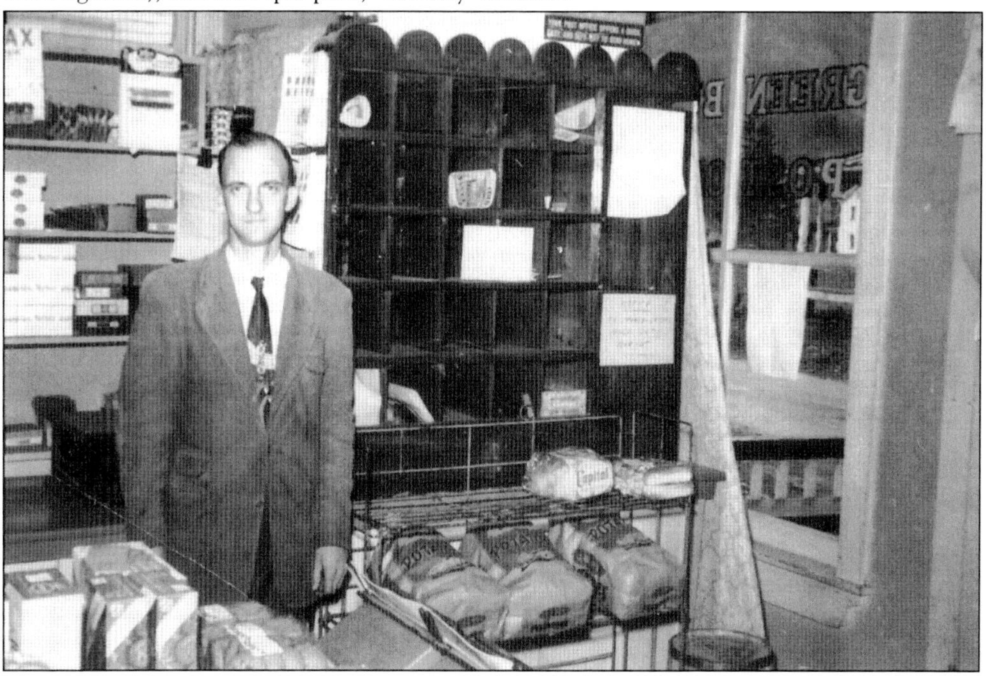

Postmaster Floyd Lamey stands at his post inside his Greenburr general store and post office on September 1, 1955. That was the last day that mail was stamped and sent from this location, but patrons continued to receive their mail there until November 15, 1955. The post office first opened on February 1, 1882, the seventh and last to be established in Sugar Valley.

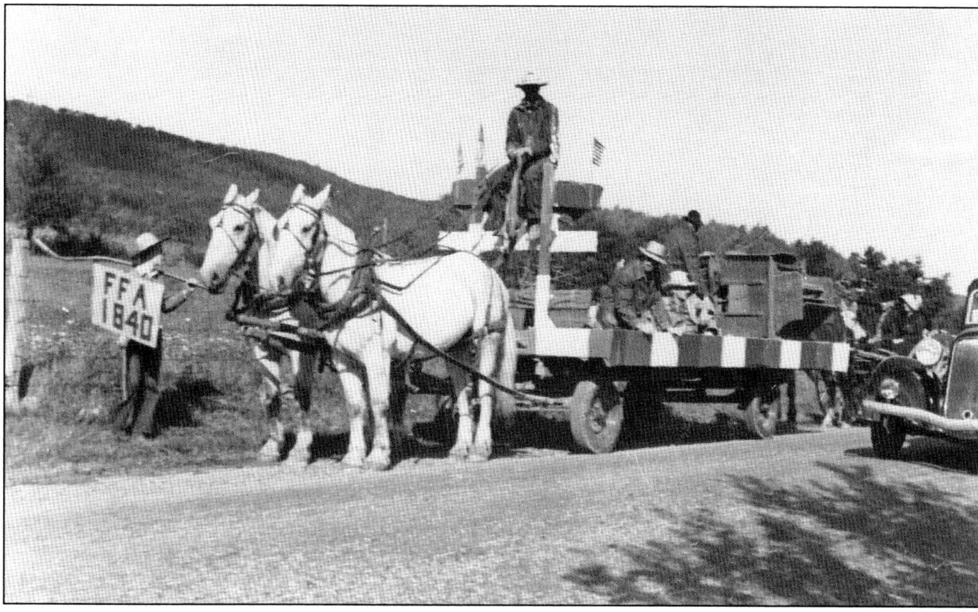

The Future Farmers of America entry in the September 26, 1940, centennial parade in Loganton, which was themed "then and now," won the prize for most historical float. Driving the team is Ellis Lesher. In the wagon, Samuel Esterline Sr. (left) and Frederick Stamm use flails on a pile of wheat. The unidentified man in the back is operating an old-fashioned fanning mill, used to separate the grain from the chaff.

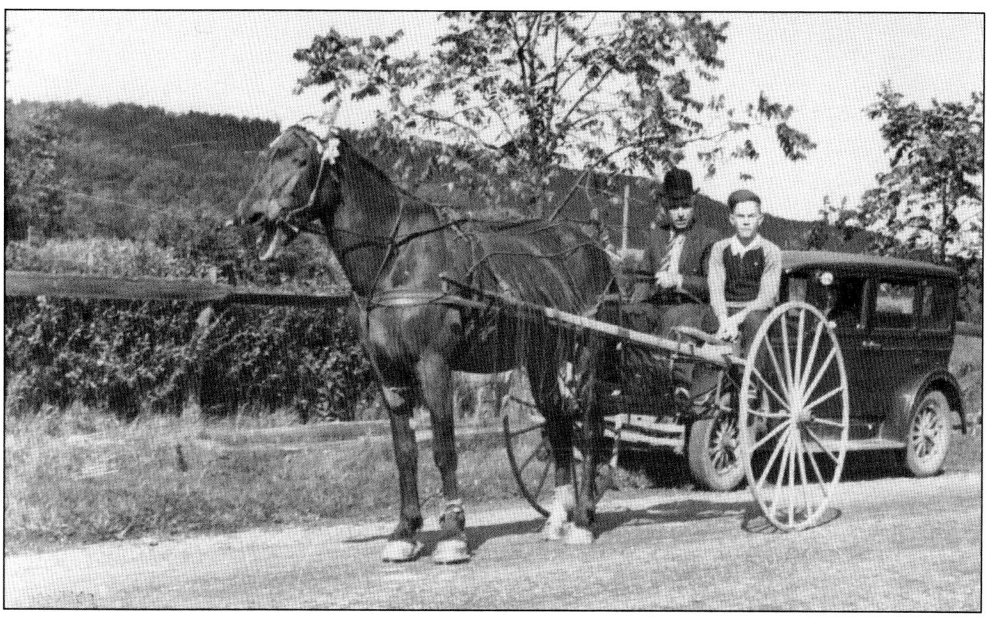

Posing for a photograph in a sulky with elaborate trappings for the horse are George Meyer (left), a retired schoolteacher at the time and resident of Booneville, and young Harold Karchner of Greenburr. During the 1940 centennial parade that same day, Meyer was accompanied by his sister Sarah Meyer, who wore her mother's old-time clothes.

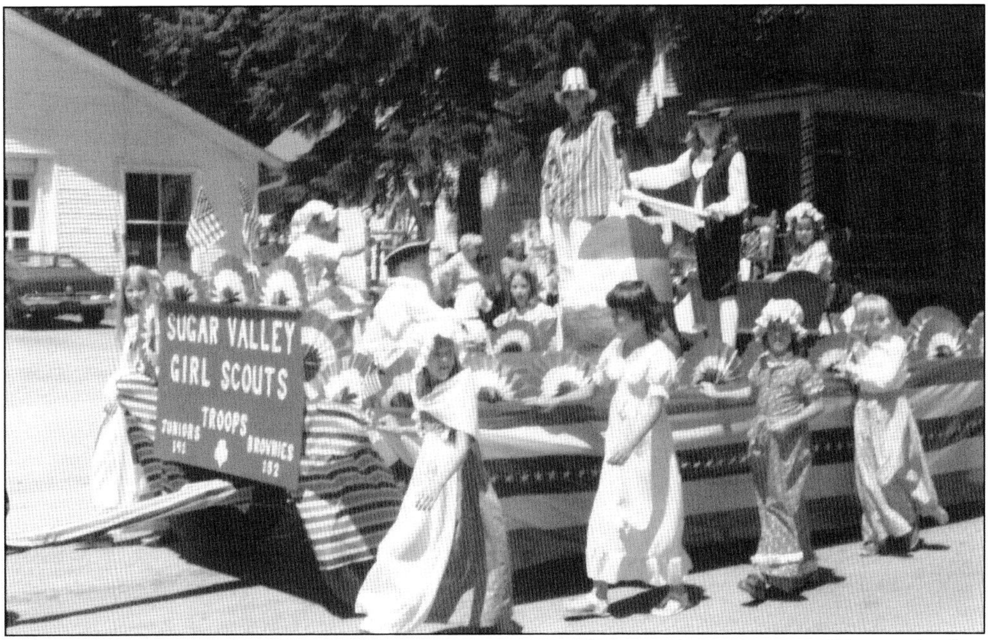

The Sugar Valley Girl Scouts had their own patriotic float in the June 12, 1976, parade that celebrated the country's bicentennial. According to the June 14, 1976, edition of the *Lock Haven Express*, "sunny skies prevailed as hundreds watched the parade the Loganton." (Courtesy of Yvonne and Steve Weaver.)

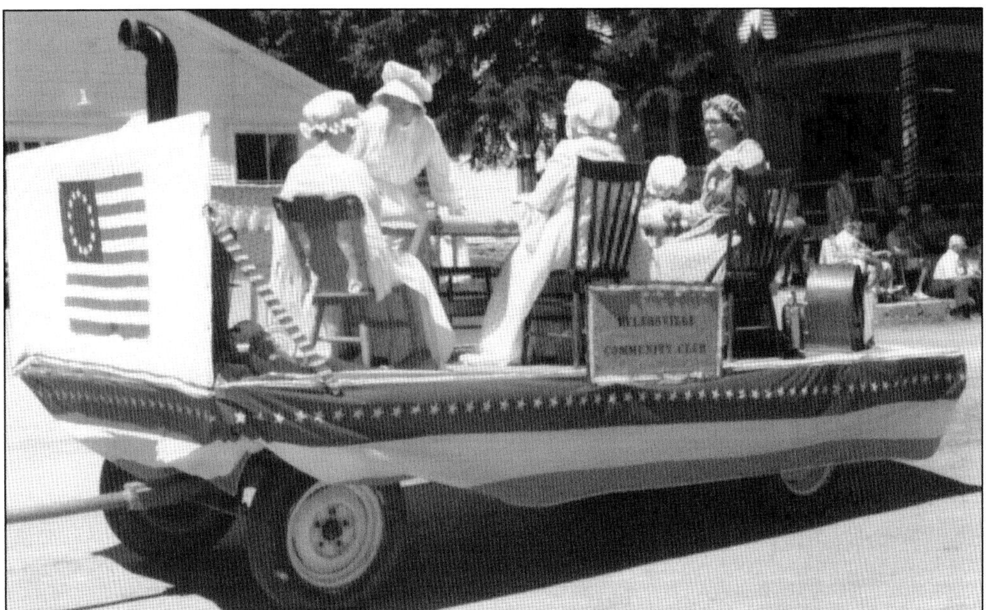

Ladies of the Tylersville Community Club are dressed in colonial garb on their float in the bicentennial parade. They won first prize in the category of historical floats. The prize for most unique float went to Daniel Schrack and his cow. Eastville's Church of the Brethren won for best float with a God-and-country theme, and Loganton's Mount Pleasant Community Church won for most elaborate float.

Seven

ENJOYING FREE TIME

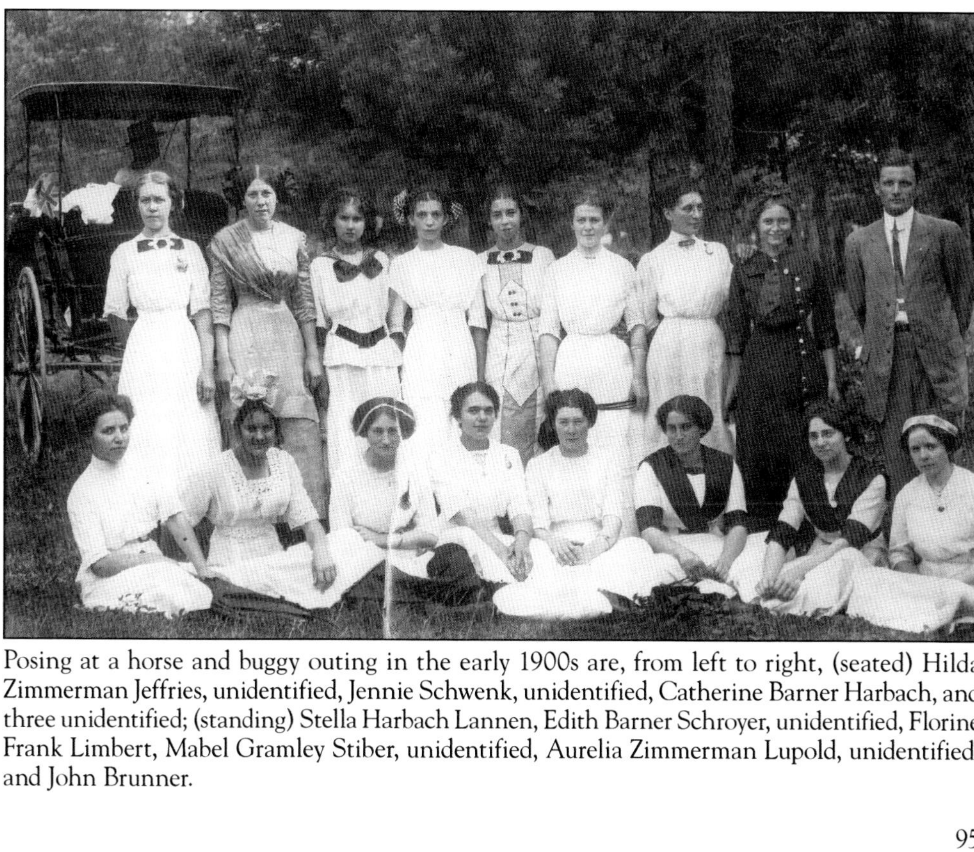

Posing at a horse and buggy outing in the early 1900s are, from left to right, (seated) Hilda Zimmerman Jeffries, unidentified, Jennie Schwenk, unidentified, Catherine Barner Harbach, and three unidentified; (standing) Stella Harbach Lannen, Edith Barner Schroyer, unidentified, Florine Frank Limbert, Mabel Gramley Stiber, unidentified, Aurelia Zimmerman Lupold, unidentified, and John Brunner.

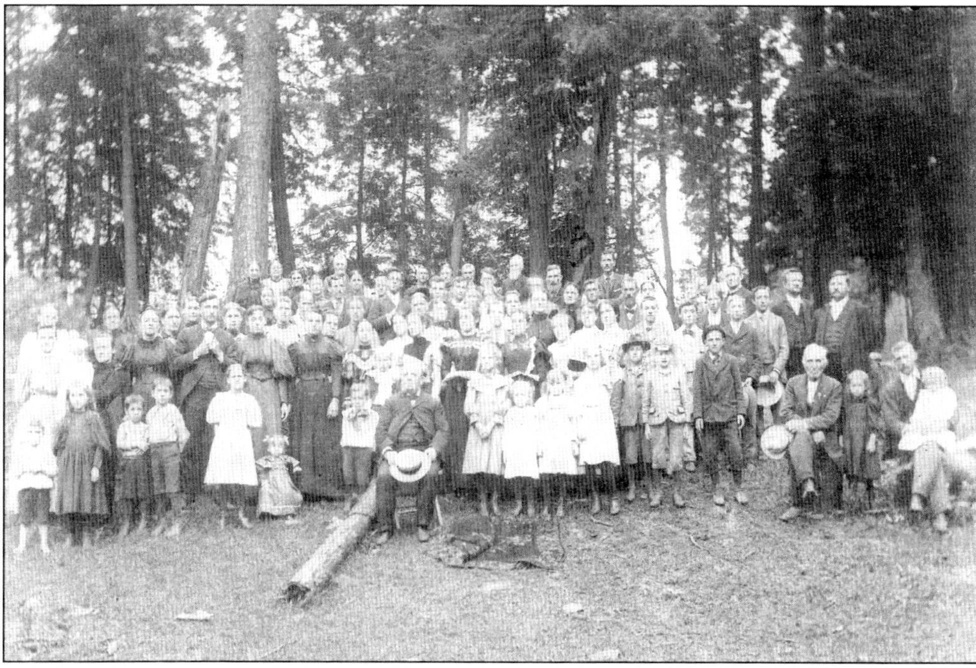

Most likely a large church group (note the two women in the center holding open books), these people are gathered at the so-called Booneville Campground on the south side of Fishing Creek between Greenburr and Booneville, probably some time in the early 1900s. It is believed that beginning in the 1880s or 1890s, Sugar Valley residents started holding annual summer church meetings and picnics there, along with family reunions and festivals.

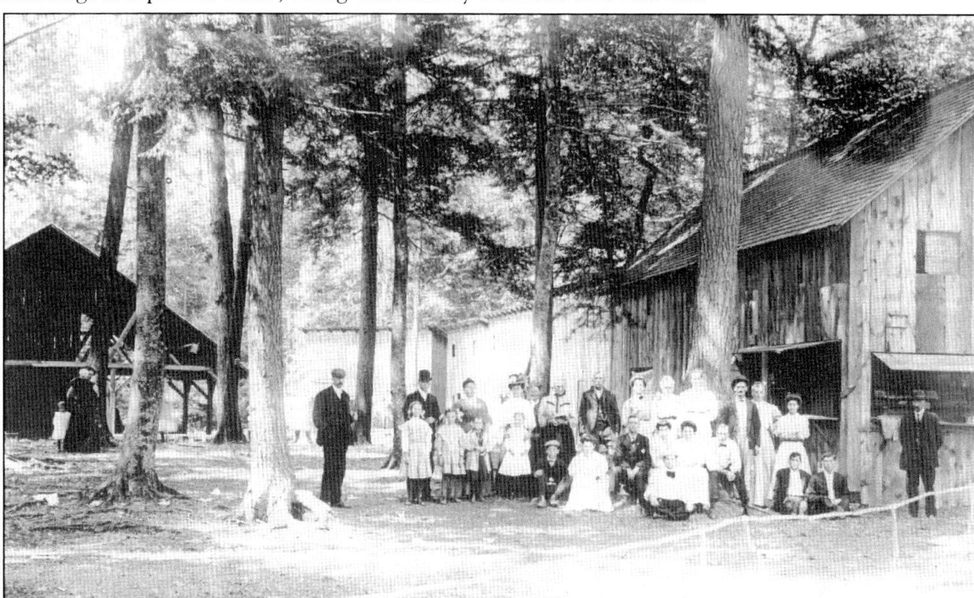

Some time before 1908, these Sugar Valley residents (again, probably a church group) pose for a photograph at the Booneville Campground. One of the pavilions erected there, mainly for religious services, was referred to as "the tabernacle" (on the far left). To this day, it contains church pews and a platform stage. Other buildings contained sleeping and cooking quarters.

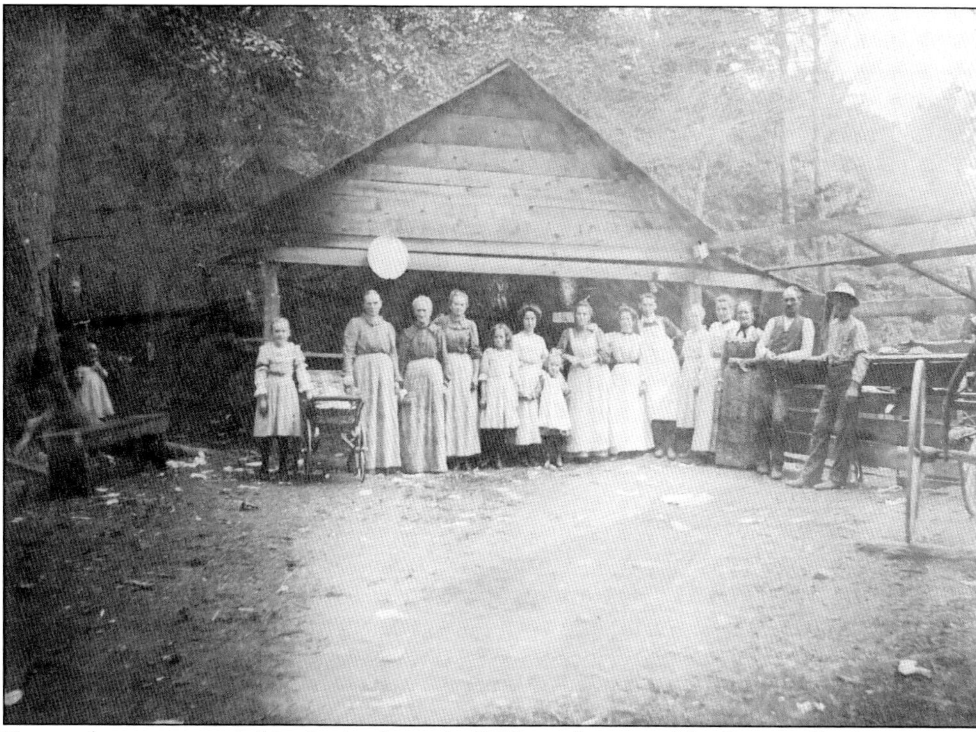

Yet another group, probably also in the early 1900s, makes use of the Booneville Campground. The recreational area remains today and is the site of an annual summertime community picnic. (Courtesy of Anne M. McCloskey.)

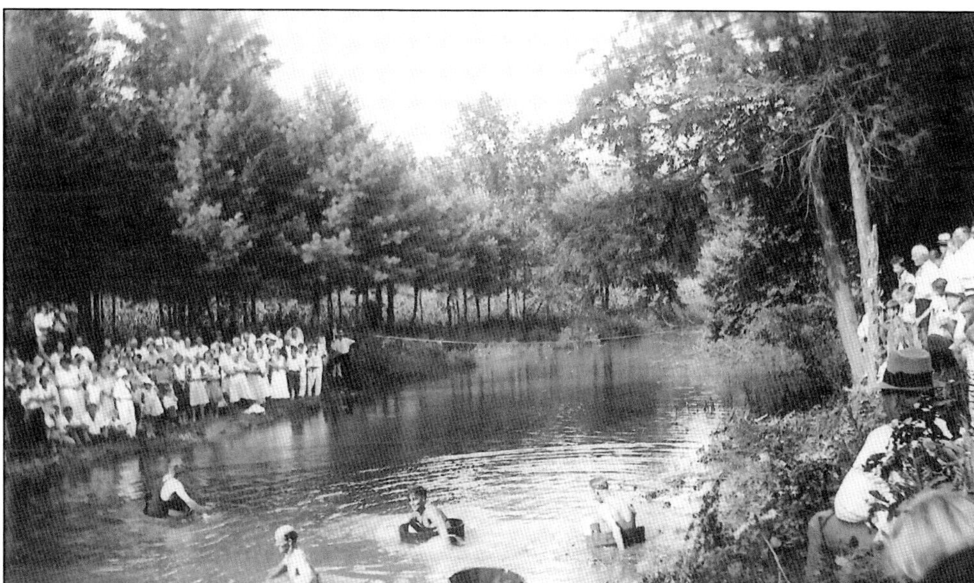

Participants and spectators, probably in the 1930s or 1940s, enjoy the wooden-tub race in Fishing Creek that was held during the years of the annual Booneville community picnic. Band concerts and ice cream socials have also been held at the grounds throughout the years. (Courtesy of John and Verna Carey.)

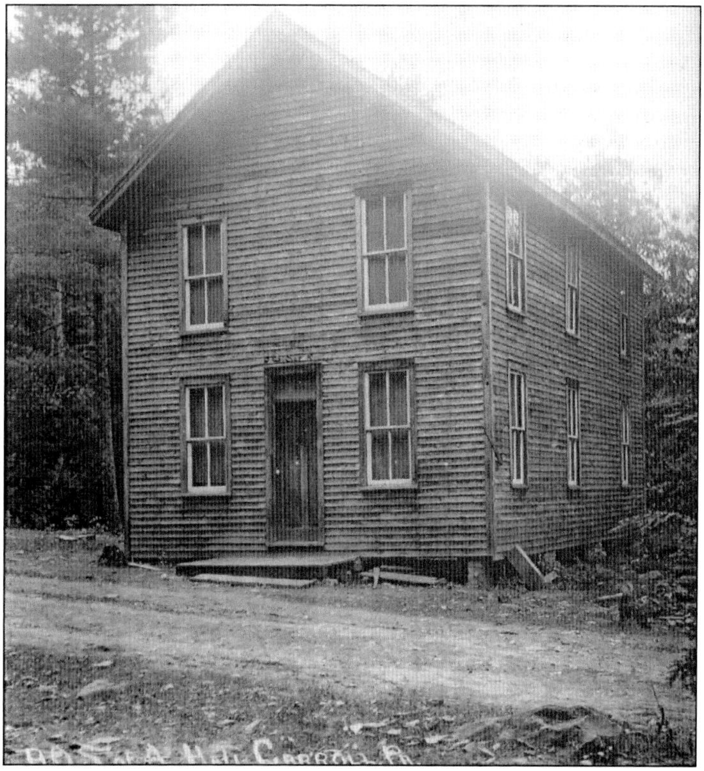

Washington Camp 520 of the Patriotic Order Sons of America met in this two-story building in Carroll. One of America's oldest patriotic and fraternal societies, the Patriotic Order Sons of America was founded in Philadelphia in 1847. After Carroll's camp disbanded, the building was sold in 1953 to Robert Causey and later became a hunting club. Loganton and Tylersville also had Patriotic Order Sons of America branches—Washington Camps 202 and 418, respectively.

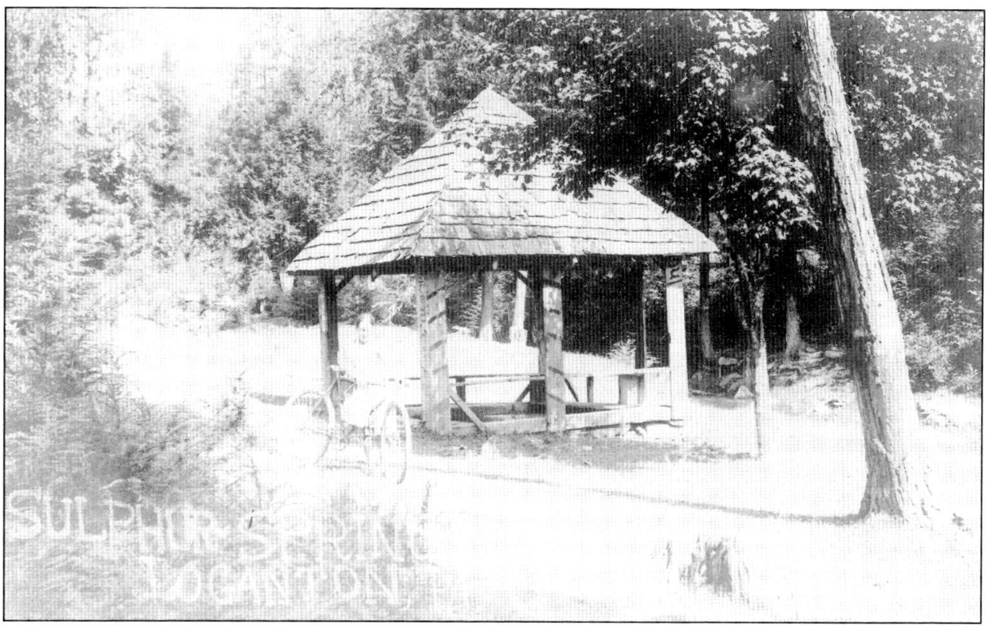

This young girl with her bicycle is at Sulphur Spring, just above Loganton, some time in the 1920s. She is believed to be Faith Currin, daughter of Daniel Scott Currin, who published the *Sugar Valley Journal* from 1884 to 1917. The spring, widely known for its reputedly medicinal mineral waters, was supposed to have been a favorite stopping place for Mingo chief James Logan back in the 1700s.

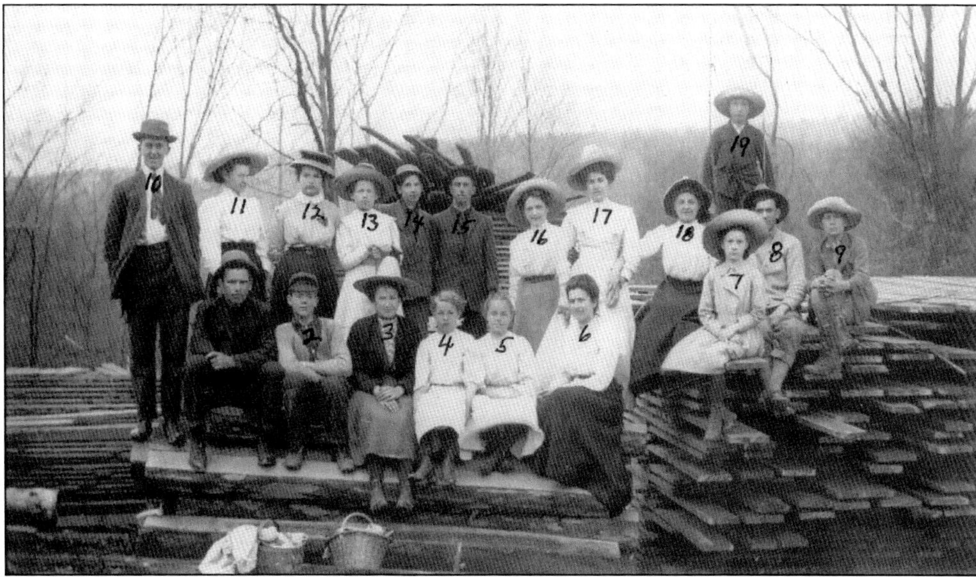

Pictured around 1910, these picnickers posed at the Cherry Run sawmill in the Mount Riansares area are, from left to right, (first row) George Meyer, Harry Greninger, Florence Weaver, Olga Overdorf, Laura Zimmerman, Sarah Meyer, Mildred Wolfe, Robert Greninger, and Ralph Welshans; (second row) Samuel Ilgen, Elizabeth Bierly, Florence Greninger, Florence Bright, Roy Strohecker, Herbert Wise, Mary Briggs, Clarie Weaver, Carrie Bierly, and Lynn Karstetter. (Courtesy of Christine Brungard.)

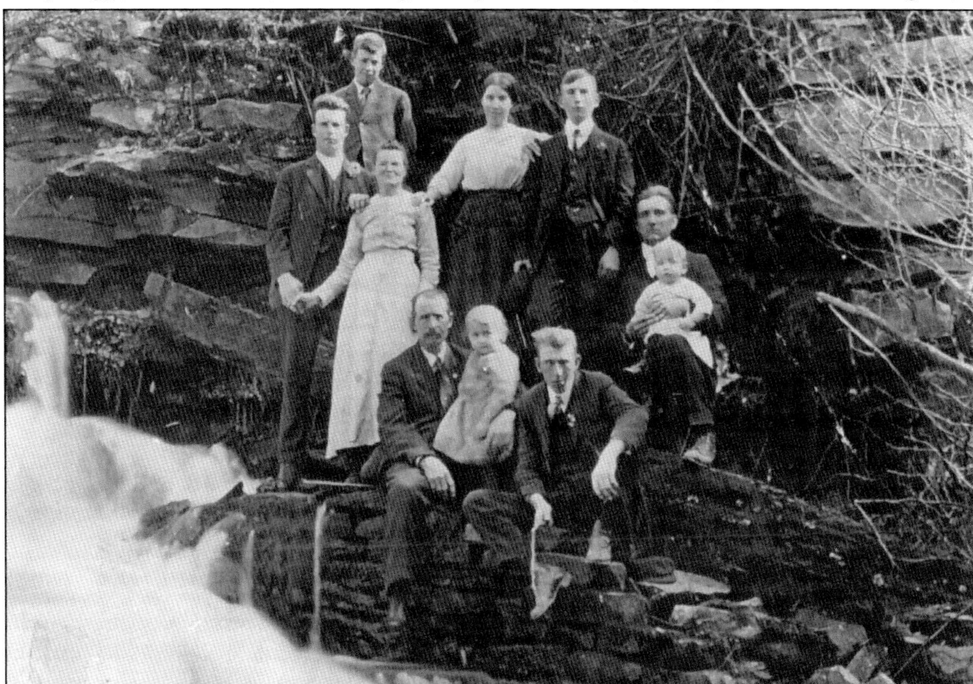

In the late 1910s, enjoying the beauty of Rosecrans Falls, located just north of the village of Rosecrans, are, from left to right, (first row) Charles Josiah Matter, Maude Washburn (toddler), and Harry Matter; (second row) Charles Dewey Matter, Sarah Matter, Clark Washburn, and John Washburn (infant); (third row) Harold Matter, Armina Matter, and Wilbur Matter.

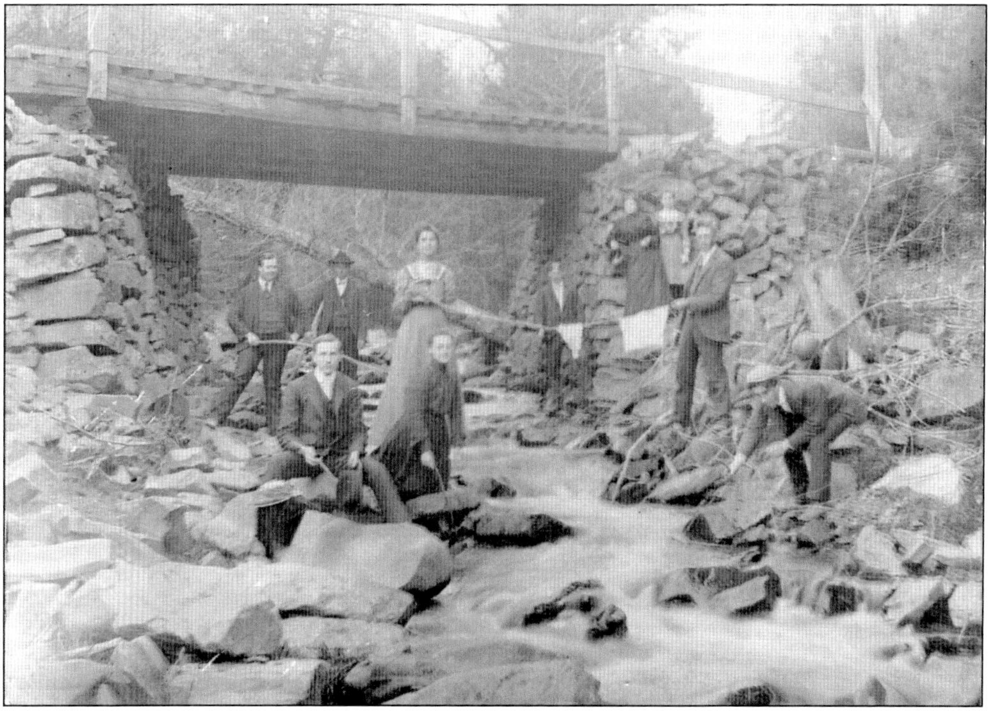

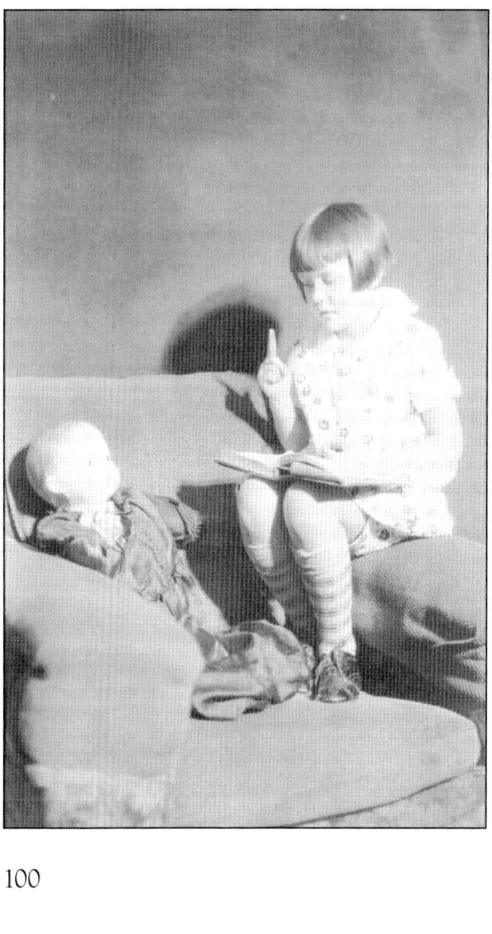

Photographed at an outing along Mill Creek not long before 1901 are, from left to right, (in foreground) James Bierly, Edna Dice, and George Gramley (bending over); (in background) Charles Wise, Daniel Wert (wearing a hat), Hattie Heller, William Weaver, Bessie Berry, Pearl Reighard, and unidentified (holding the end of the cloth-draped stick).

Kathleen Schrack reads to her doll around 1930. Daughter of Walter (the son of Emma Matilda and Ammon Schrack of Booneville) and Puella Schrack, Kathleen grew to adulthood in California, where she married Rudolph Johanson. They had two children, Gary and Kathie Jane. Kathleen Schrack Johanson died in a nursing home in Anchorage, Alaska.

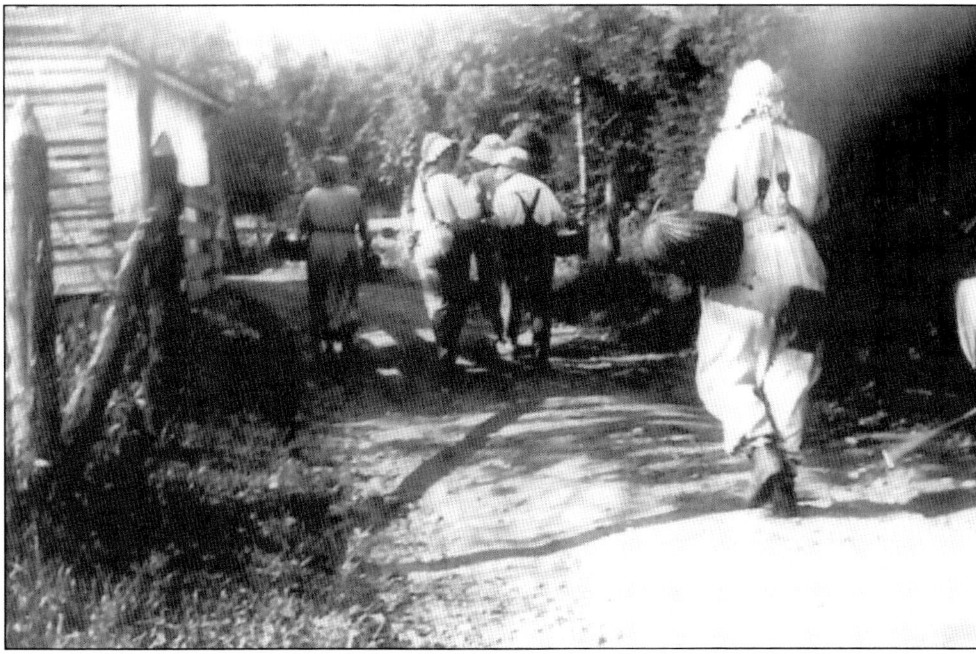

These women are off to pick huckleberries around 1910. Several years before, there had been a fire on the mountain south of Carroll that allowed huckleberry bushes to blanket the area.

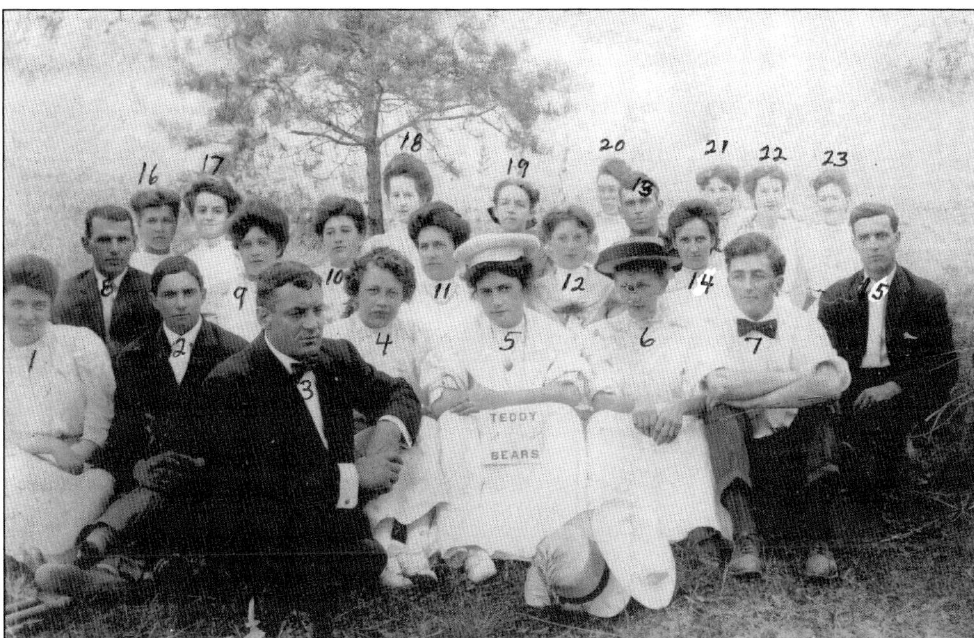

Enjoying a picnic in 1907 at Tea Spring are, from left to right, (first row) Ella Engle, Lee Herb, Joseph Hanawalt, Margaret Harter, Mary Meyers, Prudence Boone, and William Meyer; (second row) George Meyer, Emma Brungard, Mary Renninger, Sarah Meyer, Jennie Renninger, Harry Meyer, Mary Douty, and Reuben Meyer; (third row) Tacie Sheats, Carrie Kahl, Mary Sheats, Elizabeth Schrack, Tama Boob, Myrtle Morris, Ella Wise, and Euphema Brown. (Courtesy of John and Verna Carey.)

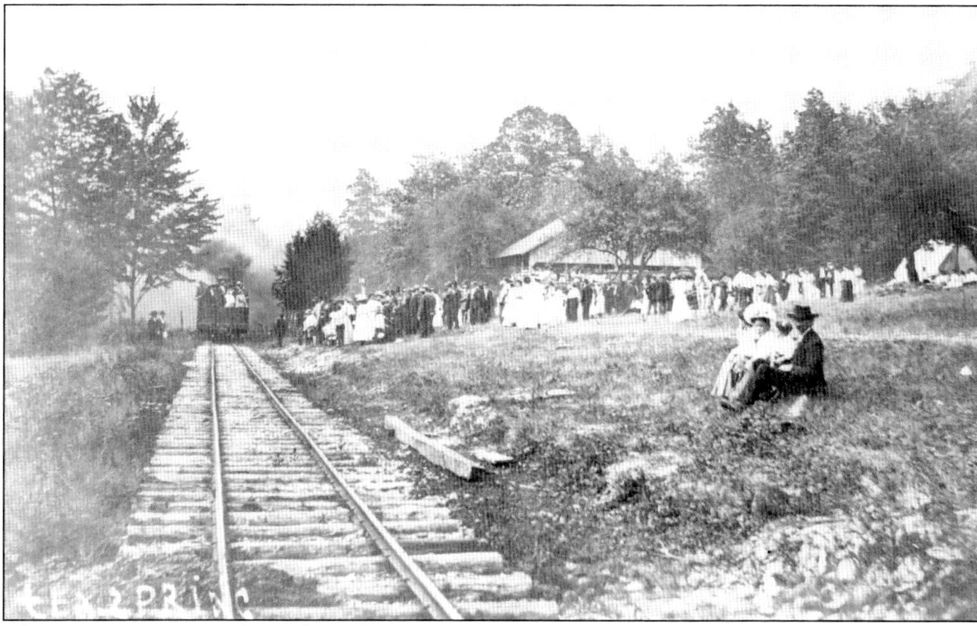

The Tea Spring stop along the White Deer & Loganton Railway was about two miles east of Carroll. On the grounds and on the train are some of the people who came to enjoy the 1908 annual summer picnic held there. Tea Spring (which drains into Sugar Valley's main waterway, Fishing Creek) was named after the variety of goldenrod that grew there, the leaves of which supposedly provided a healthy brew.

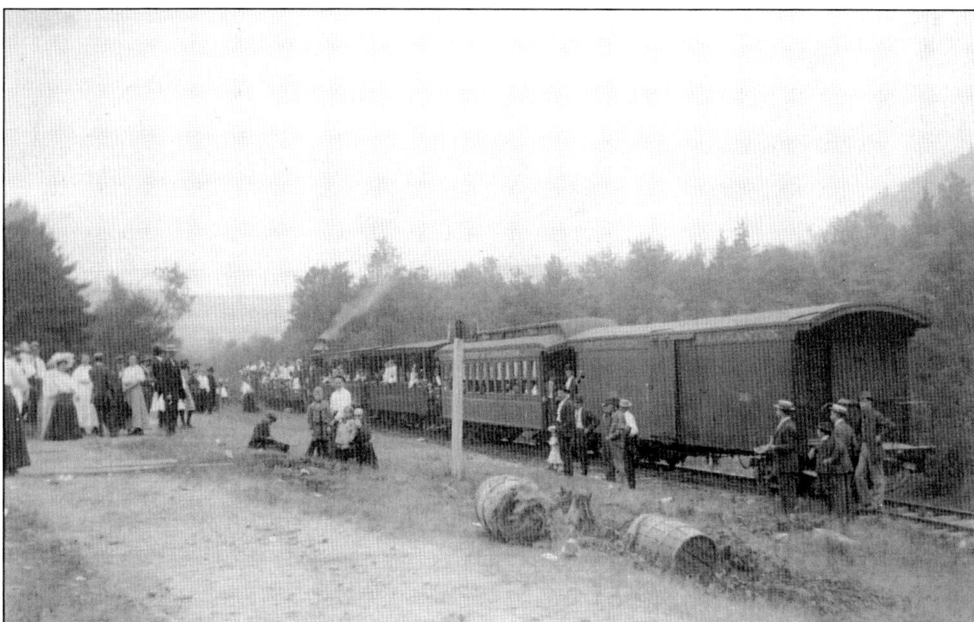

Residents of Sugar Valley traveled by a Climax locomotive–powered excursion train (on both flat cars with railings and benches and in coaches) on the White Deer & Loganton Railway one summer day around 1910 for the annual Tea Spring picnic. The family of five in the center is the Harbachs, Oscar and Anna and their three sons, (from left to right) Chester, Raymond, and Charles.

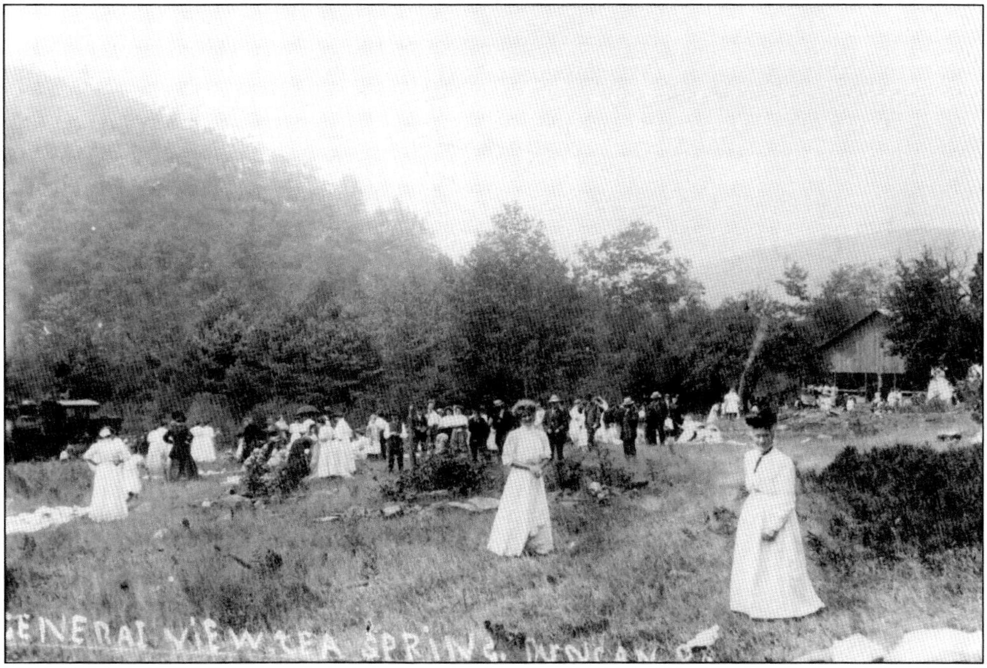

All are dressed in their finery for the 1910 Tea Spring picnic. The printed "Duncan" at the bottom of the image was the alternative name for the site. It was named after John Duncan, who began building the railroad line westward from White Deer to Sugar Valley around 1900. (Courtesy of Yvonne and Steve Weaver.)

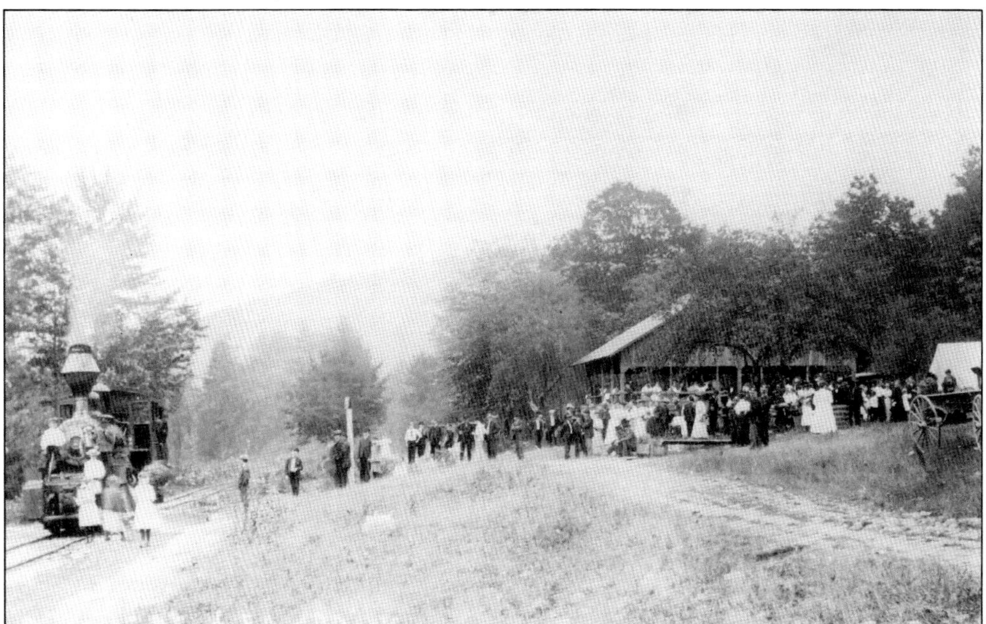

This image of the 1912 Tea Spring picnic shows a Climax locomotive on the left and a large pavilion erected by the White Deer & Loganton Railway for the convenience of the picnickers on the right. The company built a bandstand as well as a refreshment stand. To this day, the state maintains the site as a wayside area with picnic tables.

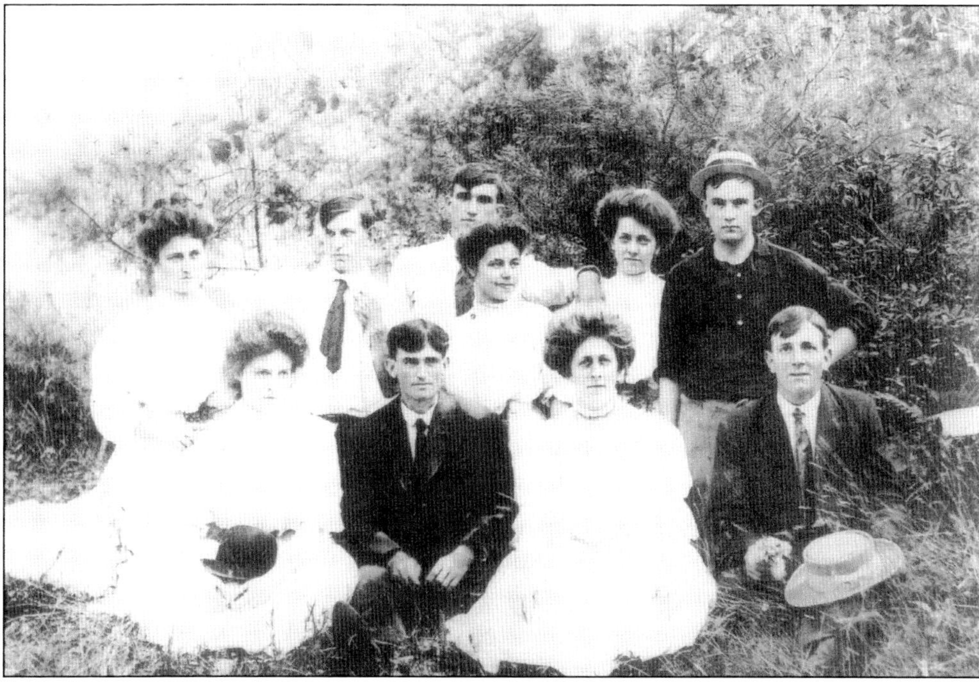

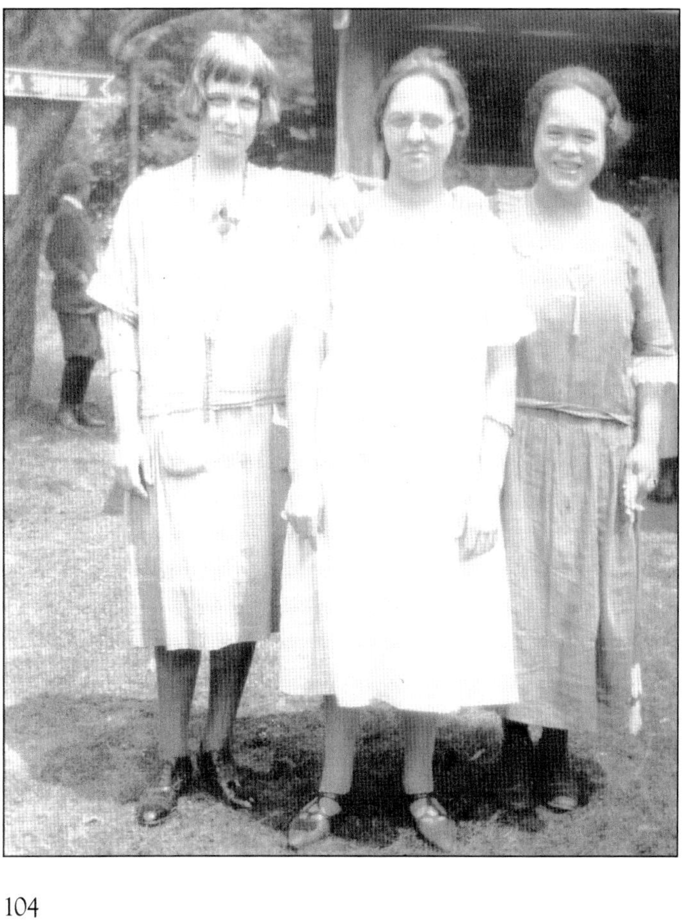

Attending a Sunday school picnic at Tea Spring around 1910 are, from left to right, (first row) Maude Haberson, William Schwenk, Mary Haberson, and Frederick Esterline; (second row) Ida Schwenk, Charles Strobert, George Strobert Jr. (in the back), Florence Berry, Nora Schroyer, and Ward Price.

These three smiling young women at Tea Spring around 1930 are, from left to right, Mabel Smith Bressler (1906–1975), Maude Beck Bartges Imes (1908–1987), and Mary E. Wolford Whipple (1907–1966).

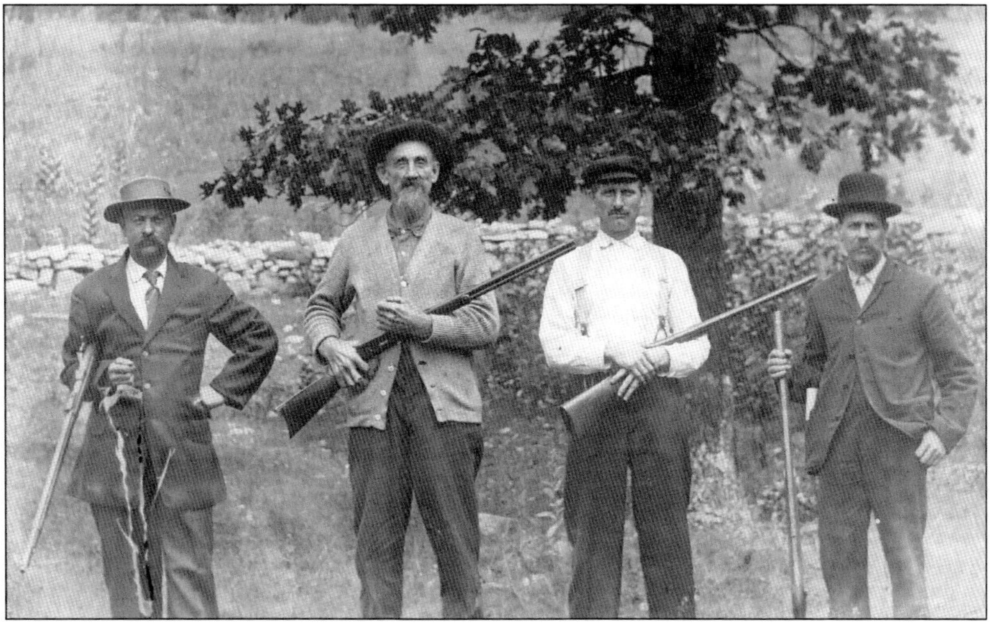

The Sugar Valley hunters in this c. 1905 photograph are, from left to right, Valentine Confer (son), Daniel Confer (father, 1827–1907), unidentified, and William Confer (son). Father and sons were farmers. William lived in a log house along the mountain above Price Cemetery (between Carroll and Loganton). He, his wife, Blanche, and his father and mother, Daniel and Judith Confer, are all buried there.

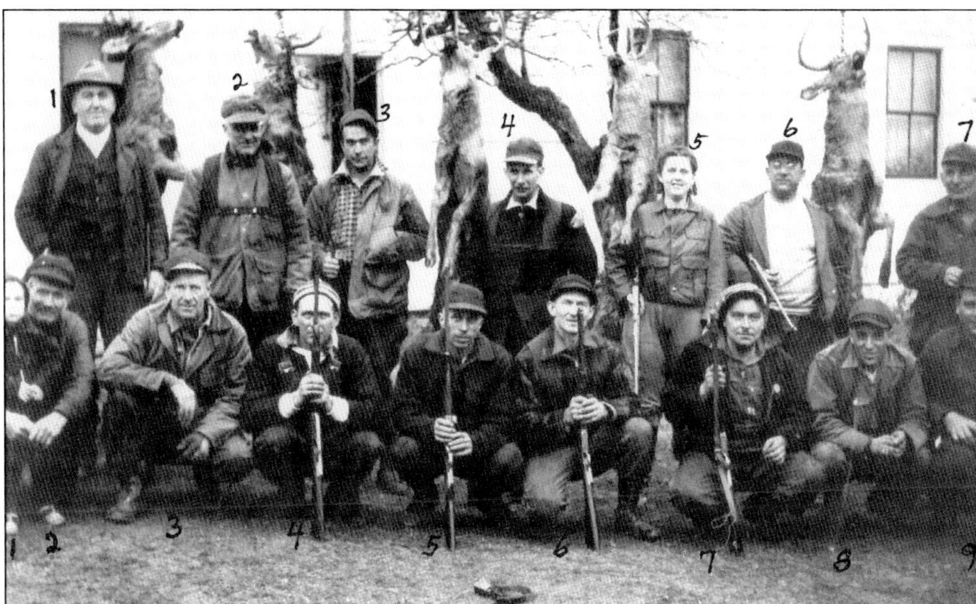

Mostly from the Booneville area, where this photograph was taken, these hunters from the 1940s are, from left to right, (first row) Samuel Greninger (boy), James Greninger, Raymond Overdorf, Clair Greninger, Herbert Wise, Roy Ruhl, Leonard Yarrison, Samuel Summers, and Boyd Yarrison; (second row) Samuel Ilgen, Reuben Meyer, Harry Welshans, Raymond Kleckner, Mary Ilgen, Patrick Welshans, and John Kleckner. (Courtesy of John and Verna Carey.)

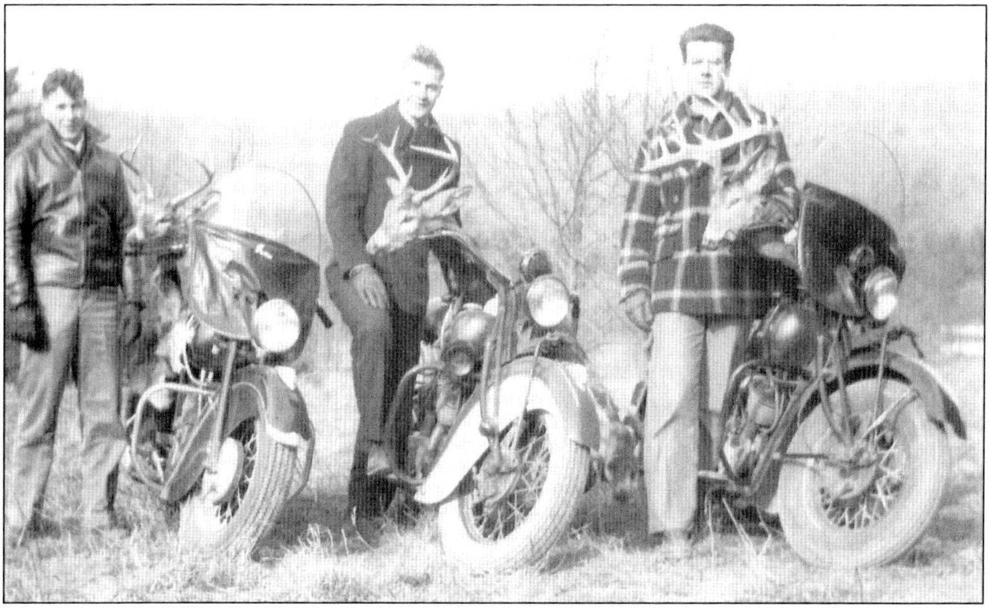

In the 1940s, three brothers pose on their "deerly adorned" Indian motorcycles (manufactured from 1901 to 1953). The riders are, from left to right, Joseph, Raymond, and Edward Heggenstaller, sons of Edward and Ida Heggenstaller. Joseph and Edward farmed. Joseph's farm was near Eastville, where the iron ore Deborah Furnace had been in the 1800s. Raymond moved to New Columbia.

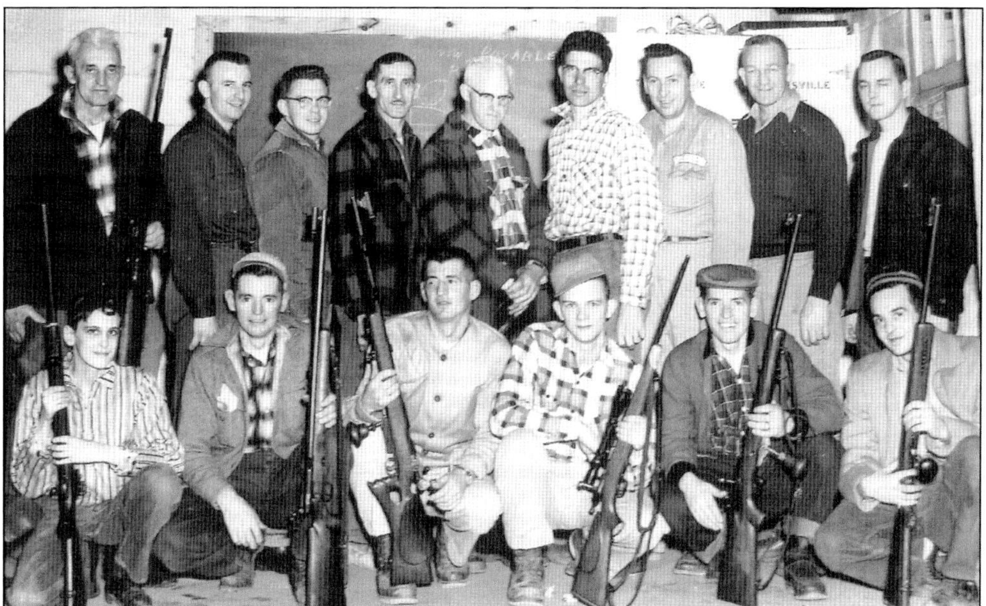

Some time in the late 1950s, the Tylersville Rifle Team posed for this photograph. The members are, from left to right, (first row) Douglas Barner, Ardell Miller, Kermit Miller, Daniel Kerstetter, Vincent Miller, and William Frantz; (second row) Torrence Miller, Robert Barner, Elmer Grieb, Floyd Barner, Ferdinand Miller, Harry Barner, Lawrence Rishel, Scott Currin, and Ronald Douty. They competed in the six-team Bald Eagle League with Loganton, Salona, Mill Hall, Castanea, and Avis. (Courtesy of Kenneth and Peggy Karstetter.)

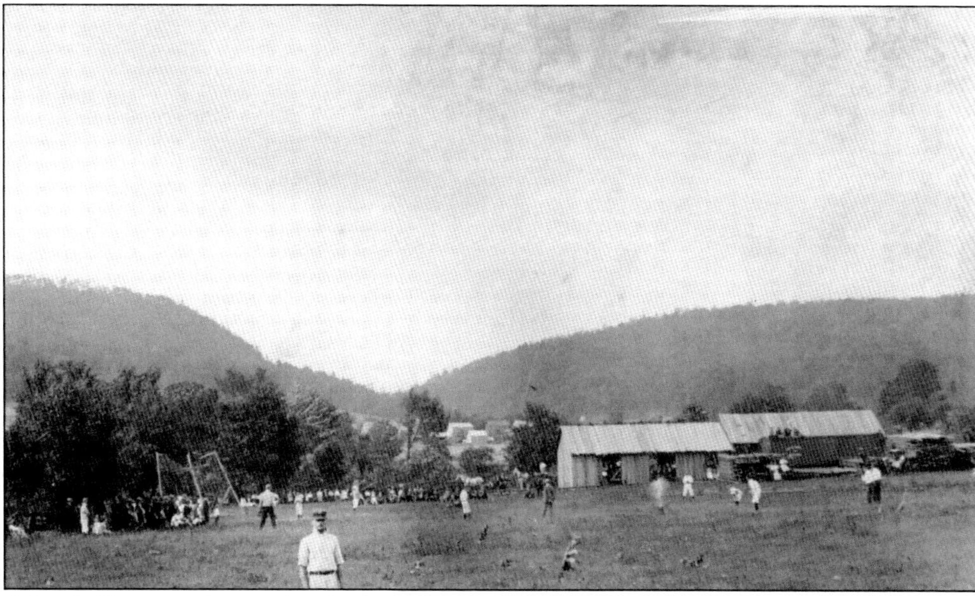

A baseball game is being played around 1910 at a ball field north of Fishing Creek, beside the sawmill and near the Loganton railroad station. John Brunner is in the foreground. Amateur inter-village games were in their heyday in the 1900s up until World War II. (Courtesy of Yvonne and Steve Weaver.)

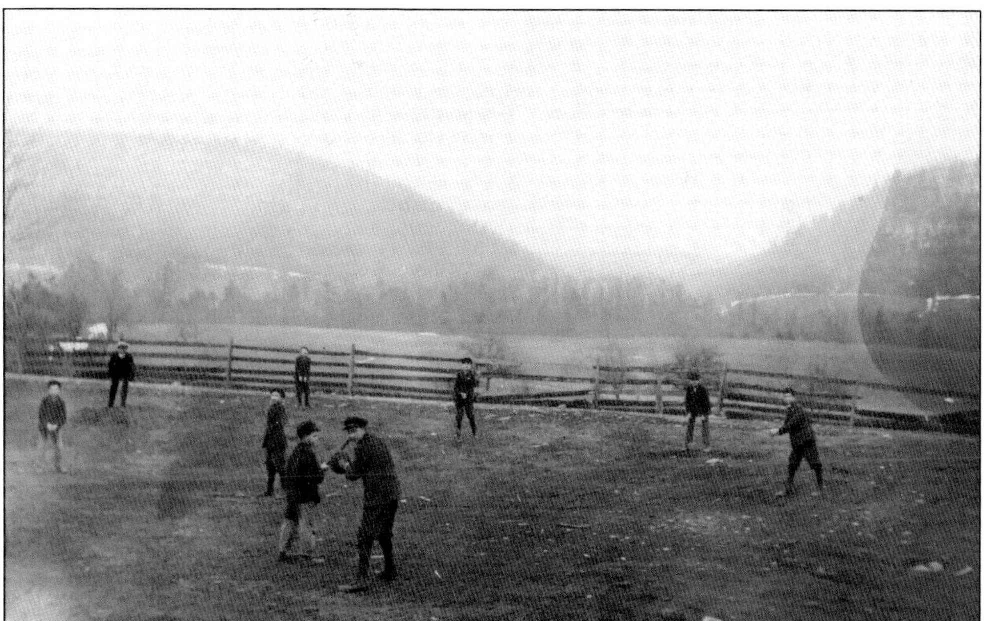

Boys in the Logan Mills school yard enjoy a game of baseball in 1912. The school was located on the south side of Fishing Creek, about a quarter-mile east of the Logan Mills covered bridge. (Courtesy of Yvonne and Steve Weaver.)

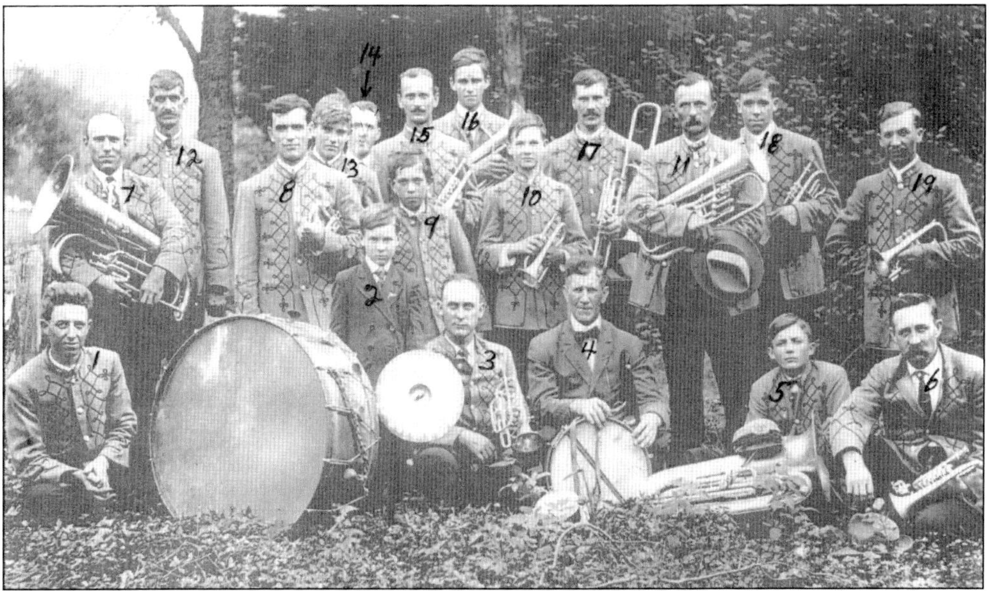

The Greenburr Cornet Band, organized in 1882, continued for more than 50 years. In this 1911 photograph, the band members are, from left to right and identified by number, (first row) Ammon Showers, Howard Lamey, Charles Brungard, Alfred Herlacher, Foster Bartges, and director Calvin C. Lamey; (second row) Edward Lebo, Reuben Meyer, Edward Tyson, Allen Lamey, and William Bartges; (third row) Perry Sheats, unidentified, Lee Lamey, Luther Best, Allen Sheats, Adam Bierly, Roy Sheats, and Cleveland Tyson.

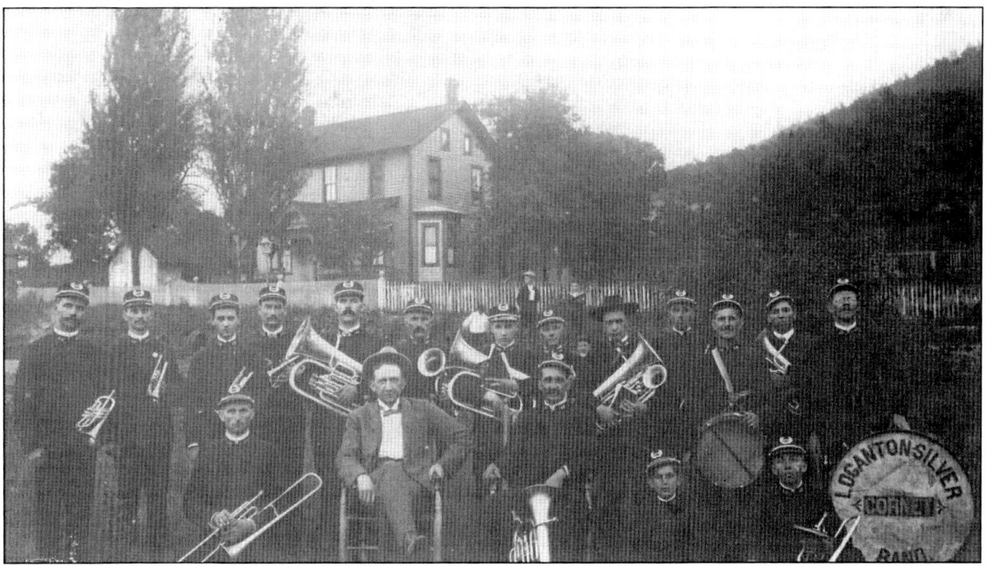

Loganton Silver Cornet Band members pose around 1918. Organized in 1886, the band played, according to its bylaws, for Loganton's Independent Order of Odd Fellows lodge, the Patriotic Order Sons of America camp, the Grand Army of the Republic post, in parades, and at "all entertainments gotten up by citizens of Logansville irrespective of religion or politics." Identified in the photograph are director Thomas Harter (seated, without a uniform), Walburn Laubach (young boy beside the drum), Luther Best (standing on the far left), and Charles Harter (in the back row, wearing a black broad-brimmed hat).

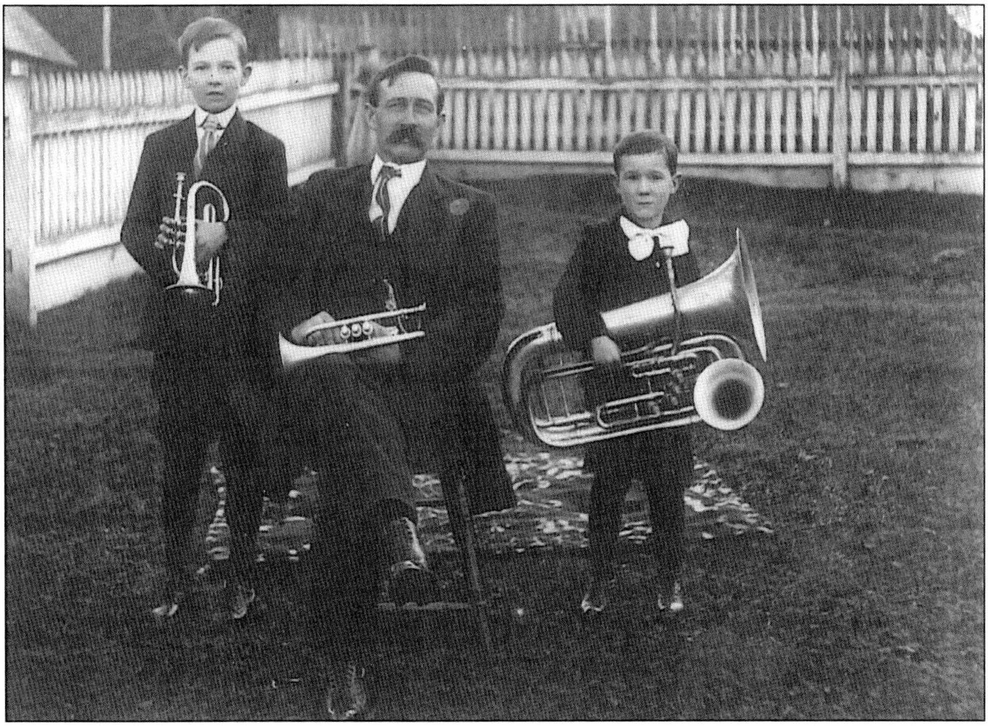

Calvin C. Lamey and sons Allen (left) and Howard pose with their brass instruments in the picket-fenced yard of their home at Bull Run around 1910. In addition to his instrumental expertise, Lamey taught singing classes in Sugar Valley.

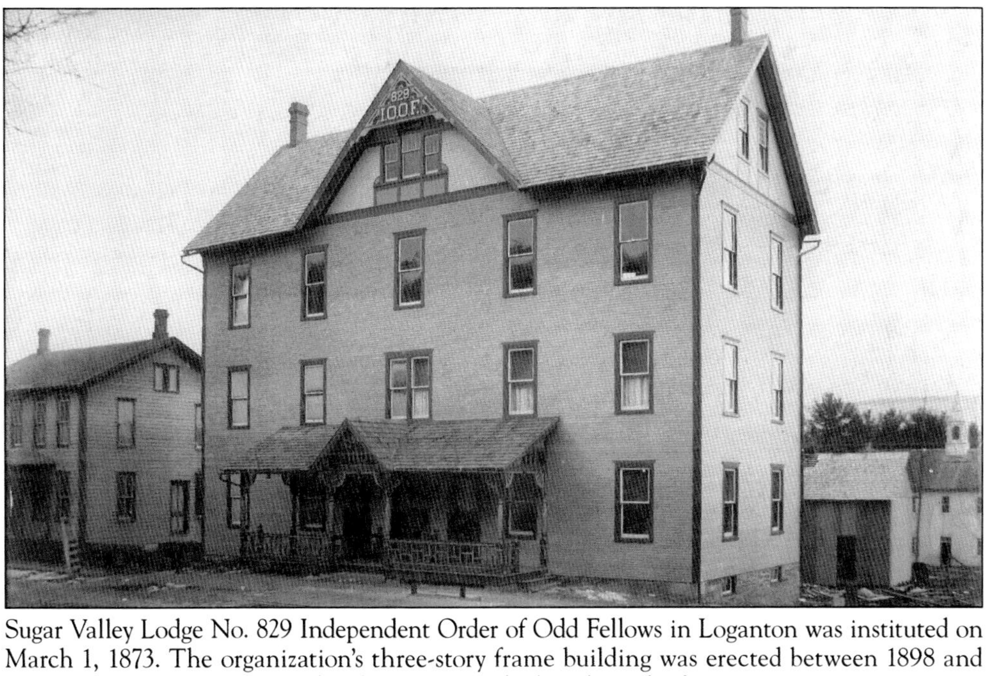

Sugar Valley Lodge No. 829 Independent Order of Odd Fellows in Loganton was instituted on March 1, 1873. The organization's three-story frame building was erected between 1898 and 1899 at the corner of Main and Hall Streets, on the lot where the former Karstetter tannery was located. The temple was destroyed in the fire of June 19, 1918.

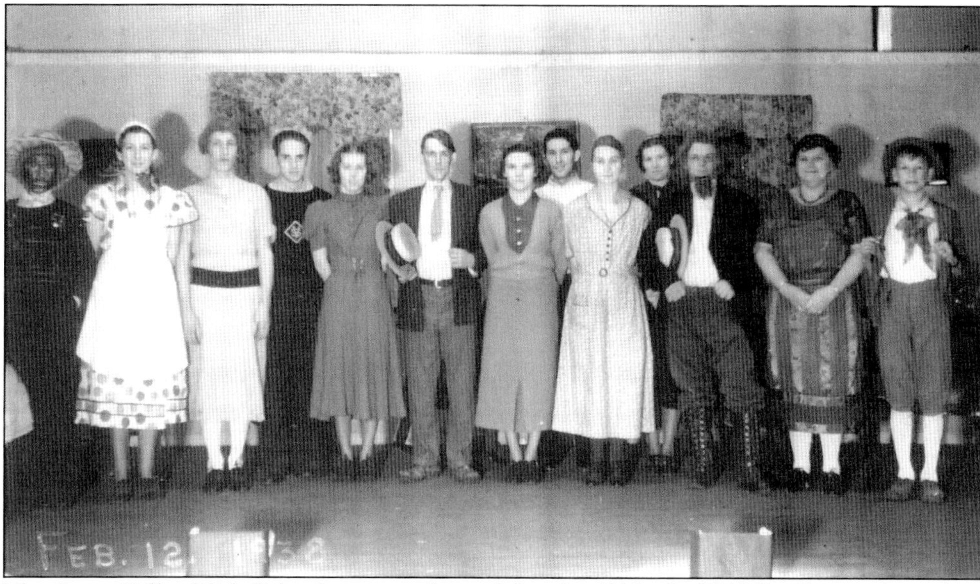

The Sugar Valley High School cast members of the play *Eddie the Wild Oat Boy* performed on February 12, 1938, at the community hall in Loganton. They are, from left to right, Harold Miller, Marian Weaver, Vance Tibbens, Charles Shaffer, Wilda Overdorf, Richard Bixel, Alice Miller, Donald Tibbens, Mildred Knarr, Marguerite Berry, Milton Shaffer, Catherine Bierly, and Guy Bierly. (Courtesy of Mildred Bixel.)

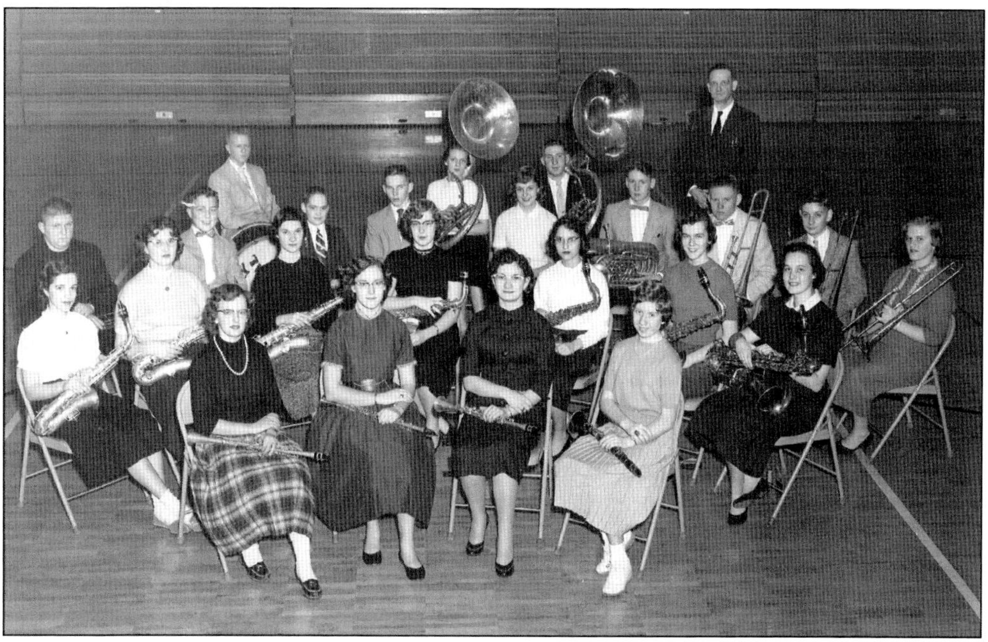

Members of the 1957 Sugar Valley High School Orchestra are, from left to right, (first row) Janice Geisewite, Laura May Truckenmiller, Julia Miller, and Gretchen Hutzel; (second row) Patricia Wians, Joann Slaterbeck, Joan Frank, Gloria Brungart, June Nicholas, Elaine Schreckengast, and Janet Lamey; (third row) Robert Welshans, William Albright, Kenneth Lupold, Leon Grieb, Peggy Grieb, Leo Klinefelter, Philip Boob, Randell Mark, and Barbara Frye; (fourth row) William Shaffer, Donna Weaver, Kenneth Roberts, and director Allen Lamey.

Eight

Posing for Posterity

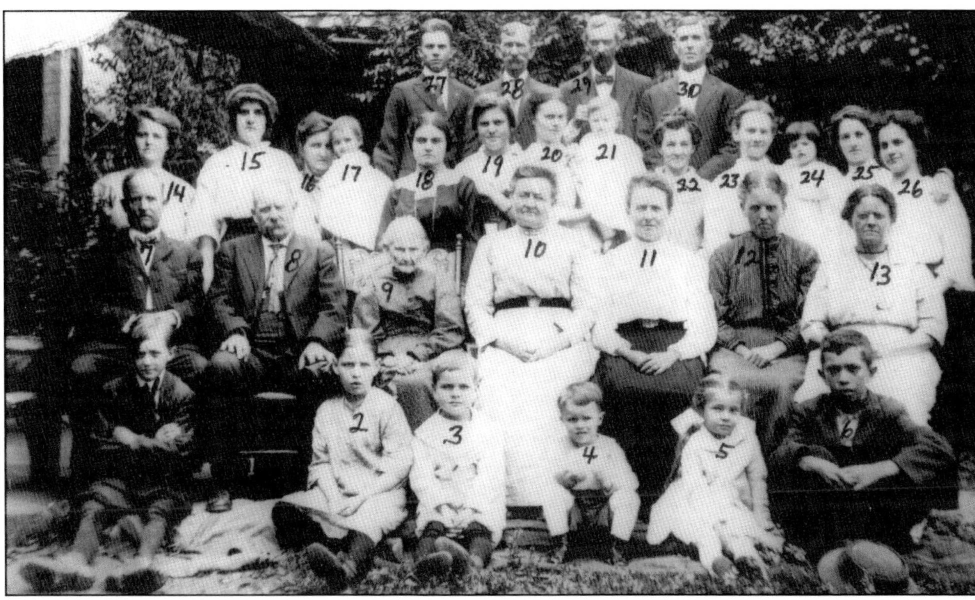

This c. 1913 reunion photograph includes, from left to right, (first row) George Kerstetter, ? Miller, ? Miller, John McCarty, Helen Tyson, and Edward Tyson; (second row) William Kerstetter, Joel Kerstetter, Anna Kerstetter, Phoebe Miller, Rebecca Miller, Emma Weaver, and Ada Wolfe; (third row) Ruth Moyer, Anna Frantz, Emma Kerstetter, Faye Moyer, Lulu Kerstetter, Eva Mechtly, Eva McCarty, Charles McCarty, Laura Tyson, Minerva Herlacher, Sylvia Morris, Mina Sheffer, and Miriam Morris; (fourth row) Roy Weaver, Israel Weaver, Daniel Tyson, and George Wolfe.

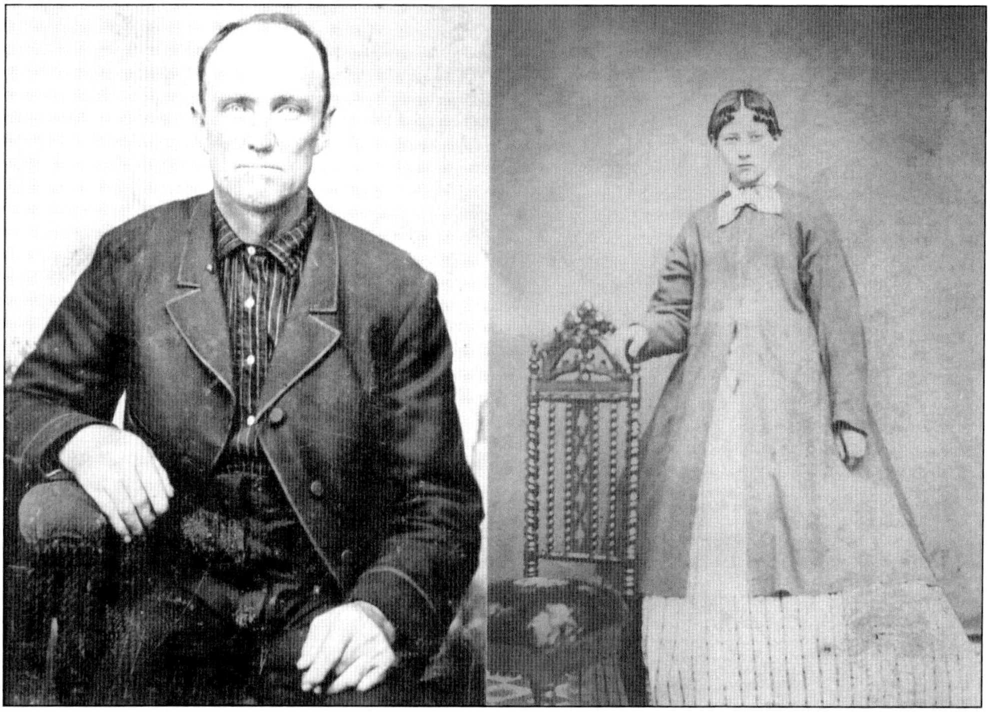

John Reighard (1843–1894) married Sarah Frankenberger (1846–1901) on January 23, 1866, at Logansville, where they lived most of their lives and raised a family of four boys and four girls. They were buried in St. Paul's Evangelical Lutheran Cemetery. Reighard was the son of Daniel and Mary Reighard. Frankenberger was the daughter of John Frankenberger (1793–1867) and Elizabeth Frankenberger (b. approximately 1806, d. 1850).

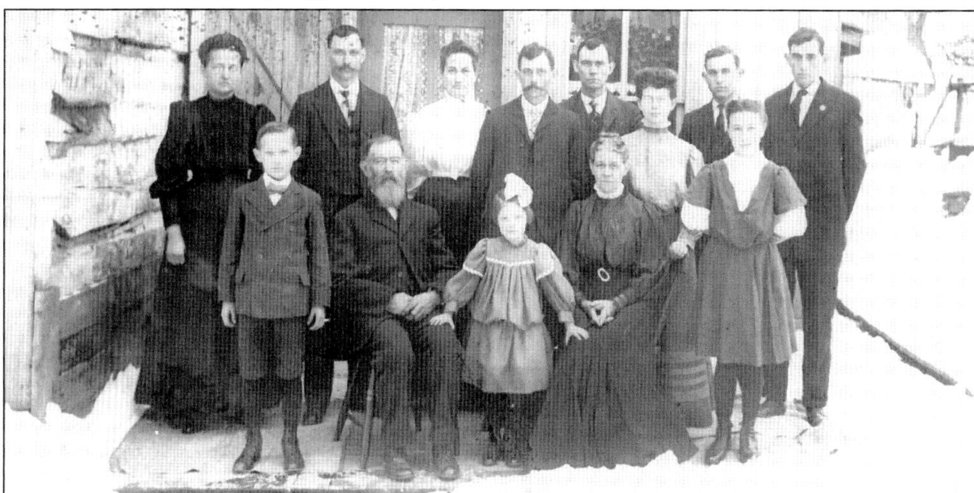

Posing in this photograph that was taken around 1908 at the Frankenberger home two miles east of Loganton, are, from left to right, (first row) Walter Frankenberger, Samuel C. Frankenberger, Emma Frankenberger Harbach Yarrison, Emma Lehman Frankenberger, and Esther Frankenberger Rockey; (second row) Ada Stamm Frankenberger, William G. Frankenberger, Mary Jane Stamm Frankenberger, Gordon Frankenberger, John M. Frankenberger, Beatrice Frankenberger Yarrison, Charles Frankenberger, and Samuel J. Frankenberger.

Pioneer John Frankenberger (1793–1867) was born in Norristown, Pennsylvania. He went on to live successively in Snyder County, Rebersburg, and finally in Sugar Valley. He was a carpenter and builder, a mechanic, a cabinetmaker, a weaver, a farmer, and an undertaker. He was married to Elizabeth Young, who bore 12 children, six of whom died of typhoid fever between 1850 and 1853. He and Elizabeth are buried in St. Paul's Evangelical Lutheran Cemetery in Loganton.

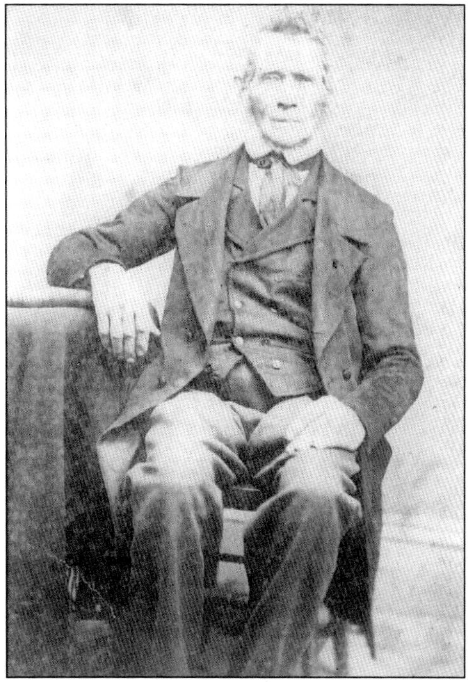

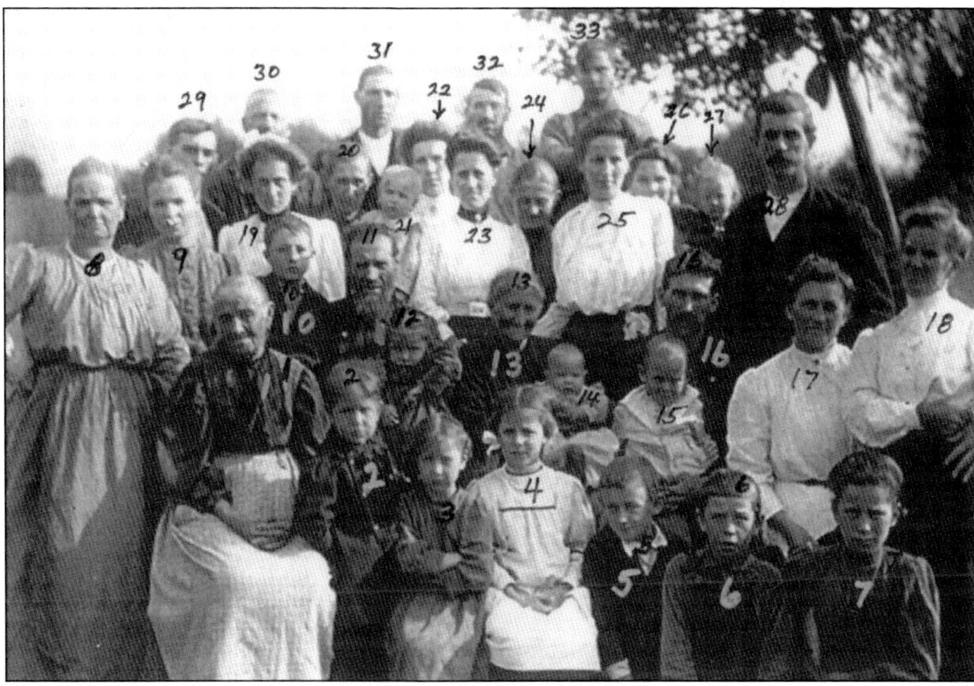

At this reunion, held around 1907, are, from left to right, (first row) D. Nevel (a Cherokee), unidentified, L. Schrack, M. Schrack, unidentified, C. Schrack, and K. Schrack; (second row) R. Duck, B. Duck, unidentified, A. Knarr, unidentified, C. Knarr, unidentified, A. Knarr, T. Knarr, E. Knarr, and A. Schrack; (third row) A. Bower, Mary Bower, unidentified, ? Knarr, Minerva Bower, S. Knarr, A. Powers, M. Knarr, B. Knarr, and J. Rine; (fourth row) unidentified, N. Bower, John Bower, Jacob Bower, and E. Powers.

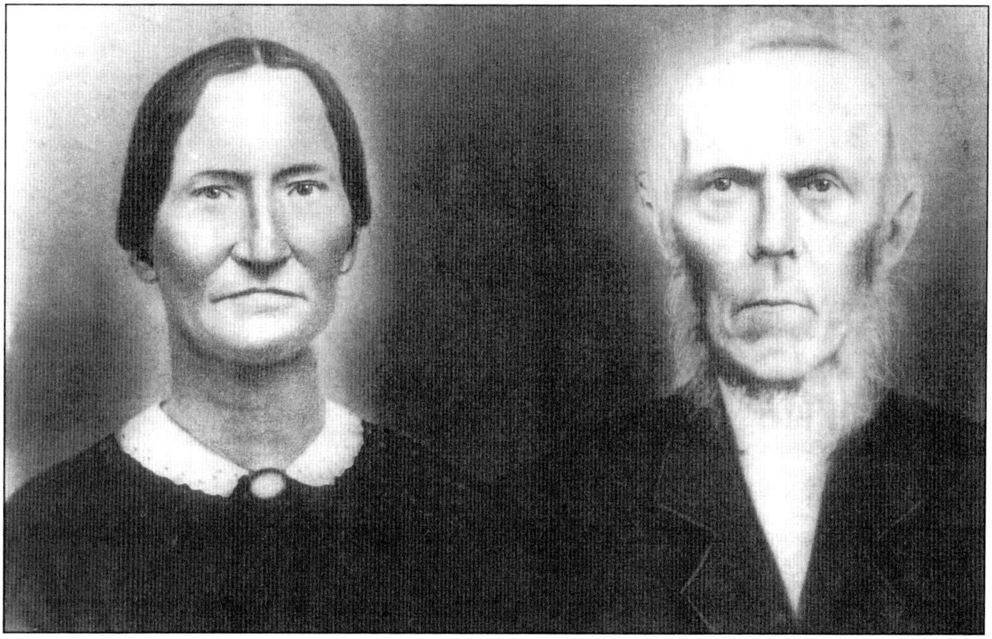

Mary Decker Lehman (1822–1899) and her husband, John Lehman (1812–1892), were both born in Wittumburg, Germany. They lived on the mountain above Carroll, farmed, raised a family of 10, and were the progenitors of all the Sugar Valley Lehmans.

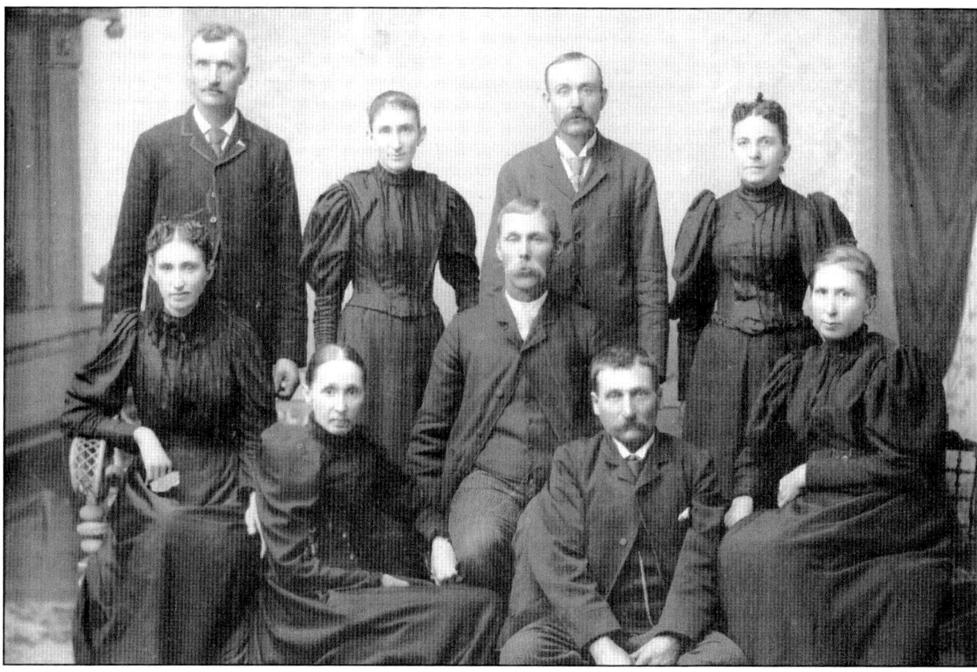

In this c. 1895 Sugar Valley photograph are, from left to right, (first row) Sarah Gramley Berry, Sabilla Gramley Penticoff, Samuel Loman, Daniel Penticoff, and Supera Gramley Loman; (second row) William Berry, Anna Gramley Harbach, Oscar Horace Harbach, and Jane Royer Gramley. All of the people in this photograph are related: Anna, Sarah, Sabilla, and Supera were all daughters of Philip and Mariah Gramley.

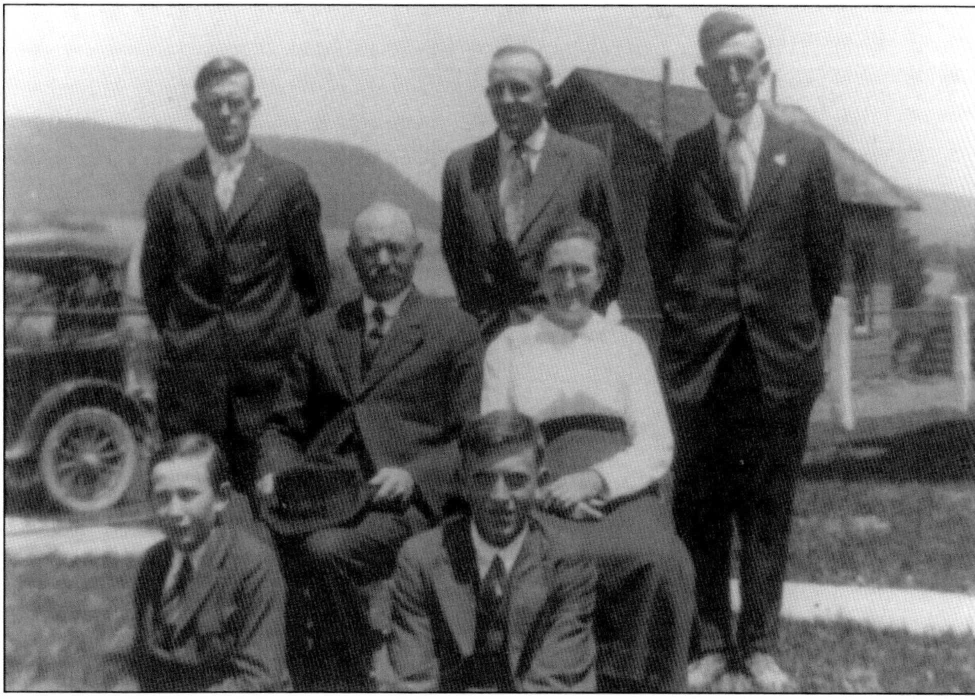

Pictured at the Harbach farm near Eastville around 1918 are, from left to right, (first row) Philip B. Harbach (1906–1952) and Glenn A. Harbach (1903–1954); (second row) Oscar Horace Harbach (1866–1935) and Anna Malizza Gramley Harbach (1869–1937); (third row) Raymond Harbach (1894–1977), Chester Harbach (1891–1968), and Charles G. Harbach (1900–1961).

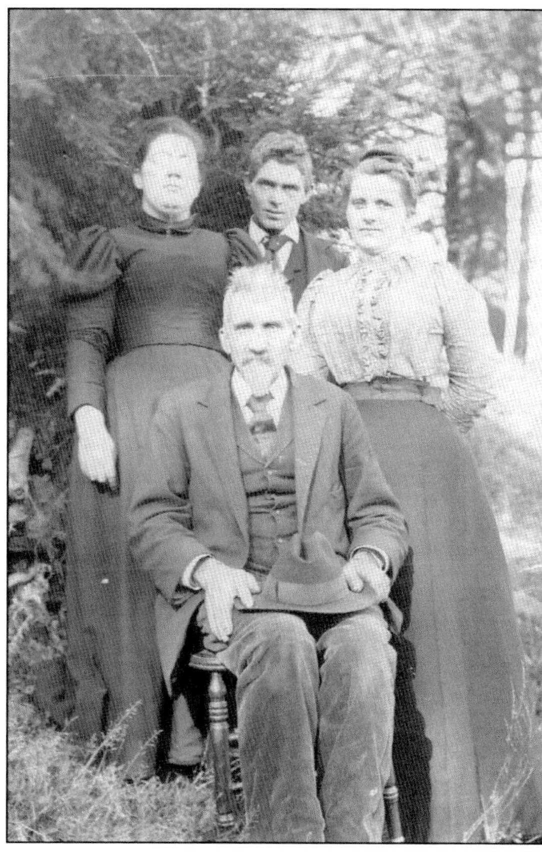

Seated is Rudolph Karstetter (1834–1907) of Booneville, a Civil War veteran whose grandfather (with the same name) was reportedly the first settler in Greene Township. His children are, from left to right, Sadie Karstetter Keister Young (1875–1940), Isaac Karstetter (1873–1963), and Alberta Karstetter Weidhahn (1871–1926). (Courtesy of Kenneth and Peggy Karstetter.)

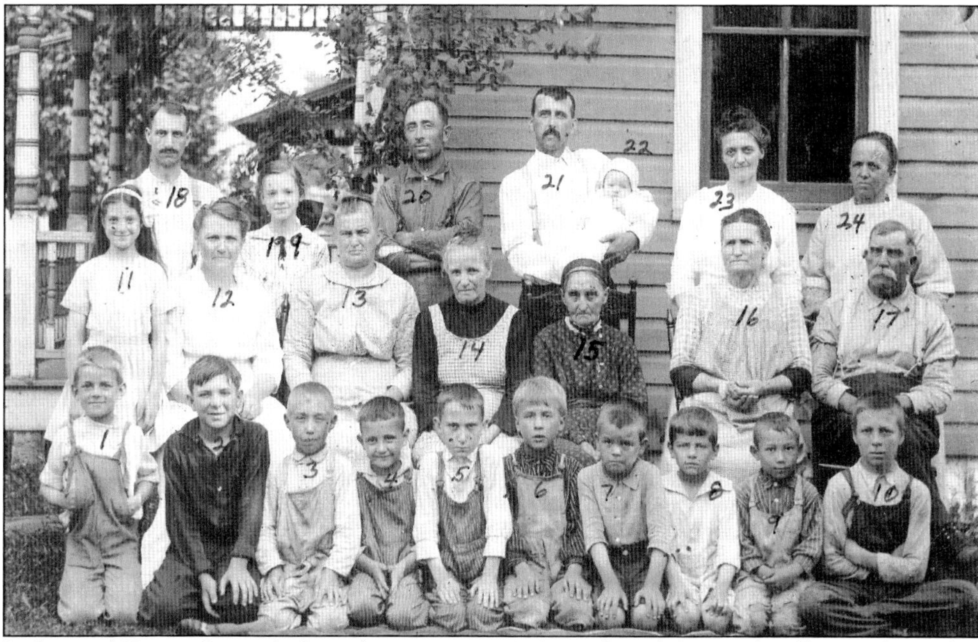

In front of Harvey Lamey's Greenburr store in 1916 are, from left to right, (first row) Gordon Adams, John Bechtol, Walter Lebo, Paul Bechtol, unidentified, Clifford Walizer, Dean Schade, Glenn Adams, Richard Lebo, and Ralph Schade; (second row) Rhea Bechtol, Mary Schreckengast, Emma Warntz, Vesta Gharet, Anna Lamey, Lydia Shaffer, and Joseph Herb; (third row) Alvin Bechtol, Mary Bechtol, Garfield Adams, Harvey Lamey, Floyd Lamey (infant), Tama Lamey, and Cora Glantz.

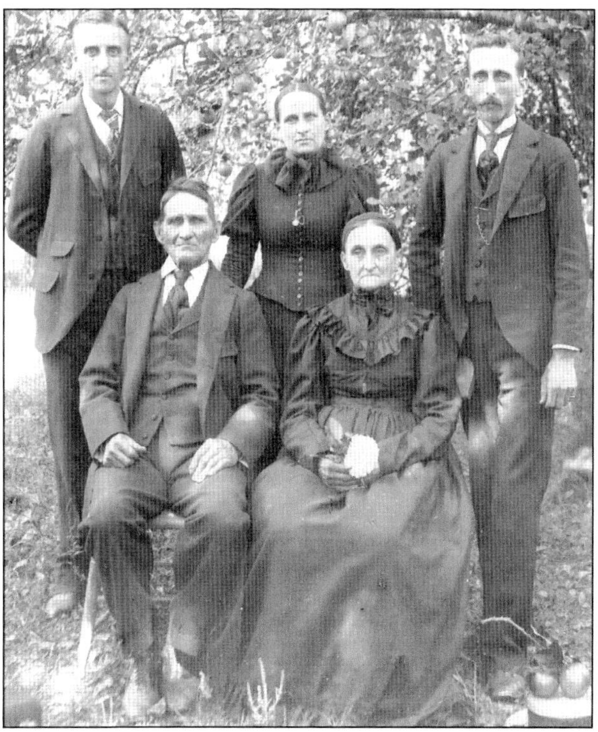

Posing in 1896, probably outside their home near Greenburr, are, from left to right, (seated) Michael Lamey (1829–1899) and his wife, Anna Bartges Lamey (1835–1917); (standing) Franklin Lamey (1874–1897), Dina Lamey Emig (1867–1942), and Harvey Lamey (1869–1953), their children. Michael was a farmer and one of the early settlers of Sugar Valley.

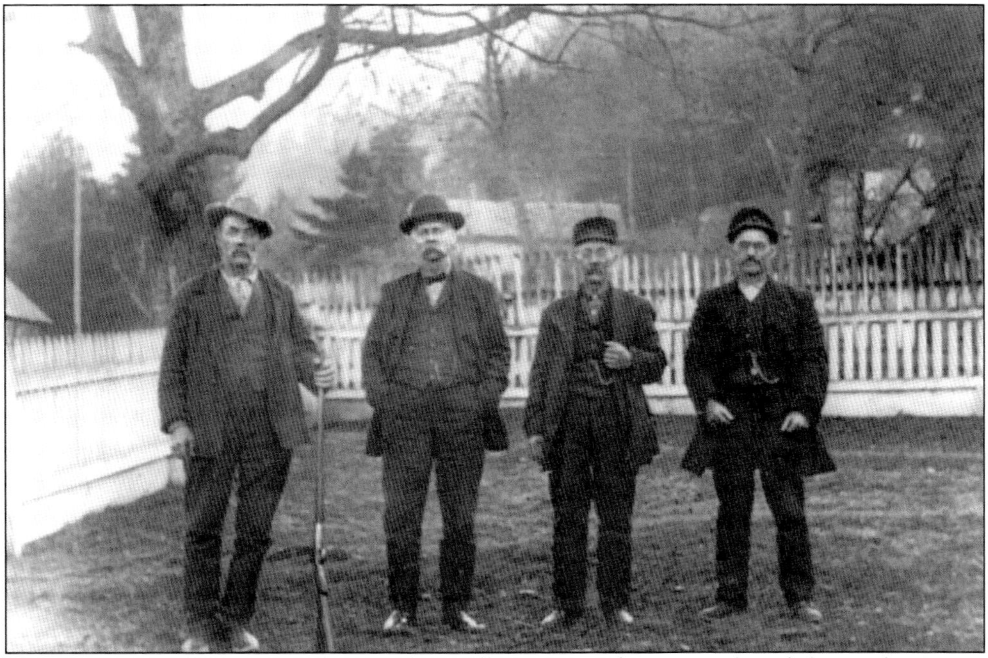

These friends and neighbors who posed at Bull Run around 1911 are, from left to right, Henry Embick (1847–1912), Noah Lamey (1852–1925), Jonathan Lebo (1849–1918), and Jonathan ?. Henry Embick was a farmer and operator of a sawmill in Bull Run. Noah Lamey was a farmer whose son Calvin and grandsons Allen and Howard all became band directors. Jonathan Lebo was a farmer.

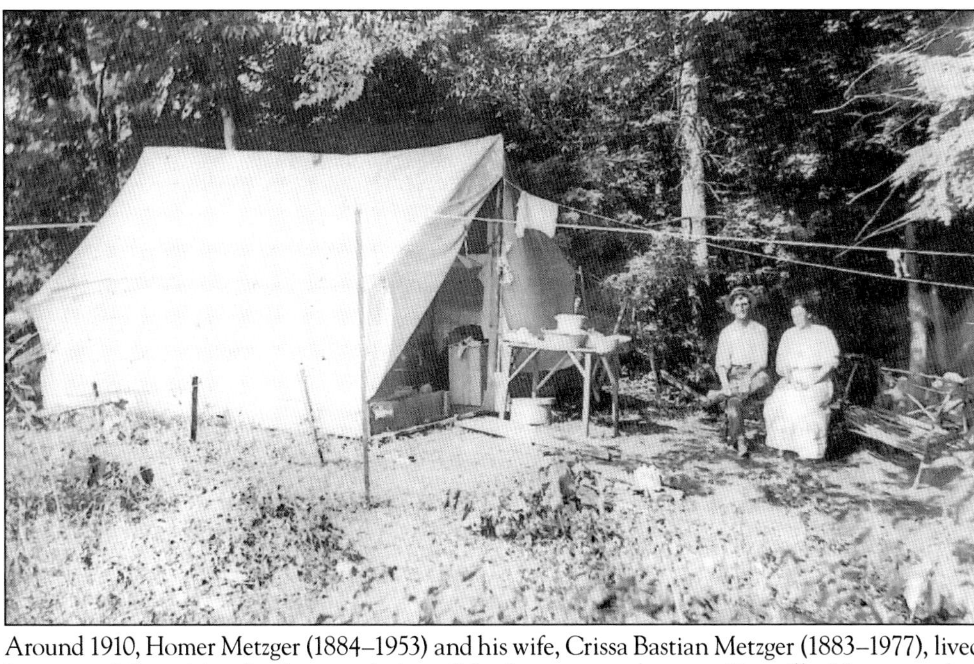

Around 1910, Homer Metzger (1884–1953) and his wife, Crissa Bastian Metzger (1883–1977), lived in a tent while waiting for the completion of the forest ranger house at Eastville. Homer worked as a forest ranger in the valley from 1909 to 1921. In 1920, he also helped put in a telephone line to Eastville. They had three sons, Forrest, Homer, and John, and one daughter, Bara.

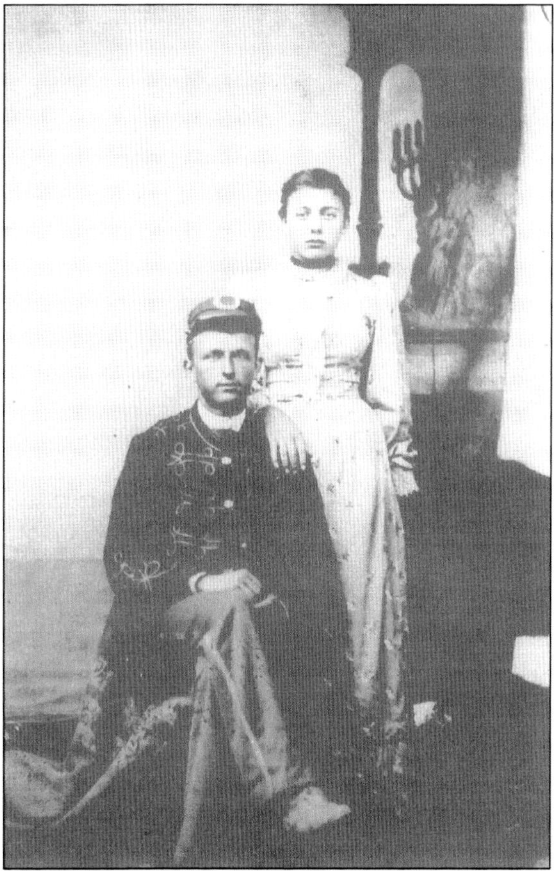

William Bartges (1872–1946), in his Greenburr Band uniform, and his wife, Frances Embick Bartges (1877–1960), pose for a formal portrait around 1905. They were married on June 1, 1895, and lived about three miles from Logan Mills at Bull Run, where Bartges ran a gristmill. William was the son of James and Susan Bartges. Frances was the daughter of Henry and Maria Embick.

Gathered together at Logan Mills some time before 1910 are, from left to right, (first row) son Jacob Bartges, father James Bartges (1843–1918), mother Jane Nestlerode Bartges (1855–1910), and daughter Ada Bartges Wolfe; (second row) son Winfield Bartges, son Edwin Bartges, son Newton Bartges, and son Ellis Bartges. James was a farmer.

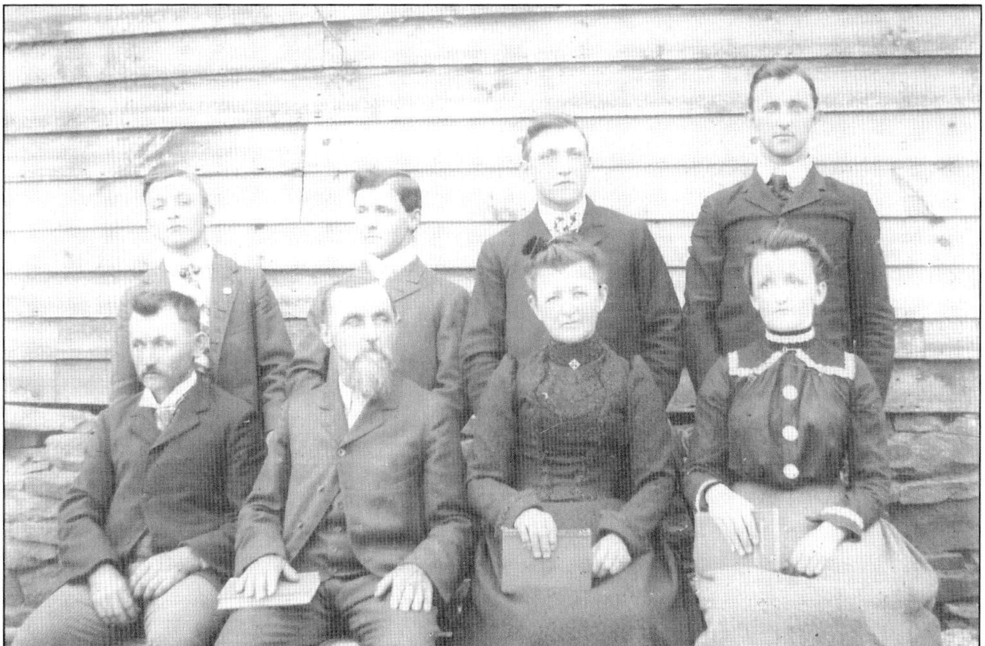

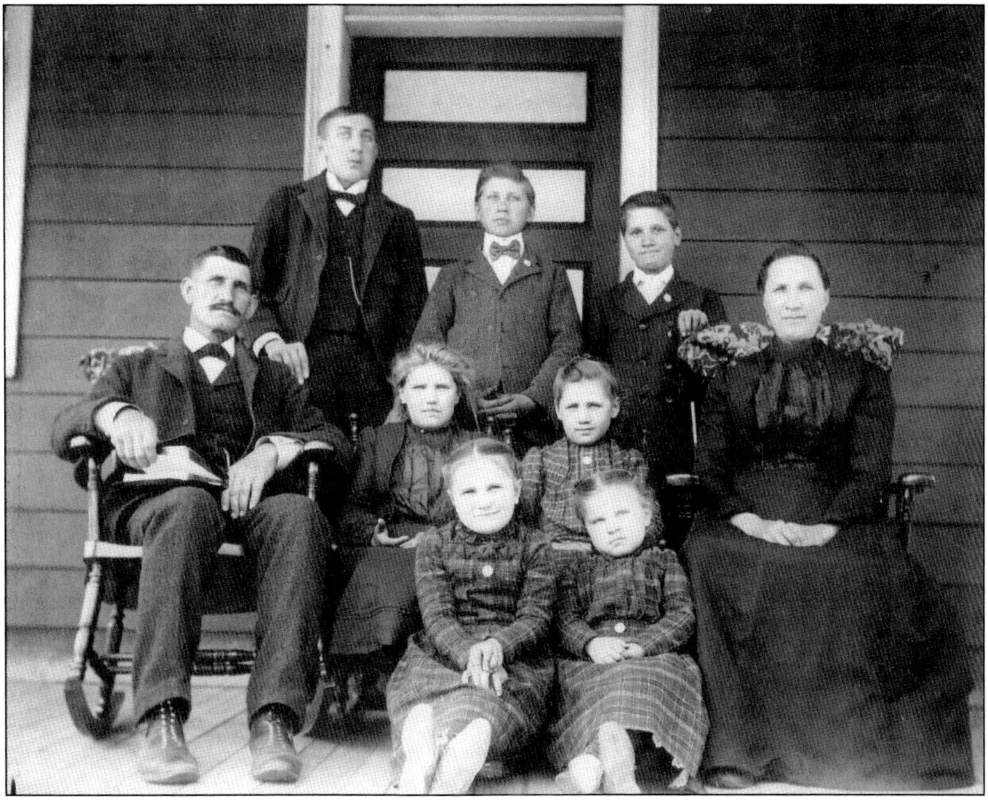

On the porch of their Tylersville home around 1900 are, from left to right, (first row) daughters Bertha and Miriam Bierly; (second row) father Rev. Adam Bierly, daughters Beulah and Verna Bierly, and mother Cordie Bressler Bierly; (third row) sons Ammon, Willis, and Roland Bierly. Adam was one of reputedly eight ministers to come from St. Paul's Evangelical Church of Logan Mills.

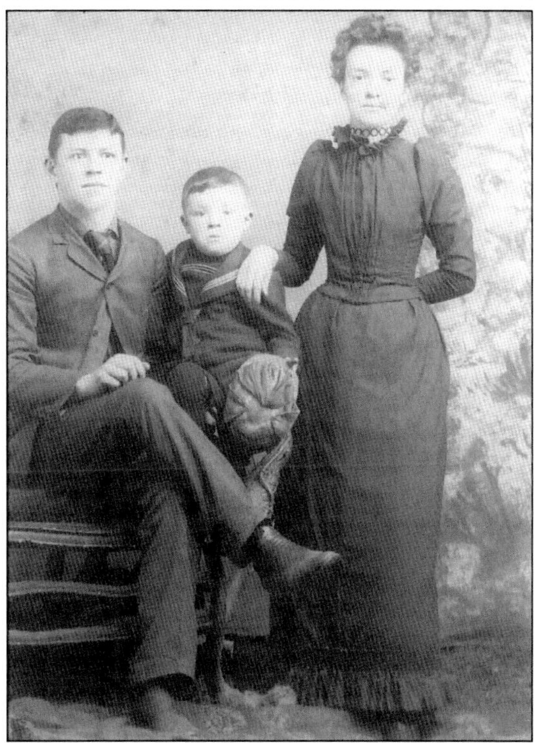

Posing around 1887 are, from left to right, Daniel Scott Currin (1865–1927), son Lee Currin, and wife Jennie Currin (nurse and midwife). In 1884, at the age of 18, Daniel founded the *Sugar Valley Journal*, becoming the youngest printer in the state. He started it as a five-column monthly, expanded it to a seven-column weekly, and continued publishing it until 1917.

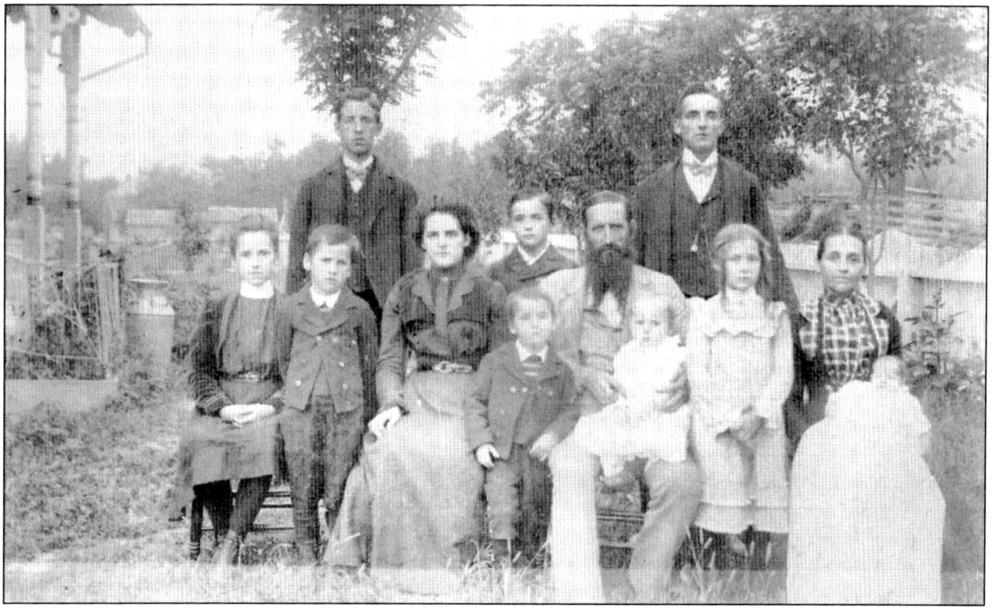

In this c. 1901 Douty family portrait are, from left to right, (first row) Mary, Lester, Elsie, Russell, father Elmer Douty (1863–1939), Walter (toddler), Laura, mother Johanna Troutner Douty (1860–1936), and Dessie (baby); (second row) George, Harry, and Reuben Douty. The family lived at Bull Run, where Elmer farmed. (Courtesy of John and Verna Carey.)

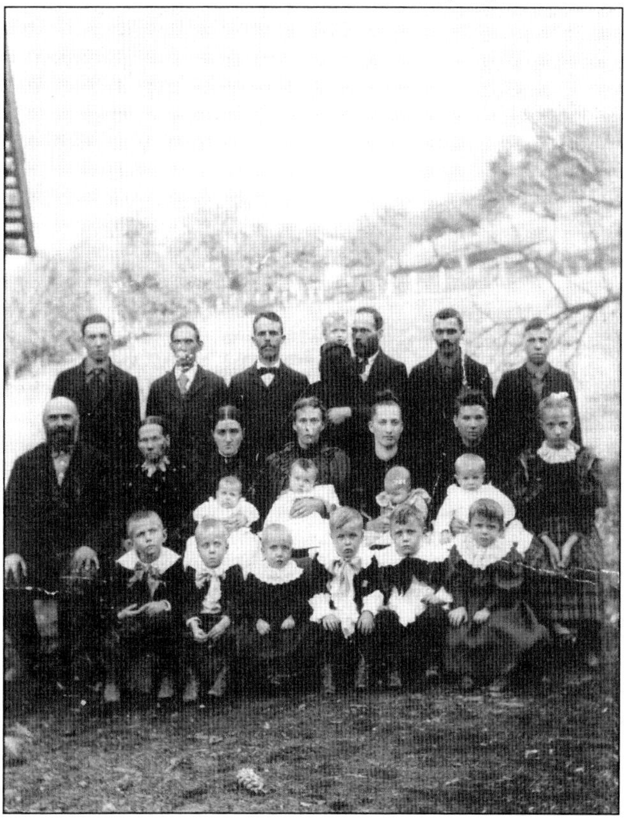

This c. 1898 Wolfe extended-family portrait at Logan Mills includes patriarch David Wolfe (who owned a sawmill) seated on the far left, and his wife, Phoebe Greninger Wolfe, beside him. Others identified in this image include (first row) Anna and Mary Bierly, the toddlers respectively third and sixth from the left; (second row) Emma Bierly, the baby fourth from the left; (third row) Bertha, Anna, and Maude Wolfe, the fourth, sixth, and seventh from the left.

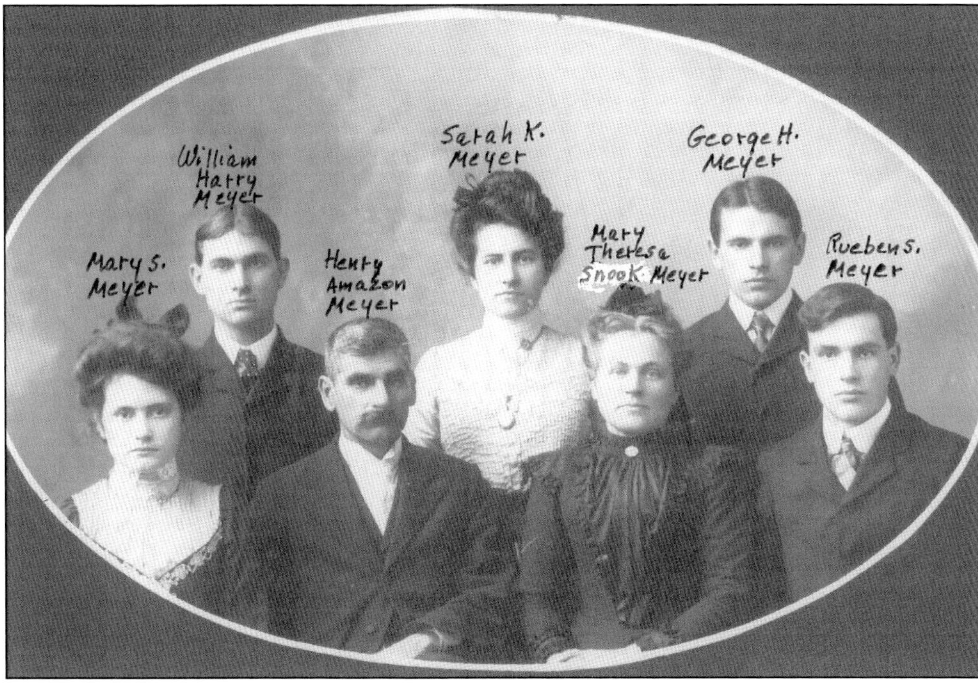

In this c. 1898 photograph are, from left to right, daughter Mary Meyer (1888–1964), son William Meyer (1880–1950), father Henry Amazon Meyer (1851–1911), daughter Sarah Meyer (1878–1954), mother Mary Snook Meyer (1856–1909), son George Meyer (1879–1960), and son Reuben Meyer (1883–1951). They lived at Booneville, and Henry operated a tannery. (Courtesy of John and Verna Carey.)

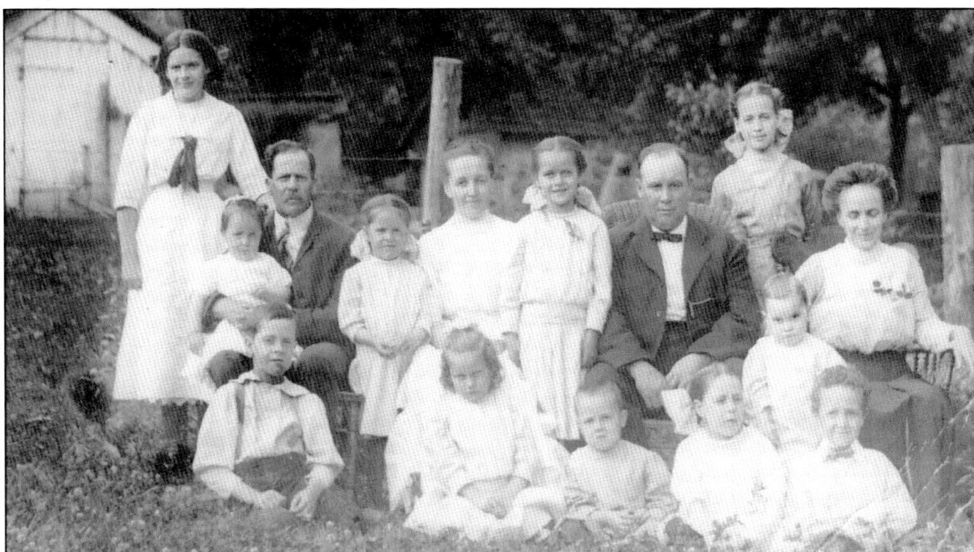

Posing in 1912 on the mountain east and above of Loganton are two families. Included in this photograph are, from left to right, (first row) Stewart Confer, Jessie Confer, Paul Robb, Leona Robb, and Harold Robb; (second row) toddler Emma Confer, William Confer, Susan Confer, Blanche Wren Confer (William Confer's wife), Hilda Confer, William Robb, toddler Lester Robb, and Virginia Wren Robb (William Robb's wife and sister of Blanche); (third row) Lydia Confer and Ruth Confer.

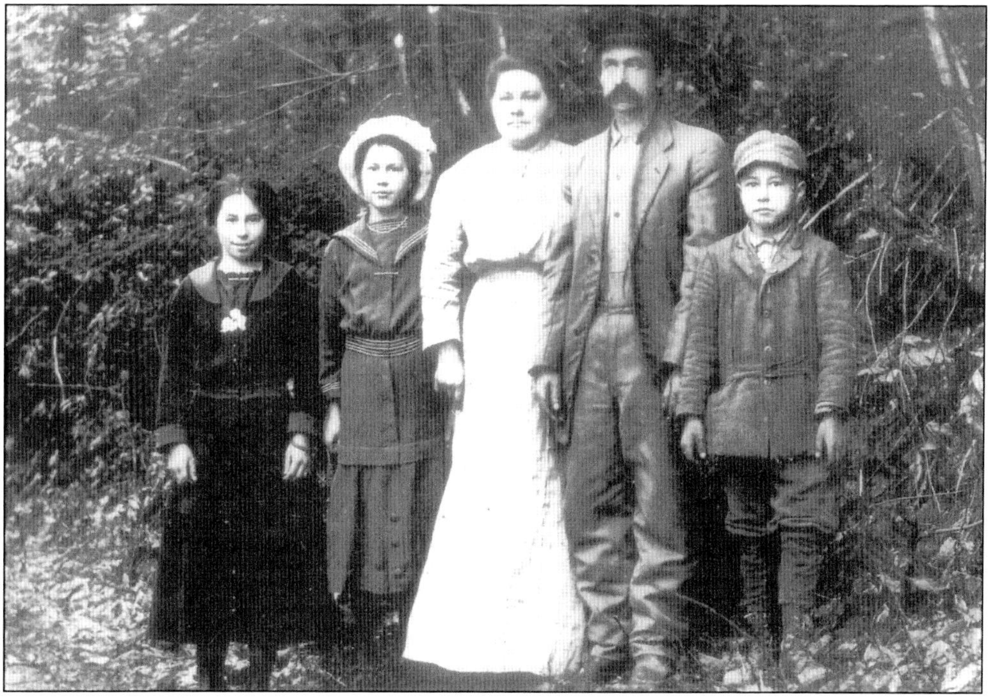

The members of the Herman family of Greenburr in this c. 1914 photograph are, from left to right, daughter Catherine, daughter Mary, mother Elizabeth, father John, and son Delbert Herman. John, born and raised in the Rosecrans area, owned a sawmill in the Logan Mills area.

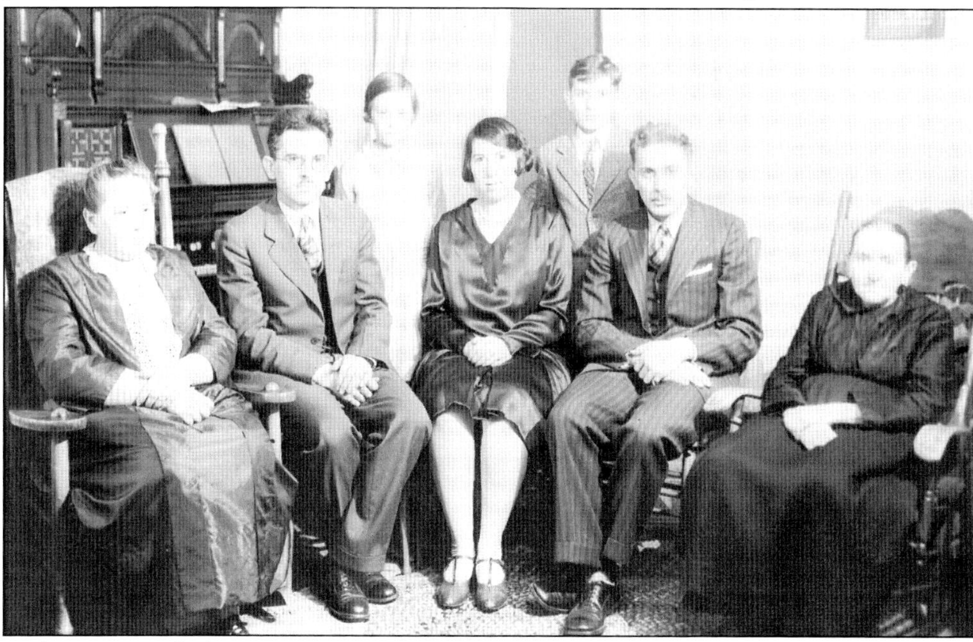

In their Booneville home around 1935, the family members in this image are, from left to right, mother Emma Matilda "Tillie" Apple Schrack (widow of Ammon Schrack), son Walter Schrack, granddaughter Kathleen Schrack, daughter Velma Schrack, son Morlin Schrack, son Stewart Schrack, and Margaret "Maggie" Jane Apple Bierly (sister of Anna Matilda).

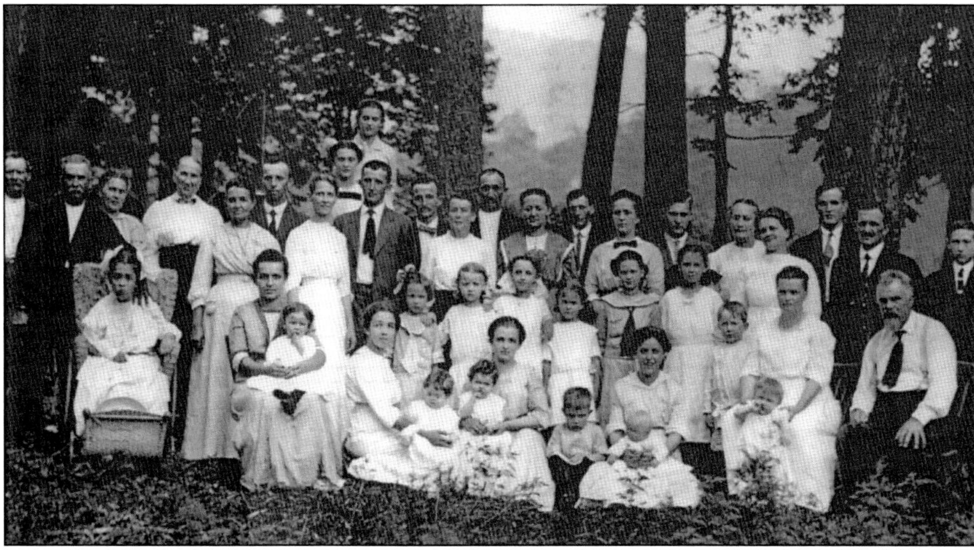

Captured in this photograph from the 1913 Stamm reunion are, from left to right, (first row) L. Schrack (in chair), L. Miller (holding A. Miller), E. Shaffer (holding Bernice Shaffer), N. Yarrison (holding Beatrice Shaffer), M. Stamm, Fae Stamm (holding V. Stamm), W. Laubach, Mary Beck Stamm (holding Heil Stamm), and H. Beck; (second row) R. Stamm, A. Stamm, Edna Stamm, R. Miller, E. Frankenberger, and Mittie Mark; (third row) J. Frankenberger, J. Schrack, G. Stamm, M. Beck, M. Schrack, Cyrus Stamm, Minnie Stamm, Martha Stamm, F. Stamm, James Stamm, Elizabeth Stamm, and Charles Stamm, A. Frankenberger, R. Miller, Margaret Mark, R. Stamm, J. Frankenberger, Mary Brown Stamm, H. Shaffer, John Stamm, and W. Frankenberger; (fourth row) M. Meyer.

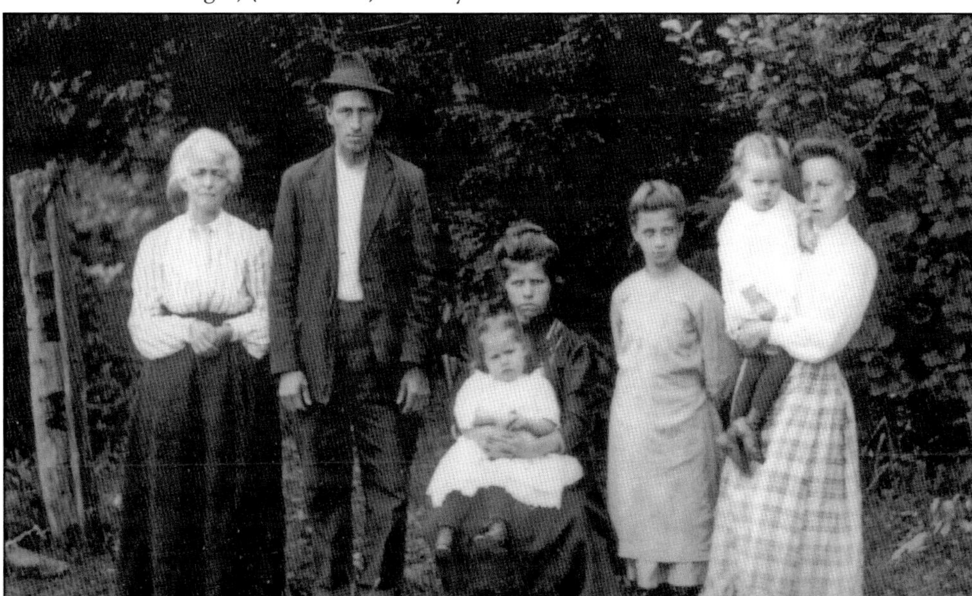

Members of the extended Trump family of Loganton posed in this c. 1913 photograph are, from left to right, Louisa Bower Trump (mother of Adam and Hanna), Adam Trump, Alice Trump (Adam's wife, holding their daughter Eva), unidentified sister of Alice, and Hanna Trump Winterrod (holding her daughter Catherine).

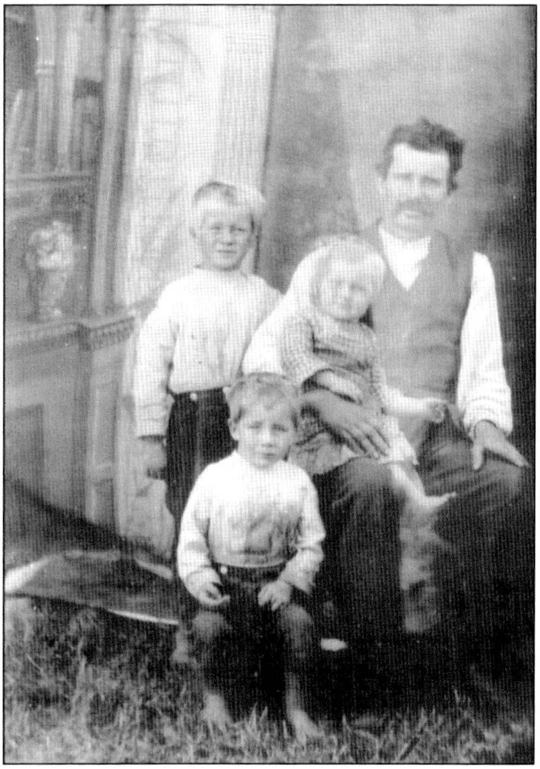

Posed for this photograph are, from left to right, Arthur, Harry, Laura, and father Samuel Motter (1850–1921). Living on top of Loganton Mountain, Samuel Motter was known as a woodsman who spent most of his time hunting, fishing, and trapping to support himself, his wife, Harriet Shaffer Motter, and their 12 children. Motter stories abound, including that he rarely wore shoes, that he had a pet bear and mountain lion, and that he walked to California and back (mostly barefoot) to claim a $2,500 inheritance from his father.

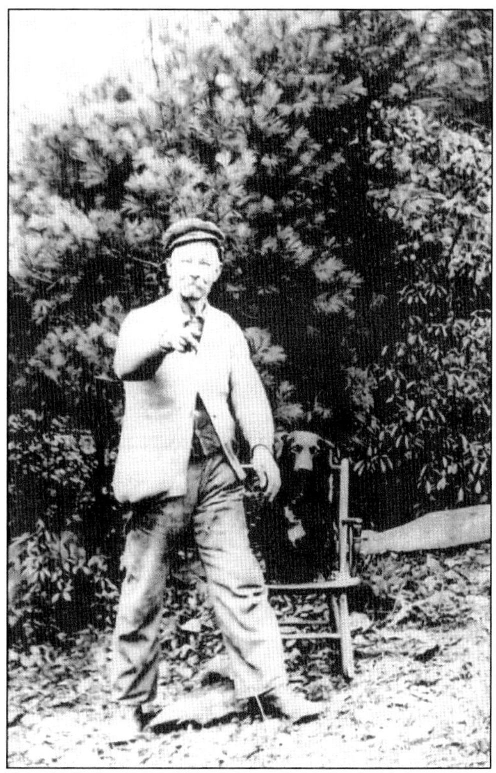

Isaac Duck (1844–1910) was a Civil War veteran who served for nine months as a private in the 195th Pennsylvania Volunteers, Company F, out of Jersey Shore, Pennsylvania. He was married to Margaret Nevel Duck (1854–1929). They lived in Loganton and raised 13 children. He was a blacksmith by trade.

Joseph Embich (1812–1893) was a farmer, logger, and shingle maker. He and his wife, Susanna Garver Embich (1813–1890), raised nine children (four boys and five girls) at their mountain home above Carroll. Their one daughter, Mariah, married noted Sugar Valley resident Charles Cyrus Harbach. Joseph and Susanna are buried in Green Grove Cemetery on Harbaugh Road, where a large sandstone marks their grave site.

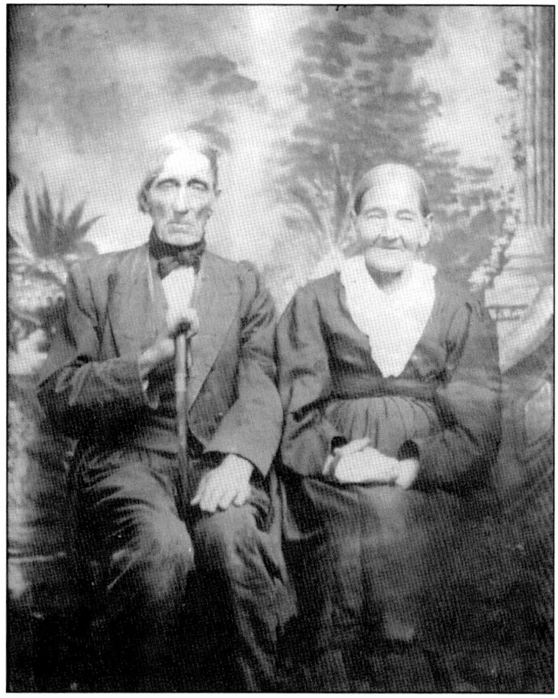

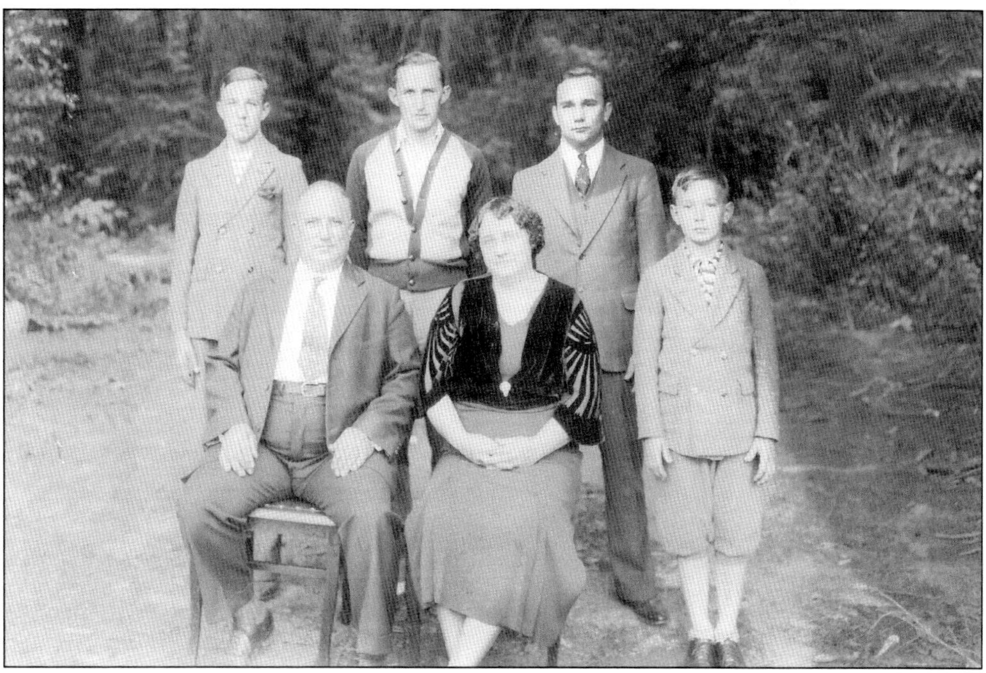

The Welshans are posed in this photograph from 1940. The family members are, from left to right, (seated) Ralph Welshans (1896–1966) and his wife, Jennie Emig Welshans; (standing) Calvin Welshans (1925–2007), Hillaire Welshans (1920–2007), Lester Welshans (1918–1994), and Elwood Welshans (1929–?). The Welshans lived in Booneville, where Ralph was the proprietor of Welshan's Grocery Store. Lester became a Church of the Nazarene minister at a number of towns in Pennsylvania.

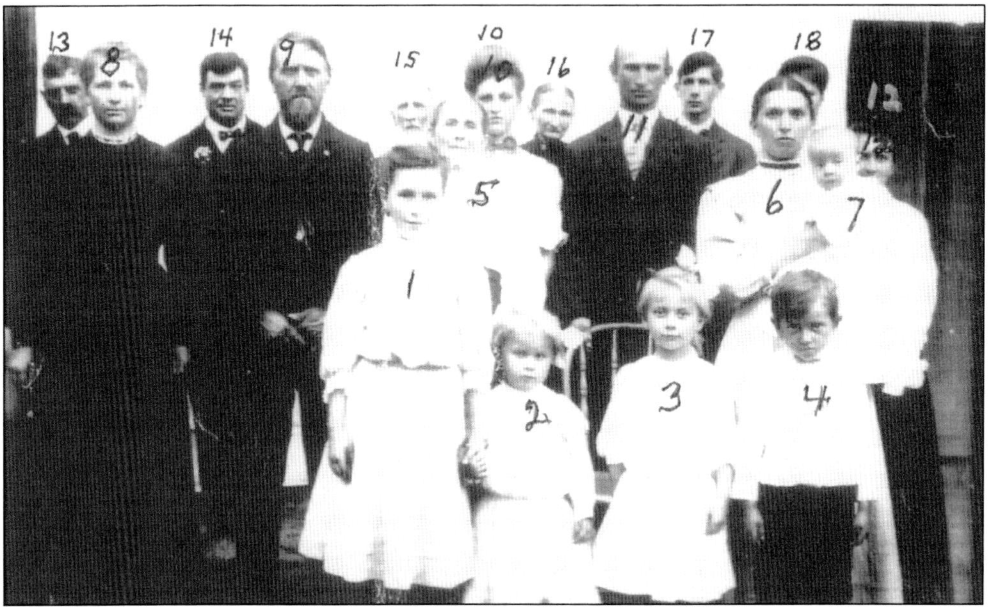

Photographed at the Walizer family reunion in Greenburr around 1908 are, from left to right, (first row) Bertha Johnson, Delilah Walizer, Lillian Walizer, and unidentified; (second row) Clara Walizer, Sarah Walizer, and Clifford Walizer; (third row) Anna Moyer, William Walizer, Cora Moyer, Newton Walizer, and Melinda Walizer; (fourth row) Sylvanus Moyer, Adam Walizer, George Walizer, Delilah Schreckengast, Wallace Walizer, and Lottie Snook.

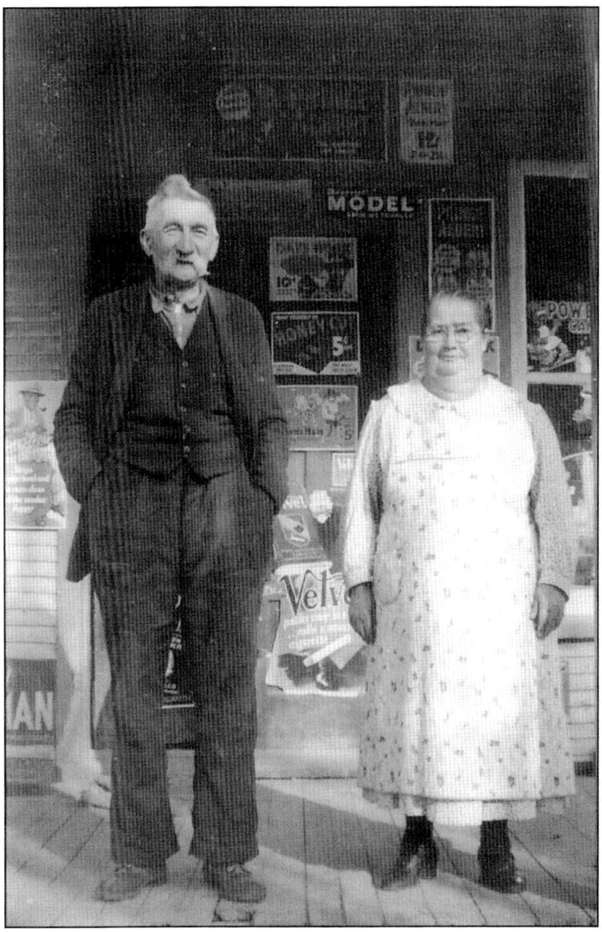

William Mesmer (1871–1954) and wife, Katie (1875–1938), stand in front of Lamey's general store in Greenburr. They rented a house belonging to Harvey Lamey along the winter road, a few yards west of the Greenburr intersection. They farmed and raised two children, Elmer and Lola.

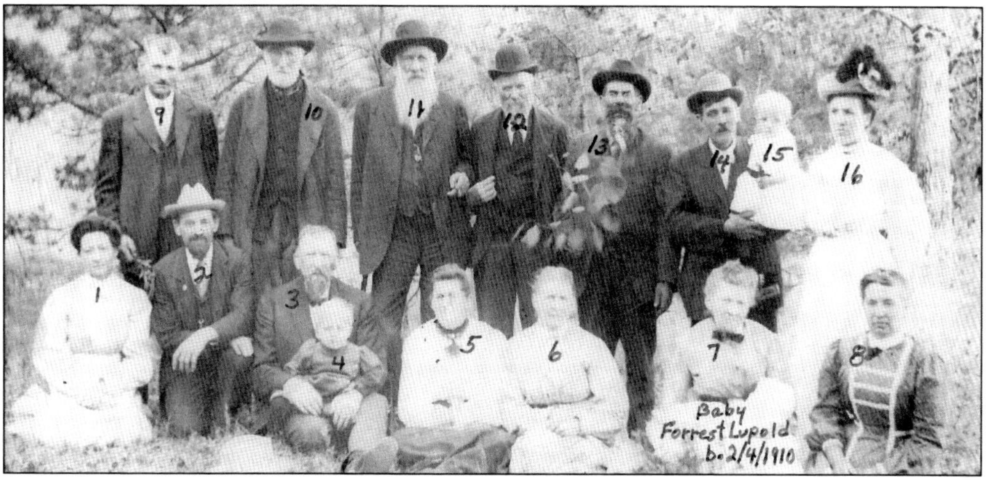

In this c. 1910 reunion photograph are, from left to right, (first row) Theressa Barner, Jeremiah Barner, Daniel Engle (holding McClellan Lupold), Charlotte Engle, Catharine Barner, Elizabeth Barner (holding Forrest Lupold), and Margaret Barner; (second row) Frank Barner, Jacob Engle, Samuel Engle, John Engle, Daniel Barner, Scott Barner (holding George Lupold), and Carrie Lupold. (Courtesy of John and Verna Carey.)

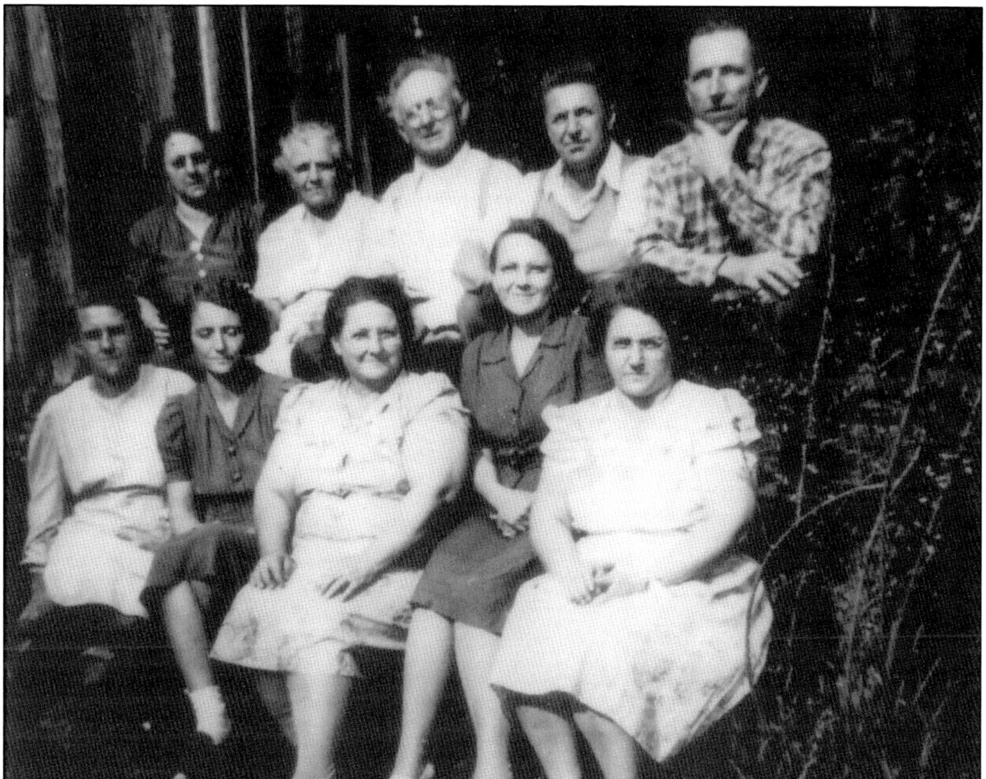

At this Cashner family reunion around 1950 are, from left to right, (first row) daughters Rilla Cashner Seyler, Vinnie Cashner, Mary Cashner Embick, Irma Cashner Shannon, and Jennie Cashner Maize; (second row) daughter Susan Cashner Jamison, mother Ada Miller Cashner, father William Cashner, son George Cashner, and son Frederick Cashner.